PC
HACKS™

Jim Aspinwall

O'REILLY®

Beijing · Cambridge · Farnham · Köln · Paris · Sebastopol · Taipei · Tokyo

PC Hacks™
by Jim Aspinwall

Copyright © 2005 O'Reilly Media, Inc. All rights reserved.
Printed in the United States of America.

Published by O'Reilly Media, Inc., 1005 Gravenstein Highway North,
Sebastopol, CA 95472.

O'Reilly books may be purchased for educational, business, or sales promotional use. Online
editions are also available for most titles (*safari.oreilly.com*). For more information, contact our
corporate/institutional sales department: (800) 998-9938 or *corporate@oreilly.com*.

Editor:	Brian Jepson	**Production Editor:**	Sanders Kleinfeld
Series Editor:	Rael Dornfest	**Cover Designer:**	Hanna Dyer
Executive Editor:	Dale Dougherty	**Interior Designer:**	Melanie Wang

Printing History:

October 2004:	First Edition.

RepKover. This book uses RepKover™, a durable and flexible lay-flat binding.

ISBN: 0-596-00748-5
[C]

Contents

Credits

About the Author

Jim Aspinwall is the coauthor and author of four books about computers and networking. His writing spans not only books but feature articles and how-to columns for a handful of PC magazines and web sites, including *Computer User*, *PC World*, and *CNET.com*. His journey into the digital world began at a humble grass roots, learning the nuances of bits and bytes as a communications system and field service engineer when raw logic was truly raw logic in the 70s and the 8008 processor was programmed with paper tape and Teletype machines. From cross-country, arm-lengthening toolbox-toting he moved to more desktop- and keyboard-bound roles in support engineering helping transition minicomputer and microcomputer systems from research labs through production to customers. Acquiring his first "turbo XT" PC in 1986 and totally baffled by a blank DOS prompt, he sought out the mentoring of a good friend to lead him gently into the PC abyss from where he has yet to surface. That mentoring led to his first collaborative work about PCs published in 1990, to his first COMDEX experience, and to his first real job working with PCs full-time for DiagSoft: supporting, testing, and marketing PC diagnostic software.

Jim's experiences (and writing about them) with the PC have been nonstop ever since: from the low-level workings of PC guts and how components, vendors, and software work together (or not), to supporting corporate clients. Jim was much of the "PC sense" behind Quarterdeck's TuneUp.com, Computer Support Technologies' RescueMe, and Aveo's Attune online PC support tools. Today he still bears the torch of trying to re-create TuneUp.com so all PC users can get expert help and tools. Jim lives in Silicon Valley, California, with his wife, Kathy, who is also working in high-tech (in fact they met through a request she made of their company help desk for remote access support to the company network). When he's not at the keyboard or hammering together some mini-remodeling project you will probably find him climbing any one of several Bay Area radio towers, installing and repairing amateur radio systems for public service/disaster communications.

Contributors

No book can begin or be completed without help from numerous resources and the keen eye of several talented individuals. A hacks book is no different, as it draws from many people and their challenges with whatever topic we're addressing. While there are many, many sharp minds who have shared knowledge and ideas towards this work, three individuals stand out as much for their unwitting role as contributors as for their constant and severe challenges to me to make this book better topic by topic and word by word:

Scott Spanbauer allowed me to write a few words with him for *PC World*, and because of his reputation and quality work I suggested he become one of the technical reviewers on this project. Not only did Scott review the heck out of what I'd written (I'm still trying to get the red ink off my monitor), he at least inadvertently if not intentionally contributed a lot of guidance, ideas, and pure hacks to this project. Look for Scott in *PC World* and other venues and enjoy!

Lincoln Spector, a cowriter when I was still writing my Windows columns, brings not only a reputation for having a keen user's-perspective eye but a tremendous sense of personality to technical subjects. I wanted Lincoln on-board as another technical editor, and I got that and much more. Adding a hack suggestion here and there, he also had questions about other possible hacks and spawned more and better entries. If you get a chance, thank him for his contributions and do look up his "Gigglebytes" columns!

Brian Jepson of O'Reilly turned out to be more than a project editor, and I swear he encouraged Scott and Lincoln to be merciless with their reviews, and then joined right in with them at my expense, but to the betterment of this work. Having good editors is both a blessing and a curse, but all for the better. They make you work your butt off and then hand you back clean, polished, presentable material you don't mind showing your friends and family, can be especially proud of when it appears on store shelves, and be happier still when someone takes a copy off the shelf and home with them. Brian contributed more than editing and project management; he contributed several hacks of his own and greatly refined the ones I humbly submitted.

Acknowledgments

First, to my friend Rory, whom I met over ham radio. He taught me what a PC is and what to do with it, providing knowledge and whetting an appetite no one else could. We took a leap of faith together concocting our first PC book, *The PC Users Survival Guide* (M & T Books). (I think his response to my "We're going to write a book about this" was "Who's we?") We made it through another project, *Troubleshooting Your PC* (Wiley), breaking new ground for all involved, driving inspiration, and creating a momentum that anything is possible, doable, and enjoyable. I carry that spirit of friendship with me every day and am blessed to know such a good person. No amount of "thank you's" can ever fully express my gratitude, but I do thank you very much!

Kudos to Mike Todd, another early mentor and PC community builder. Working with Mike on The Source and other early online systems gave me a sense of belonging and worth to the greater worldwide community of PC users and technology. Today others manage and participate in spin-off communities, but Mike is a pioneer who truly created the first online PC forums. He deserves unique credit for a lot of what has become the helpful PC community spirit we enjoy on the Web today. That community spirit has been apparent in two of our collaborative PC works with Rory, of which we are very proud. I am quite thankful for the opportunity to work with and be inspired by such talents.

Speaking of pioneers, there is Gordon Kraft, founder of DiagSoft. Gordon had the guts and tenacity to gather together some of the sharpest programmers around and literally create the PC diagnostic and utility software business we all benefit from today. He also had the fortitude and tolerance to take me into the fold and let me be a little crazy in our efforts to support our customers and create exciting new products. PC support by remote control was fermented in our minds and created at our hands. Gordon didn't exactly create a PC monster in me, but he did feed and nourish it. While he's been hoping to "capture my brain on disk" (the PC skills part, that is), I'm still trying to sort it all out and index it. Hopefully I've done well with this work.

For further inspiration, and for trying to keep my name on the cover of something on store shelves besides the *National Enquirer*, Judy B deserves armloads of credit and appreciation. As my acquisitions editor she literally handed me two previous book projects, *IRQ, DMA & I/O* (MIS:Press), a brain dump of PC configuration references, and *Installing, Troubleshooting and Repairing Wireless Networks* (McGraw-Hill). No one seems to buy or read either of them, but they were fun projects made most enjoyable by her upbeat encouragement and friendship throughout.

Along the winding, wandering journey of my PC "career" have been many exceptional, talented, skilled, motivating, and inspiring people: the "crews" at DiagSoft and Quarterdeck, two of the finest software companies ever; the people behind the ideas of further automating tech support and PC help at TuneUp.com, CST, and Aveo; the amazingly sharp and inspired but I think as yet unfulfilled talent at Phoenix Technologies/Award Software who make the code that starts our PCs every day; and all of the vendors and products in between Acronis and Xircom. Every one of you gives us something to challenge us and something to accomplish every day that we use our PCs. And, of course, to the millions of users around the world, from the hundreds I fix PCs for (and the ones I do it with—Marina, Richard, Kevin, Jeremy, Philip, Nopporn, and David) every day to those who correspond occasionally by email seeking answers. The PC significantly changed at least a part of our world; I'm just here trying to make some of it better.

Significant acknowledgment goes to Robert Luhn, one of my editors of several years with Computer User and CNET, someone I consider a good friend and certainly a generous mentor in encouraging, promoting, and extending my usefulness as a writer. Without Robert's insight, suggestions, recruitment, and probably no small selling job, this book and many of my other contributions to PC users would not have been possible. Thanks for believing in me!

Last and certainly not least, in fact perhaps the greatest credit goes to my wife, Kathy. She must think I stretched this project out as an excuse to avoid the growing list of home improvement projects, but honestly I didn't. She "signed up" for only a couple months of me living in my "cave," paying more attention to my herd of keyboards and PC parts than anything else, but little did she or I know that my editors and tech reviewers were determined to get the best and most out of me. I hope you know how much I appreciate you and how proud I am to have you in my life!

Preface

More, better, faster, cheaper, easier, cooler, safer. All of these and more capture our desire to understand and get the most out of the investment we've made in our PCs. From making a PC boot faster, to improving its reliability, to using multiple operating systems, to being able to recover quickly when something goes wrong, the PC hacks in this book will improve your PC experience and make you a lot more computer-savvy.

Why PC Hacks?

The term *hacking* has a bad reputation in the press. They use it to refer to someone who breaks into systems or wreaks havoc with computers as their weapon. Among people who write code, though, the term *hack* refers to a "quick-and-dirty" solution to a problem or a clever way to get something done. And the term *hacker* is taken very much as a compliment, indicating that someone is being *creative*, having the technical chops to get things done. The Hacks series is an attempt to reclaim the word, document the good ways people are hacking, and pass the hacker ethic of creative participation on to the uninitiated. Seeing how others approach systems and problems is often the quickest way to learn about a new technology.

How to Use This Book

You can read this book from cover to cover if you like, but each hack stands on its own, so feel free to browse and jump to the different sections that interest you most. If there's a prerequisite you need to know about, a cross-reference will guide you to the right hack.

Since you'll be hacking your PC, and it probably contains all your data, never more than ever are you most strongly encouraged to follow three basic tenets of PC ownership: back up, Back Up, and BACK UP! While we won't intentionally lead you through a hack that will harm your system, life with a PC is not a matter of *if* your system will crash, but *when*. Backups, system restore points, software and hardware installation disks, and printouts of hard-to-remember or obscure details are very handy to keep safe but close at hand should you need them.

Pay careful attention to the details and precautions for each hack. Not all hacks will work with all PCs or installed hardware. After you've done your backup it will be to your benefit to gather all your manuals and driver disks or visit the web sites for your PC and peripheral vendors to get current documentation and drivers.

If you do not know all the details of your system—video, network, sound, mouse, printers, scanner, etc.—download, install, run, and print the results from a comprehensive system information utility program. SiSoftware's Sandra is quite comprehensive and readily available from *http://www.sisoftware.net*. This information will help you decide if your PC, add-ins, or peripherals qualify for a particular hack or not.

If your PC or any of its components are under manufacturer's warranty, you should think twice or three times about the impact of hacking on it. If a hack could void your warranty, you probably want to wait until the warranty expires before trying it.

Armed with these considerations and preparations, start with the aspect of your PC that bugs you the most—a slow hard drive, sluggish boot-up, choppy video, or a lingering I/O port problem—and dig in to the appropriate chapter.

How This Book Is Organized

Whether you are a hard-core techie, just learning the ropes of building and tinkering with your own systems, or trying to figure out why Widget A does not work with Widgets B, C, D, and so on, there is a hack in here for you. You will find a hack for every aspect of your PC from power supply to mouse port, video to network connections, and have the chance to learn a lot about each section of a PC along the way. It has been my goal to help make your PC more reliable, economical, and effective whether it is five years or five days old. Without dwelling too much on the past and the foundations that make the PC what it is today, you will discover subtle nuances, and maybe a few "trade secrets," that will dispel common PC myths about how things work, or don't, and why. Each major element of a PC and specifics about them are covered in the following ten chapters:

Chapter 1, Basic System Board Hacks

This chapter covers the intricacies of normal and quirky system board behavior, dealing with boot-up passwords, boards that won't boot, booting faster, BIOS upgrades, and adding or changing a boot-up graphic.

Chapter 2, Basic System Board Setup

From how to get into your BIOS setup program to what to do when you get there, the subtle and not-so-subtle aspects of what all those BIOS parameters do and cannot do. Master those drive, I/O port, Plug and Play, and power management parameters with ease.

Chapter 3, CPU Hacks

This chapter is where the heart of your PC starts racing. This is where you determine if you have a CPU and system board you can overclock, learn how to choose components that can be sped up, and how to turbocharge them. You'll also see how to improve the cooling of your CPU so it will stand up to turbocharged speeds.

Chapter 4, Memory Hacks

A fast, stable CPU will meet its first speed bump if you haven't got enough RAM or if the RAM you have is chugging along like a snail. You need to feed your CPU, operating system, and data enough RAM to let the system achieve its potential, and here you'll find recommendations for how much is enough and how much can be too much. RAM can be sped up and optimized to match your CPU byte for byte once you learn and apply the right parameters to get it off the starting line and handling all those speeding bits.

Chapter 5, Disk Hacks

Hard drives used to be easy. Either you had one or you didn't. When you got one, all you had were limited options for installation and configuration. In this chapter you'll see all of the options in today's PCs, hard drives, and operating systems, which offer dozens of combinations of capacity, performance, partitioning, formatting, and filesystems to suit your needs and learn how to select, install, and configure a proper storage system.

Chapter 6, Disk Drive Performance Hacks

Choosing the right hard drive system reduces the PC's most significant bottleneck—disk storage performance. This chapter shows you all those hard drive ratings and parameters, then how to get the most out of what you have with simple cabling changes, operating system parameters, and interface and drive upgrades.

Chapter 7, Video Hacks

What you see may not be all you can get. Today's PC viewer wants video quality that meets or exceeds that of full-motion high-definition television. PC gamers yearn for maximum frames-per-second performance. "Frames are life," especially when fighting the visually superior, ultra-agile Galactigons wielding only a K-Bar knife and an early year 2021 model focused gamma-laser torch. If you can't see them coming to get you then you cannot stop them. Fast video is one of a handful of aspects that define high-quality video—you want smooth textures, crisp edges, vibrant colors, and no hint of pixels or choppiness. Choosing the right video card by the numbers and then cranking the numbers up is what this chapter is all about.

Chapter 8, I/O Device Hacks

Get out the soldering iron and magnifying glass, or keep the one you have warm from performing our CPU hacks. Seriously, we cut a few wires in one crafty hack in this chapter, then we're back to switches, jumpers, BIOS, and Windows parameters to make sure your PC configuration follows the PC BIOS and Plug and Play rules for getting more and conflict-free I/O ports.

Chapter 9, Boot-Up Hacks

If you're not happy with just one operating system then this is the chapter for you. In here are hacks covering everything from DOS to Linux, and several ways to allow your system to shift "personalities" nearly on the fly.

Chapter 10, Configuring a New PC

This is our "pro" chapter. Most PC problems are preventable with a little tender loving care. No, scratch that: with a lot of deliberate proactive, protective, preventive, and preemptive measures. From virus protection to firewalls to backups, you'll see how to cover yourself against common PC predators and recover from the damage they can cause. Apply these hacks to all your PCs, new or old, and you'll be glad you did.

Conventions

The following is a list of the typographical conventions used in this book:

Italics

Used to indicate URLs, filenames, filename extensions, and the names of directories/folders. For example, a path in the filesystem will appear as *C:\Windows\System32*.

Constant width

> Used to show code examples, the contents of files, and console output, as well as the names of variables, commands, and other code excerpts.

Constant width bold

> Used to indicate text that should be typed by the user.

Constant width italic

> Used in code examples to show sample text to be replaced with your own values.

Color

> The second color is used to indicate a cross-reference to other hacks within the text.

You should pay special attention to notes set apart from the text with the following icons:

> This is a tip, suggestion, or general note. It contains useful supplementary information about the topic at hand.

> This is a warning or note of caution, often indicating that your money or your privacy might be at risk.

The thermometer icons, found next to each hack, indicate the relative complexity of the hack:

 beginner   moderate   expert

Using Code Examples

This book is here to help you get your job done. In general, you may use the code in this book in your programs and documentation. You do not need to contact us for permission unless you're reproducing a significant portion of the code. For example, writing a program that uses several chunks of code from this book does not require permission. Selling or distributing a CD-ROM of examples from O'Reilly books *does* require permission. Answering a question by citing this book and quoting example code does not require permission. Incorporating a significant amount of example code from this book into your product's documentation *does* require permission.

We appreciate, but do not require, attribution. An attribution usually includes the title, author, publisher, and ISBN. For example: "*PC Hacks* by Jim Aspinwall. Copyright 2004 O'Reilly Media, Inc., 0-596-00748-5."

If you feel your use of code examples falls outside fair use or the permission given above, feel free to contact us at *permissions@oreilly.com*.

Disclaimer

Much of the information contained in this book is based on personal knowledge and experience. While I believe that the information contained herein is correct, I accept no responsibility for its validity. The hardware designs and descriptive text contained herein are provided for educational purposes only. It is the responsibility of the reader to independently verify all information. Original manufacturer's data should be used at all times when implementing a design.

The author (Jim Aspinwall), contributors, and O'Reilly Media, Inc., make no warranty, representation, or guarantee regarding the suitability of any hardware or software described herein for any particular purpose, nor do they assume any liability arising out of the application or use of any product, system, or software, and specifically disclaim any and all liability, including, without limitation, consequential or incidental damages. The hardware and software described herein are not designed, intended, nor authorized for use in any application intended to support or sustain life or any other application in which the failure of a system could create a situation in which personal injury, death, loss of data or information, or damages to property may occur. Should the reader implement any design described herein for any application, the reader shall indemnify and hold the author, contributors, O'Reilly Media, Inc., and their respective shareholders, officers, employees, and distributors harmless against all claims, costs, damages and expenses, and reasonable solicitor fees arising out of, directly or indirectly, any claim of personal injury, death, loss of data or information, or damages to property associated with such unintended or unauthorized use.

How to Contact O'Reilly

We have tested and verified the information in this book to the best of our ability, but you may find that features have changed (or even that we have made mistakes!). As a reader of this book, you can help us to improve future editions by sending us your feedback. Please let us know about any errors, inaccuracies, bugs, misleading or confusing statements, and typos that you find anywhere in this book.

Please also let us know what we can do to make this book more useful to you. We take your comments seriously and will try to incorporate reasonable suggestions into future editions. You can write to us at:

O'Reilly Media, Inc.
1005 Gravenstein Highway North
Sebastopol, CA 95472
(800) 998-9938 (in the U.S. or Canada)
(707) 829-0515 (international/local)
(707) 829-0104 (fax)

To ask technical questions or to comment on the book, send email to:

bookquestions@oreilly.com

The web site for *PC Hacks* lists examples, errata, and plans for future editions. You can find this page at:

http://www.oreilly.com/catalog/pchks

For more information about this book and others, see the O'Reilly web site:

http://www.oreilly.com

Got a Hack?

To explore Hacks books online or to contribute a hack for future titles, visit:

http://hacks.oreilly.com

## CHAPTER ONE

Basic System Board Hacks
Hacks 1–10

With the exception of your PC's unhackable power supply, hacking your PC starts with the lowest level of detail within your system board—from how fast the clock is that makes the CPU tick to how the I/O bus is configured for your hard drives and peripherals. Hacking starts with the *Basic Input/ Output System* (BIOS) setup program, which affects the CPU, memory, chipset, and peripherals.

While some PC users think in terms of exotic mice, expansive flat-panel LCD screens, and high download bandwidth speeds, there are myriad mysteriously-named parameters and features within the system BIOS. These parameters may control everything from CPU and memory clocking to I/O device configurations and system passwords. The right amount of parameter tweaking at the BIOS level can squeeze another few million-instructions-per-second (MIPS) or microseconds of faster video or hard drive performance out of the bones of your system.

Of course, like anything functional, the right bones or foundation elements have to be in place—in this case reliable and capable system components (CPU, chipset, and memory) and a BIOS, the essential innards of any PC, that can be tweaked. Tweaking or hacking a system board is done with software settings in the BIOS setup program, hardware jumpers, or dual-in-line-package (DIP) switches, so you must have the manual for your system board handy to be able to locate the correct jumpers and switches. I recommend you also have a small flashlight handy so you can see, as well as a pair of needle-nosed pliers to move jumpers around, and the right screwdriver to be able to get into your PC's case. Other than these tools, all you need is a steady hand and attention paid to the keystrokes needed to navigate your PC's setup program.

Before you hack the system board, CPU, BIOS, peripherals, or operating system, there are a few basic things I need to cover to get you out of any trouble you can get yourself into with the hacks in this and subsequent chapters. Hacking your system BIOS has potential dangers: one slipup and things can quit working. Fortunately there are some easy ways out of most mistakes made at this level of system hacking.

Your PC's system board typically comes to you "factory fresh" without any tweaks or parameters set to abnormal values. Once you start reconfiguring the system, almost anything can happen—from not being able to boot up at all, to partial boot and system crash, to partial boot and all else is pending a password you forgot or never knew. These hacks will get you around a couple of common mistakes and problems that will inevitably come up as you work with numerous PCs.

HACK #1   Lock Others Out of Your Computer

Lock out unauthorized users from tinkering with your BIOS or even starting the operating system.

Of course, the opposite of a password that keeps *you* out of your system is a password that keeps *others* out of your system. The BIOS in some PCs may provide no password protection at all, a single password that controls access to BIOS setup and allows the system to boot up, or two passwords—one for access to BIOS setup (a Setup or Supervisor password) and bootup, and the other to control access to booting up only (a User or Boot password). To set a password for your system, look in the setup menus for security settings, as shown in Figure 1-1.

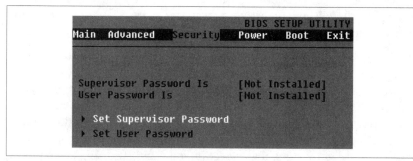

Figure 1-1. BIOS and boot passwords can protect you from hackers

A User or Boot password keeps the system from booting up—a measure of intrusion and system hacking protection. A System or Supervisor password keeps lurkers out of your BIOS settings, and keeps them from changing the User/Boot password.

If you are going to set a User or Boot password, be sure you also set a Setup or Supervisor password so the BIOS settings and boot password cannot be changed and so someone cannot set a Supervisor password to keep you out of the system, requiring you to bypass the BIOS password [Hack #2]. Because there is a back door, the only way to prevent attackers from circumventing the password is to use a case that can be locked shut with a key or a locking cable.

HACK
#2

Bypass the BIOS Password

Recover from a CMOS memory-affecting virus or work around a boot-time password by making BIOS forget all it once knew.

A PC goes through a process when it is first turned on: the Power-On Self-Test, or P.O.S.T. Some system boards provide security measures [Hack #1] that demand a password before beginning the P.O.S.T. process or allowing you into the BIOS setup program.

The original IBM-PC (1981) did not provide any security measures or a BIOS setup program; all it had was a P.O.S.T. If you needed to configure a PC, you did it with switches and jumpers. A program to set up the system BIOS and configuration did not come along until the IBM-PC/AT (1984), and it had to be run from a special boot-up diskette. The idea of providing a user interface and access to the system configuration settings within the BIOS did not come along until about 1986. Today no PC system is made without this valuable built-in setup feature. Eventually, the security feature of password-protecting access to the system came along.

If, after turning on your PC, you are prompted for a password instead of greeted with a fancy logo screen or the technical gibberish that suggests the system is getting ready to let you use it, then a security feature has been turned on that we call a "pre-boot password." Without the right password to get past this point, the system is basically dead in the water—game over, do not pass go and collect $200—unless or until you reset the BIOS setting. But how do you do that without getting past the password to the setup program?

This hack is also very effective for putting the system board back into "factory stupid" mode where it knows nothing about your system components and forgets all of your parameter tweaks. This is very useful if you've performed a hack that renders the system unbootable or unstable.

Bypass the BIOS Password

The goal is to get the system to forget that it needs a password and forget what the password was. The password data is stored with the rest of the system configuration data in a small amount of memory that is kept alive using a small battery or internal power cell. To clear out the data, you need to remove the power from this memory element. This means the system will also lose any system configuration that was saved. You'll need to later reconfigure the system parameters so you can boot your operating system.

For this and many subsequent hacks, you will be working with electrical components inside your PC. We want you to get through the entire book and enjoy your computer for a long time without risk of electrical shock or component damage. When the cover is off your PC and you are removing or adding components—be they add-in cards, RAM chips, CPUs, or fans—especially when you are handling the screws to hold things in place, *ALWAYS* turn the PC's power *OFF* and *unplug the power cord* from the back of the PC.

Disconnecting the power cord removes the risk of exposure to high voltages and accidentally turning the power to the system board on. Disconnecting the power cord also allows the PC chassis to become ungrounded, which reduces the potential difference between any static charge in your body and the chassis so static shocks are less likely.

It is also recommended that you use an anti-static wrist strap connected to the PC's chassis for further protection of delicate electronic components.

To perform this hack you will need:

- A #1 or #2 Phillips-head screwdriver, or (less likely) a T-15 TORX driver or a 1/4" hex nutdriver, to open the case
- Needle-nosed pliers if you are working with jumpers
- A small flashlight or headlamp

With tools at hand, perform the following steps:

1. Turn the PC off (this means a total shutdown, not merely standby or hibernate mode) and disconnect the AC power cord.

2. Remove the cover from your system (this step may require tools, undoing a thumbscrew, or flipping a latch or two).

3. Refer to the user manual for the motherboard to find out how to "reset CMOS" memory. You may also find a label for specific jumper or switch settings marked on the system board.

4. Change the switch setting or jumper position to a specific position or remove the jumper entirely as prescribed in the manual to clear or reset the CMOS memory.

5. Wait 20–30 seconds for the memory to clear out from lack of power.

6. After 20–30 seconds put the switch or jumper the way it was before for normal use.

7. Reconnect the power cord and start up the system to see if the settings have changed to defaults.

8. Shut the PC down, disconnect the power cord, replace the cover, reconnect the power, and power up the PC.

9. Enter the BIOS setup program to configure the system as needed. This may include setting the date and time, selecting disk drive parameters, and selecting which devices the system uses to boot up with first.

If your system does not have a "reset CMOS" jumper or switch , the only option is to locate and remove the coin-style battery cell (or on some very old PCs, the battery pack), as shown in Figure 1-2, that provides the power to the CMOS memory.

Figure 1-2. System board with coin-style battery used to retain CMOS memory

Follow Steps 1 and 2 above, locate the battery, and remove it. Leave the battery out of the system for 20–30 seconds, replace it, and start up the system. The CMOS memory in some systems may retain settings longer than others. If the CMOS memory does not clear and you're still stuck, you may need to leave the battery out for several hours before reinstalling it.Once the system is able to perform P.O.S.T. and to start booting up the system, you will need to get into the Setup program for the BIOS and make a few basic adjustments, such as:

- Setting the date and time
- Selecting auto-detect or manually setting specific parameters for IDE hard drives
- Setting the boot-device order—diskette drive, hard drive, CD-ROM, etc.

If you expect to perform more hacks with jumpers, switches, cables, chips, or disk drives, you'll probably find it convenient to leave the cover off your PC, but beware: we do not want to cause more trouble than we're trying to solve. You could be exposing yourself to dangerous voltages (inside the power supply) or exposing the internal wires and connections to disk drives and plug-in cards to your tools, screws, and other wires that could come in contact with them. At this stage, spilling your favorite beverage or dropping your tools anywhere inside the PC chassis is not advised.

> You may find one of many possible "backdoor" passwords for your BIOS that allow you access to the system setup program and bypass boot passwords at either of two web sites: *http://www.labmice.techtarget.com/articles/BIOS_hacks.html* or *http://www.pwcrack.com/bios.shtml*.

HACK #3 Recover a BIOS That Won't Boot

Recover from hacking your BIOS into an unbootable state by starting from scratch with safe defaults for the BIOS settings.

The P.O.S.T. was designed to do many things, from taking inventory of the system components to testing them. Through years of PC development the P.O.S.T. has been modified to accommodate many new and special features of system boards, new CPUs and chipsets, a variety of disk drive types, myriad Plug and Play devices, and USB ports, as well as when the BIOS turns over control to which type of bootable device and operating system. Adding the ability to configure various settings has put the BIOS and P.O.S.T. at risk of tampering and corruption.

If your PC simply will not leave P.O.S.T. and start to boot up an operating system, or if it begins to boot up an operating system but you're getting "no operating system found" or memory errors, or the operating system locks up before you've had a chance to use it, chances are something is amiss in the

BIOS settings. It's possible that your system BIOS has gotten really confused by an odd system or power glitch, configuration settings you changed such as overclocking or memory timings, or even a rare CMOS-attacking virus.

Your best bet under these circumstances is to reset the BIOS into a "safe" or default mode, one without special tweaks, adjustments, timing changes, and so forth. You have two choices to effect a default configuration of the BIOS. The first is to clear the BIOS configuration memory [Hack #2] so that things start up fresh with no unusual settings.

 Access to the BIOS setup program varies widely between different BIOS vendors and system board makers. You may see a hint like "Press F2 to enter Setup" appear on your screen as the system runs through P.O.S.T., or the proper key combination may be hidden behind the PC maker's graphic logo at startup. Refer to your system's manual or to Table 1-1 for access to the most common BIOS setup programs.

This hack provides another way, which is relevant if you can access the system setup program, by whatever magical combination of button pushing or keystrokes is appropriate for your system board. Table 1-1 shows typical keys used to access the setup program for various systems' BIOS.

Table 1-1. Typical keystrokes used to access BIOS setup programs

System maker/BIOS brand	Keystrokes to enter setup
American Megatrends/AMI BIOS	<ESC>
Award BIOS	<DEL>
COMPAQ	<F10>
Dell	<F2>
Gateway	Varies by brand of BIOS
HP	<F1>
IBM	<F1>
Intel	<F2>
Phoenix	<F1>
Miscellaneous/Various	<Ctrl>+S
	<Ctrl>+<Alt>+S

Once you have entered the BIOS setup program, you're going to be looking for a menu selection or key to press to set factory or "safe" defaults for all of the parameters. In some versions of Award BIOS this may be done using the

F5 or F6 keys. Figure 1-3 shows a Phoenix BIOS for an Intel system board for which the safe defaults can be restored by pressing the F9 key.

```
←→       Select Menu
↑↓       Select Item
Tab      Select Field
Enter    Select ▶ Sub-Menu
F9       Setup Defaults
F10      Save and Exit
ESC      Exit
```

Figure 1-3. The F9 key resets the BIOS to default (safe) settings

If there is no single keystroke to set all of the parameters to defaults, you will have to accomplish this the second way, by checking each and every parameter and changing them all to default or "auto" settings. Some setup programs provide some very terse "help" on the screen to give you an indication of what the setting should be. If the setup program is of no help, you should refer to the manual that came with your system board or documentation on the manufacturer's web site. If all else fails, you will need to take extreme measures [Hack #2].

You may have to make some minor adjustments in the BIOS settings to allow the system to boot up properly, and if you wish to continue tweaking after that, change only one setting at a time and make note of what you change each time so you can determine which tweak causes the problem. The technical term for this process is *trial and error*!

Boot Faster

HACK #4

Some of the stuff your computer does at boot time is of no use. Disable those features to boot faster.

The system BIOS does a lot of work in the P.O.S.T. phase before it gets your system to the point where it reads boot-up information from a disk drive to load an operating system. Some of the things that happen in P.O.S.T. have nothing to do with system performance other than impeding the process of getting to the operating system to run your applications. Intel, AMD, AMI, Award/Phoenix, and the PC manufacturers were aware of this waste of time, evaluated the events involved, and in many cases took steps to reduce the number of items and the amount of time the startup process takes. To that end there are a handful of changes you can make in order to boot up faster:

Disable Extended Tests

Many systems offer the option of allowing an in-depth test of system memory and components (an extended test) or zipping through the system and getting to bootup as quickly as possible. With RAM as reliable and economical as it is (and having so much of it) and having Plug and Play operating systems like Windows and, to some extent, current versions of Linux, the Quick Test mode is more than adequate, and preferred for faster boot times. This parameter is shown in Figure 1-4 and specifies the depth, and thus the time involved, for testing system RAM and finding and checking the basic components of the system—COM and LPT ports and such.

```
                                  BIOS SETUP UTILITY
 Main   Advanced    Security    Power   Boot   Exit


    Quiet Boot                   [Disabled]
    Intel(R) Rapid BIOS Boot     [Disabled]

    Scan User Flash Area         [Disabled]
    After Power Failure          [Stays Off]
    On Modem Ring                [Stay Off]
    On LAN                       [Stay Off]
    On PME                       [Stay Off]
    On ACPI S5                   [Stay Off]
```

Figure 1-4. Settings for the fastest P.O.S.T.

Configure Drive Detection

Most BIOSes provide the capability to automatically search for, identify, and configure different types of drives across four possible IDE and Serial ATA connections. This parameter setting usually shows up as AUTO in the IDE configuration choices. If you leave the parameter for all four possible IDE or Serial ATA devices set to AUTO, your BIOS will waste a lot of time searching for nonexistent devices. For faster boot times set the parameter to NONE as shown in Figure 1-5 for any unused interfaces and connections that have nothing attached to them.

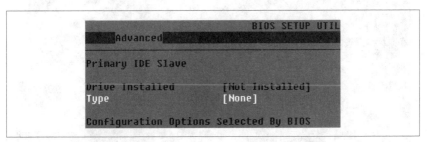

```
                                  BIOS SETUP UTIL
      Advanced

 Primary IDE Slave

 Drive Installed          [Not Installed]
 Type                     [None]

 Configuration Options Selected By BIOS
```

Figure 1-5. Set any unused IDE devices to NONE to speed boot time

User BIOS Regions

This parameter, if it exists in your setup program, instructs the BIOS to search upper DOS memory (between 640 KB and 1 MB) for the existence of additional BIOS extension code. Such code exists on SCSI host adapters and on network cards that provide the ability to boot from a network server. Most PC users will never encounter a SCSI interface, nor systems configured to boot over a LAN through a network card, so there is no need to set this parameter to anything but No, Off, or Disabled and save yourself a couple more seconds at boot time.

Display a Boot-Time Graphic

Many computers will display a graphic at boot time. Make it one of your own.

Intel and most of the PC OEMs want to remind you who made the system, so they have built in a boot-time graphic as seen in Figure 1-6. Boot-time graphics are an alternative to the technical bits and bytes that have traditionally appeared on PC boot screens. Displaying the graphic takes extra time in order to load up the graphic image stored in the BIOS memory chip and configure the video to display graphics. As techies are interested in faster performance, product logos are not of much interest.

Figure 1-6. An Intel boot-time graphic hides the technical details of P.O.S.T.

If your system BIOS is stored in FLASH RAM (instead of a conventional old-style EPROM), it may be possible to load your own graphic into the BIOS chip. To perform this hack you need a BIOS that supports boot-time graphics and the appropriate software programs to make the changes and write them into your BIOS FLASH ROM chip. Most implementations of Award BIOS Versions 4.5 and up support boot-time graphics display. You will need a couple of software programs, as follows:

- A graphics program to either create a new graphics file or convert an existing one to a 640×480×16-color uncompressed BMP graphic file for display at bootup (I didn't say it would or had to be an impressive graphic, just a graphic file)

- The appropriate *AWDFLASH.EXE* program for your system board (from the manufacturer's web site)

- A program to add the graphics file to your BIOS—either the CBROM program from *http://www.stormpages.com/crazyape/cbrom.html* or AwardMod through *http://sourceforge.net/projects/awardmod/*.

With these tools available, proceed through the following steps to use CBROM to modify your BIOS file:

1. Make or obtain a bootable DOS or Windows 95-Me startup diskette.

2. On a blank diskette, copy the *AWDFLASH.EXE* program (approximately 28 KB), the CBROM program (78 KB) and your graphics file (approximately 16 KB), with enough room for two copies of your BIOS (256 KB each).

3. Boot up with the diskette from Step 1. When you finally get a DOS prompt, change diskettes so the diskette of Step 2 is in the diskette drive.

4. Run the AWDFLASH program and follow the instructions to make a copy of your BIOS file on the diskette. Exit the AWDFLASH program back to the DOS prompt.

5. Make a copy of the BIOS file you just saved so you'll have two copies— one to tinker with and one as a backup file.

6. Run the CBROM program to merge the graphic file into the BIOS file, substituting the appropriate filenames in a single command line as follows:

   ```
   cbrom yourbios.awd /logo yourlogo.bmp [Enter]
   ```

7. Run the AWDFLASH program and follow the instructions to load your new BIOS file into the BIOS FLASH ROM.

8. Remove the diskette from the drive and restart the system to enjoy your new boot-up look.

If you choose to use the AwardMod program, which runs in Windows, follow Steps 1–5 above, skip the rest, and then follow these steps:

1. Restart your system to Windows and run the AwardMod program, shown in Figure 1-7.

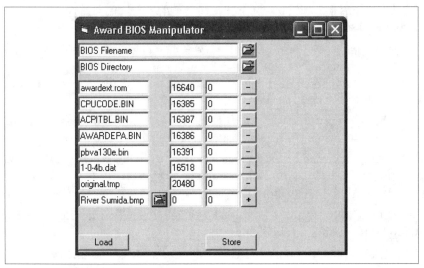

Figure 1-7. The AwardMod program lets you see which feature modules are in your BIOS and add your logo

2. Select the BIOS filename and directory (on the diskette), and then click the Load button to begin working with the BIOS file.

3. At the bottom of the listing you'll see an open file folder icon. Click this icon and browse to find and open your logo BMP file. The filename will appear in the listing.

4. Click the Store button to merge the logo into a new BIOS file and save it, then exit the program. Make sure the new BIOS file is on the diskette.

5. Replace the diskette with a bootable diskette, and then reboot the system to DOS.

6. Switch to the diskette with the FLASH program and new BIOS file.

7. Run the AWDFLASH program and follow the instructions to load your new BIOS file into the BIOS FLASH ROM.

8. Remove the diskette from the drive and restart the system to enjoy your new boot-up look.

The logo-replacement process involves rewriting a major portion of the data stored in the FLASH ROM containing your BIOS. Replacing the original startup graphic with your own certainly adds a bit of class to your system and identifies you as the "creator" of your PC, but it is not without risks.

Make sure you use a stable AC process power source with an Uninterruptible Power Supply (UPS) and that nothing disturbs the system during the FLASH process or your BIOS will be destroyed **[Hack #10]**.

Be sure to make a backup of your BIOS using the appropriate FLASH ROM tools provided by your system board maker before hacking into logo land. You'll need the backup file to load the original BIOS back into the system if you make a mistake.

HACK #6 Configure Boot Device Order

Don't wait for the floppy disk or CD-ROM to time out before the system boots.

One advantage of modern BIOS and hardware capabilities is that they allow you to boot up from something other than a diskette or hard drive. BIOS can now fetch and run an operating system from an appropriately capable and configured LAN adapter or a bootable CD-ROM. You can tell the BIOS which devices it should try to boot up from, and in what order.

For a faster boot time you probably want your hard drive to be the first device in the list, as shown in Figure 1-8, ignoring the presence of diskettes or bootable CD-ROMs, although some BIOSes will detect the presence of a bootable CD-ROM and offer the option of booting off the CD regardless of the boot device order you set. Skipping the process of looking for a bootable diskette or CD-ROM by telling the BIOS to boot from the IDE hard drive first can shave anywhere from a few seconds to tens of seconds off your boot time.

```
1st Boot Device        [IDE-HDD]
2nd Boot Device        [ATAPI CDROM]
3rd Boot Device        [Floppy]
4th Boot Device        [Disabled]

▶ IDE Drive Configuration
```

Figure 1-8. Booting from your IDE hard drive first saves time

If you do choose to put the hard drive first in the boot order, you will not be able to boot up from a diskette or CD-ROM. You can come back to this parameter to change the boot device order to boot from a device other than the hard drive, as shown in Figure 1-9, when you need to run a diagnostic program, load a new image onto the hard drive using a program like Symantec's GHOST, or reinstall the operating system.

```
1st Boot Device         [ATAPI CDROM]
2nd Boot Device         [Floppy]
3rd Boot Device         [IDE-HDD]
4th Boot Device         [Disabled]

  ▶ IDE Drive Configuration
```

Figure 1-9. A typical first boot device configuration

If you want to boot from a drive connected to a USB port, you must have a BIOS that supports booting from USB ZIP, USB FDD, USB HDD, or alternate devices as one of the boot options.

Set Your Clock Back

HACK #7

Avoid or test date- and time-related features of your programs by setting the system clock back or ahead in the BIOS.

Setting the system date and time backwards or forwards is one way to see how a program behaves on different dates, ensure that a scheduled event runs, or make sure a program expires when it is supposed to.

> This hack is most useful for testing purposes only. In normal use it is not practical to hold your system clock back or force it forward because scheduled events such as backups, virus scans and updates, file records, and data such as email arrival and send times will become very confused and may not function properly.
>
> This hack will probably not let you bypass the expiration dates of trial software, Windows XP activation, or other rights-management technologies, as many of these programs keep track of radical time setting changes or number of uses in the registry or protected files. I certainly do not advocate such deceptive practices.

You might think that waiting until the operating system is done loading and then using the date and time functions at a DOS prompt or within Windows would be sufficient to fool a specific program, but some programs may not be easily fooled from within Windows.

Don't wait for the operating system; make these time-altering changes in the BIOS setup program to ensure that the operating system starts with the date or time you want—date and time setting is a basic function within setup. Be careful of changing the date if you're going to run your real, live accounting software (or other time-specific programs you rely on) or you could end up unbalancing the books.

If you are using the Windows Time service or one of many "atomic clock" programs to obtain an accurate date and time from one of the many online time servers, be sure to disable these in Windows before resetting the date and time in BIOS. Follow these steps to disable the Windows Time service:

1. Go to Start→Control Panel→Administrative Tools.
2. Double-click Services.
3. Scroll down to find Windows Time and either double-click on the service name or right-click and select Properties.
4. At the "Startup type:" box, select Disabled.
5. Click OK to save the value and close the dialog.
6. Restart your PC, and then enter the setup program and adjust the date and time to suit your needs before restarting Windows and running your application or tests.

Avoid the Legacy USB Option

Save yourself from boot-up delays and Windows device detection confusion.

The Legacy USB setting tells the BIOS and operating system to detect and enable USB keyboards and mice in the absence of normal PS/2-port devices. Setting this parameter to Yes, On, or Enabled is important and necessary if you have only a USB keyboard and mouse and need to use them in non-Windows operating systems, such as DOS, OS/2, some self-booting diagnostic/maintenance programs, or the early stages of some Linux setups.

If this parameter is on or enabled and you use a normal PS/2-port connected keyboard, with no USB-connected keyboard attached, Windows 95 and 98 may hang up looking for a USB keyboard that does not exist. Disable or turn this setting off, or you could be fighting with the system for a long time and it will probably win. Your system may also boot up faster if it does not have to waste time looking for a nonexistent device.

If you have a conventional or PS/2 keyboard and mouse, you never need to enable this capability. For Windows 98SE, Me, and XP, which have native USB support built in, you need to make sure this parameter is set to No, Off, or Disabled as shown in Figure 1-10.

```
Audio Device              [Enabled]
LAN Device                [Enabled]
Legacy USB Support        [Disabled]
```

Figure 1-10. Disable Legacy USB Support unless you need to use a USB keyboard in DOS, OS/2, or Linux

Legacy USB is one sadly misunderstood parameter. With USB 2.0 being the current new USB standard, don't be misled into thinking this has something to do with USB 2.0 ports supporting "old" USB 1.1 devices—it does not.

HACK
#9   Hack an Unhackable BIOS

You may be able to find a BIOS upgrade to work around that unhackable, squeaky-clean OEM BIOS.

By this point you may have discovered which feature hacks your BIOS supports, if any. Your PC may contain a "dummied-down" BIOS that provides very few setup options to choose from, while a truly hackable BIOS will give you parameters aplenty.

Most "no name," "white box," do-it-yourself PC system boards come littered with hackable bits through switches, jumpers, or the BIOS. These boards are the subject of the majority of hacks, overclocking, modifications, BIOS upgrades, and just plain "geeking out" on what a PC can be made to do. You'll get hours of enjoyment fiddling with every bit and parameter you can find and perhaps encounter hours or days of frustration if one of your hacks causes you to lose data or massive quantities of that soft, furry stuff atop your head.

If you've got an "OEM system"—one with a recognizable and sustained brand name such as Compaq, Dell, Gateway, HP, IBM, NEC, Sony, or Toshiba—chances are you will not find any parameters worth hacking on—you've got a "dummied down" BIOS.

The unhackable BIOS exists for one very simple reason: the manufacturer wants this PC to work for the broadest, simplest set of PC users. In other words, it does not want to have to bear the cost of support calls related to hacked BIOS settings. Completely understandable if this is a family PC but very frustrating if you're a real techie and wish to experiment.

All hope may not be lost. Many vendors use the same or a similar version of system boards that you can get off the shelf or by mail order. For instance, I have an HP Pavilion system that uses an Asus A7V-M and by coincidence an individually boxed Asus A7V I bought to build into my own case. The HP

Pavilion A7V-M board uses a "dummied down" Award BIOS, while the boxed board uses a fully hackable Award BIOS. The "dummied down" BIOS in the HP does not allow me to change CPU or memory timing, which are critical to the overclocking hacks "Control CPU Clock Speed from the BIOS" [Hack #25] and "Set the CPU Multiplier" [Hack #27].

BIOS upgrades can afford you the benefit of new hacking capabilities, provide fixes to known bugs, or provide support for newer features and hardware such as larger hard drives. Furthermore, these upgrades may come with bootable CD-ROM support that may not be included in the original BIOS.

If the P.O.S.T. display for your system board does not show either the AMI, Award, MR BIOS, or Phoenix brand name as appears in Figure 1-11 when it boots up, you're probably stuck—no hacking allowed. If you do see the brand name of the BIOS you may be in luck, as you may be able to take advantage of this Hack by getting an upgraded BIOS from Unicore at *http://www.unicore.com*.

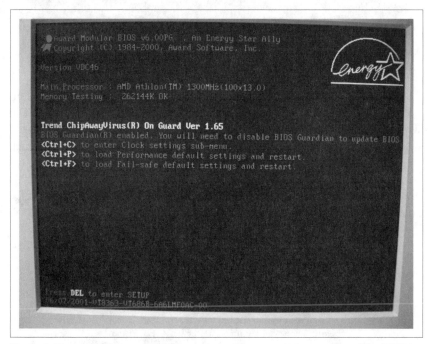

Figure 1-11. A typical Award BIOS boot screen. The true version number of the BIOS is shown in the lower left corner

Unicore provides a small program they call the BIOS Agent that can sniff out details of your present BIOS. They also have a list of tips to identify your

BIOS if their program cannot do it. The best way to identify your Award BIOS is from the absolute version number that appears at the bottom of your screen at boot time, as shown in Figure 1-12. You can press the Pause/Break key on most PCs to stop the system from booting up so you can copy down this information. From that information, their sales department can tell you if they can provide an upgraded BIOS, and perhaps what additional features you might get with it.

Press **DEL** to enter SETUP
06/07/2001-VT8363-VT686B-6A6LMFOAC-00

i key   Exit

Figure 1-12. The BIOS version number information for a PC with Award BIOS

The unfortunate part of getting a new BIOS from Unicore is that you cannot merely download the BIOS code and upload it into your PC as you can with BIOS updates from the motherboard maker. A Unicore BIOS upgrade will come to you in the mail already installed on a memory chip, which reduces the chances of someone pirating their work. If your system board's BIOS memory chip is soldered onto the board, as shown in Figure 1-13, or is not mounted in a chip socket, as shown in Figure 1-14, you will likely not be able to purchase a BIOS upgrade from Unicore.

You may notice two sets of numbers referring to the version of Award or Phoenix BIOS running your system. The number at the top of the screen—like 4.51, 6.0PG, etc.—is a gross representation of the base BIOS code set used to create the specific BIOS version you have. You will need to locate and note the longer multicharacter number that indicates the specific version for your system board. For Award BIOS this number is almost always displayed in the lower-left corner of the screen. For Phoenix BIOS this number typically appears near the top of the screen with other system board manufacturer's information.

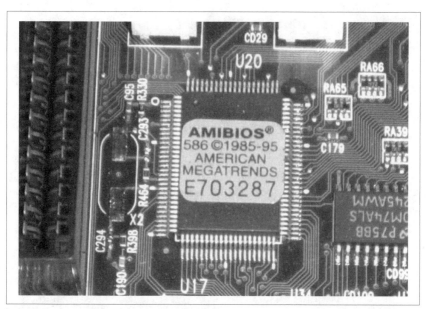

Figure 1-13. This AMIBIOS chip is a FLASH ROM that cannot be removed from the board; it can only be updated electronically

Figure 1-14. A replaceable/upgradeable socket-mounted Award BIOS chip (note CMOS memory battery and CMOS reset jumper above chip)

Upgrade Your Flash BIOS

#10 Resolve system-level bugs and overcome feature limitations by upgrading your BIOS.

Sometimes only after a product gets to market and is used in a lot of different situations can a vendor learn of problems or limitations. Nearly every system board and PC system on the market undergoes at least one significant revision of the BIOS after the product has been released for sale.

Most of us think nothing of seeking out the latest patches and updates for our application software and hardware drivers in hopes of solving a problem, gaining a feature, or boosting performance, but rarely do we think of updating the software and internal drivers that make our system board tick—the system BIOS.

I highly recommend visiting the web site of the manufacturer of your PC system or system board, or even Unicore's web site, to learn what the latest revision of BIOS is for your PC and the issues the revision addresses. You may find one or more clues that can help you solve problems or gain new or proper functionality of your system for a few minutes of browsing and downloading time.

> Do not bother visiting the BIOS makers' web sites looking for BIOS updates. AMI and Award/Phoenix supply only the tools and services for system-board and PC-system makers to create their own BIOS code specific to each individual system board.
>
> You wouldn't think of calling Microsoft, makers of the Visual Studio program development tools, about support or upgrades for software made by Adobe, Intuit, Symantec, or other software makers who use the Visual Studio tools. Nor would you call Sears about problems with your house built with a Craftsman hammer. And so it is with the BIOS companies.
>
> A good resource for identifying your system board is the *http://www.motherboards.org* web site.

In most cases, except getting a BIOS upgrade from Unicore, getting a BIOS update and the software program to load the update into your PC are free from every system board and PC maker's web site. Since many of the devices you add to a system after the initial purchase are too new to be known to or supported by system board vendors, BIOS upgrades are issued to fix anything from an all-out serious bug that prevents some aspect of the system board from working, to enhancing the detection or size of certain types of disk drives, to adding extra support for Plug and Play or power management functions. These items should be spelled out in a *readme* or BIOS revision description file associated with the particular BIOS version you download.

Updating the system BIOS involves overwriting the BIOS code currently stored on the system board and replacing it with new code. This process has the potential to render your system board useless if there is an error or interruption while the update is occurring. If the BIOS file you download is incomplete or corrupt in any way, you will not be able to properly load the BIOS into the system board.

Part of the overall BIOS upgrade process should include backing up the current BIOS onto disk. If your system does not behave correctly after the upgrade, you can flash it with a new good BIOS file or use the original backed-up BIOS file to go back to a known good state.

Depending on your motherboard's capabilities, you may or may not be able to recover from a flashing accident. Intel provides a downloadable recovery BIOS, which can recover certain Intel motherboards after a failed BIOS upgrade. You can locate your recovery BIOS by visiting *http:// downloadfinder.intel.com*, navigating to your motherboard, and selecting the recovery BIOS, if one is available.

A typical BIOS file is either 128 or 256 KB in size, though some may be as large as 2 MB, depending on features. The typical BIOS file, along with the program for updating your system board, both fit on a single 1.44 MB DOS-bootable formatted diskette. If you lack a diskette drive for your system, as may be the case for a laptop PC, you can also use a bootable CD containing the BIOS file and update program.

Some BIOS upgrade programs are available for use under Windows, which, although convenient and more user-friendly, has the risk of failing due to a crash, conflict, or other instability within Windows. I recommend using a DOS-based BIOS upgrade program if it is available.

Some BIOS update programs create their own bootable diskettes and execute the upgrade process automatically so you need only supply the diskette. Once you have downloaded the BIOS file (usually a .BIN file extension type) and BIOS update program to your hard drive, follow the instructions provided with the upgrade (likely proceeding from Step 8 below) or all of the following steps to update your system's BIOS.

Be sure your computer is plugged into a UPS (Uninterruptible Power Supply). All it takes is a power outage during a BIOS upgrade to render your motherboard useless.

1. Prepare a formatted DOS boot diskette. Any version of DOS should do, but making a DOS 6.22, Windows 95, 98, or Me startup diskette would be most common. You can also make an MS-DOS startup disk using the format program in Windows XP, downloading boot diskette images from *http://www.bootdisk.com*.

2. If in Windows, double-click My Computer, then double-click the A: drive.

3. In DOS or Windows, delete the following files from the diskette to make room for the BIOS files:
   - All *ASPIxxxx.SYS* files
   - All *BTxxxxxx.SYS* files
   - *OAKCDROM.SYS*
   - *RAMDRIVE.SYS*
   - *EBD.CAB*
   - *SMARTDRV.EXE*
   - *CONFIG.SYS*
   - *AUTOEXEC.BAT*

4. Copy the specific BIOS (*.BIN*) file to the diskette.

5. Copy the BIOS upgrade program to the diskette.

6. Restart the PC with the diskette in the drive so the system boots from the floppy. You may need to change the boot device order **[Hack #6]** first.

7. At the DOS prompt type in the name of the BIOS upgrade program and press the Enter key to run it. You should be presented with a text menu of options.

8. One of the options should be to copy the existing FLASH ROM BIOS to disk as a backup—do this. (Often the upgrade process will automatically prompt to copy a backup of the BIOS to disk.)

9. Select the option to program the new BIOS file into the FLASH ROM. If you are presented with the option, and you did not already make a backup of the existing BIOS, do so now.

10. Follow the prompts to upgrade your BIOS. In some cases, you will need to provide the name of the new BIOS file and let the program copy the file into the FLASH ROM.

11. When the programming process completes, remove the diskette from the drive and then restart the PC. If your computer displays the BIOS version at boot time, you should notice the new BIOS version appear on screen.

12. Go into the BIOS setup program. Verify or set the date, time, and other parameters you're familiar with and then restart the PC. You're done with the BIOS upgrade.

Do not forget to check the web site of your video card, disk drive, printer, and USB-connected product vendors for any BIOS or firmware updates for these devices.

Basic System Board Setup
Hacks 11–18

This chapter covers the things the BIOS was meant to do—detect and configure devices that interact with the core PC, basic input and output (I/O) devices, and connections to the outside world. You will also see emphasis on when it makes sense to switch from older I/O devices to new.

You're on a mission to ensure that PCs are properly configured, and you need to be armed with the knowledge and tools to carry out that mission. If you fail, you may lose any chance of improving the performance and capabilities of your PC and all further hacks may be a waste of time.

I/O devices are either contained within the system board or are optional devices plugged into slots or external interfaces connected to the system board. Their misconfiguration can interfere with more essential functions, such as those of the disk drive, display, keyboard, and mouse.

Unless you're tinkering with a really old XT- or AT-style system board (see Figure 2-1), your PC is probably built around an all-in-one ATX-style system board with an Intel Celeron; Pentium I, II, III, or 4; or AMD Athlon or Duron CPU. It probably provides the basic I/O ports: PS/2 keyboard and mouse ports, USB ports, at least one serial/COM port, and a parallel/LPT port. If it's a *legacy-free system*, it may only have USB and perhaps FireWire (IEEE 1394) ports. Various system boards include built-in sound, video, or Ethernet adapters too—lacking only a disk drive, monitor, keyboard, and mouse to be a complete PC.

With an older AT-style system, the I/O ports for your peripherals—COM, LPT, video, sound, and network—may be provided by various plug-in cards, using either 8- or 16-bit slots or perhaps even a PCI slot.

For newer systems, such as the ATX-style system board shown in Figure 2-2, I've foraged through the BIOS setup programs to dig up a series of hacks that, while not necessarily improving performance, can help you prevent conflicts between devices now and as you add more features into your system.

Figure 2-1. An older no-frills mini AT-style system board with non-PS/2 keyboard connection and lacking any built-in I/O

Figure 2-2. This newer ATX-style system board includes all of the basic I/O you'll need: PS/2 ports, USB, COM, LPT, game port, and sound

The setup features in most BIOS versions, even the OEM/name-brand PC systems, allow you to tweak the basic I/O port settings so you can enable, disable, and reconfigure ports to create a known, stable setup and work around some mistakes Plug and Play can make as you add more features into the system.

HACK #11   Step Away from the Legacy Device

The technology police are knocking at our doors, subjecting us to techno-modernization. We can and will be able to move along and pretend nothing exciting has happened.

As the Borg proclaim in many *Star Trek* episodes, "Resistance is futile. You will be assimilated." So will you find emphasis on moving PC I/O capabilities and devices as far away as possible from legacy technology. ISA technology is bigger, bulkier, and fraught with more configuration complexities and conflicts than the vendors and their support people ever imagined, and it's been more than a bit frustrating for millions of PC users as well. The best way to avoid the rest of this chapter and a lot of frustration and to gain a lot of performance and reliability is to disconnect, remove, disable, and replace all of your legacy devices with PCI, PCI-X, AGP, USB, or IEEE-1394 products.

With systems that provide enough 8- or 16-bit ISA slots (typically the black-colored edge connectors on your system board) to allow you to fill the system up with a lot of ISA devices, it is not unusual to run out of IRQs (Interrupt Request lines), limited resources that the CPU uses to address devices. Over the past few years the number of ISA slots on any given system board has decreased (often to zero) while the number of PCI slots (typically white edge connectors) has increased, and even the number of PCI slots is decreasing as more common functions (network, video, sound) have been built onto the system board. PCI devices do not have the same problems with IRQs that ISA cards have: PCI devices can share IRQs, and modern motherboards can assign IRQs dynamically (with ISA, you usually have to set a jumper on the card).

Finding any new 8- or 16-bit ISA I/O device to expand your system for more external peripherals at a computer store may be next to impossible, and you may be challenged to find documentation on how to configure any of the older boards you come across. Vendors have switched to PCI, and most peripherals have moved from using serial or parallel I/O to USB or IEEE-1394, which are beginning to make the PCI bus for external devices obsolete as well.

Expanding the I/O capabilities of a laptop computer almost certainly forces you into using products based on PC Card (formerly known as PCMCIA), or external USB or IEEE-1394 devices. Many newer laptop computers lack serial or parallel ports, forcing you to purchase USB-to-serial or USB-to-parallel adapters in order to use your older peripherals or connect to the console or terminal ports on routers, switches, and other devices.

Eventually new PCs will lack serial and parallel ports, and PCI slots will be replaced with PCI X and AGP. Many systems are being shipped without diskette drives, preferring rewritable CD-ROM and DVD drives. Even the old style 40-pin IDE drives and IDE interface is giving way to serial ATA interfaces. All this to reduce system complexity, size, cabling mazes, power requirements, cooling requirements, and hardware support burdens. Save yourself a few headaches and gain the advantages of performance and reliability with new PCI- or USB-based hardware.

HACK #12 Manage Devices

Take control of device configuration.

One of the basic functions of the PC's BIOS is to identify and provide access to a variety of core components and I/O devices, whether they are embedded on the system board or plugged into an I/O card slot. Core components include the CPU, memory, internal system clocks and timers, and the I/O bus itself. Simple I/O devices supported by every BIOS include the keyboard, mouse, video adapter, I/O ports (serial, parallel, USB, and/or FireWire), and disk drive adapters. All of these devices have very predictable but limited places to be, including:

- Preset and expected hardware addresses (to access and get data to or from the device)
- Interrupt Request (IRQ) signals so devices can tell the CPU and programs they need attention
- Direct Memory Access (DMA) request and acknowledgment signals for devices and the CPU to communicate with each other, allowing high-speed data transfers directly to and from device memory

The earlier, or legacy, BIOS dealt with the hardware as provided, and the hardware configurations were preset or manually altered using switches and jumpers. When all you had were simple I/O devices, configuring a PC was manageable but admittedly not easy for those not inclined to get inside a PC and work with wires and jumpers. As PCs got more popular, more and more nontechnical users were exposed to them, and configuring a PC started to become a major frustration and technical support nightmare for PC vendors. As technology advanced, users wanted more, faster, and better things from the PC. The simple, aging, and slow I/O devices and limitations of the PC and BIOS had to be rethought.

To be able to advance, the PC had to change, but because so many people and companies had so much invested in the PC hardware and software status quo, any new PC technology had to accommodate the old as well as the new. The goals of any technology advances were based on experience and history, leading to the following goals for PCs:

- Detection, recognition, and cooperation with any ISA devices [Hack #11]
- No hardware-based configuration—everything must be software-configurable
- Automatic device detection, identification, and configuration, whether a new device is added or an existing one is removed
- Avoidance of duplication, overlap, and conflicts with address, IRQ, and DMA signals
- Notification to the operating system of hardware changes

Fast-forward through a few less-than-successful PC technology changes like the VESA Local Bus (VLB), IBM's MicroChannel Architecture (MCA), and the Enhanced Industry Standard Architecture (EISA), and you come to the long-standing period of current technologies. These include the Peripheral Component Interconnect (PCI) I/O bus, Advanced Graphics Port (AGP), Universal Serial Bus (USB), and IEEE-1394 (aka FireWire, aka i.Link)—and more recently Serial ATA and PCI-X data buses.

None of these current technologies would have been possible or flourished if it were not for significant changes and additions to the PC BIOS—specifically, creating and adding what is known as Plug and Play capabilities.

The Plug and Play spec is available for download from Microsoft's web site (*http://download.microsoft.com/download/whistler/hwdev3/1.0/WXP/EN-US/ pnpbios.exe*). It makes an interesting read if you're into technical jargon and hardware and software interactions. Amidst all of the technical and process jargon, the most salient content you will find is that Plug and Play BIOS first looks and acts like the old BIOS: it detects the presence and configuration of any legacy devices (configured by hardware switches, jumpers, or software programs that flip virtual switches in the device) in the PC and reserves those configuration settings to avoid having them used by Plug and Play devices. After discovering legacy devices, Plug and Play BIOS determines the configuration of Plug and Play devices. It evaluates what it finds for any changes to hardware settings—the addition or subtraction of devices—to determine if it should initiate automatic configuration of the new device or any previously existing devices to make sure every device has a nonconflicting configuration.

You may encounter a Plug and Play device, or its device driver, that simply insists on using the resources of an existing device, ignoring a legacy or other Plug and Play device that is using the resources.

This problem might be corrected by reconfiguring the settings for the new device with Device Manager [Hacks #75, #76, and #77]. Reconfiguring a device does not take effect until the system is restarted and Windows accepts the new configuration based on updated Plug and Play BIOS data.

The Plug and Play specification does not tell you exactly how or why Plug and Play BIOS or various Plug and Play devices work. The actual implementation of Plug and Play is somewhat left up to interpretation by the programmers and engineers at dozens of vendors. Without hard and fast rules to go by, the resulting BIOS and hardware implementations can vary and affect the experiences you will have adding and configuring devices for your PC.

Plug and Play devices come in a variety of flavors, specifically, those that may only report their configuration but cannot be reconfigured, which is typical for fixed resource system board components, and those that can both report their configuration and reconfigure themselves to avoid conflicts.

There have been reports of early implementations of Plug and Play devices that supposedly reconfigure themselves but, in fact, only report their configuration and will not budge a single bit to avoid conflicts. Video cards, as a basic system device, are usually not reconfigurable and should not tell the BIOS that they are reconfigurable.

If you plug in a new PCI network adapter and suddenly find that either the network adapter is not recognized or that your PCI video card no longer works, you have probably encountered a bug in the firmware code in one of the devices. The only remedy is to find out from the manufacturer of both devices if a firmware upgrade exists to solve this problem and upgrade the adapters, or to change to another model or brand of either card.

Improving Your Odds with Plug and Play

Plug and Play is not perfect. Trying to accommodate the needs and wishes of dozens of hardware and software makers in arriving at a single set of BIOS functionality that would support and dictate the capabilities of PCs for many years could not have been an easy task. Plug and Play is quite amazing, but could do a lot more for all of us. Instead it has specific limitations in what it can do. These limitations will become apparent as you deal with the PC's I/O system, connect devices to it, and see how operating systems deal with it all together.

Functionally, a Plug and Play BIOS pits devices against one another in a race against time to fight for available resources. A Plug and Play BIOS automatically determines which devices can change configuration, allows each device to settle on a configuration, and then stores the data to present these devices to the operating system. True Plug and Play devices are supposed to work with the BIOS to figure out device settings that do not conflict with already-configured devices and *set devices* (legacy devices and settings that absolutely cannot be changed, such as keyboards, mice, timers, CPU numeric processors, and disk drive interfaces). Unfortunately, some Plug and Play devices do not play nice: they do not have the ability to be reconfigured during bootup to work around already-configured devices because they are not fully compatible with Plug and Play. This happens quite often with a combination of cheap network cards and some video cards, or when mixing cheap and name-brand network cards in the same system.

If you get lucky and don't have your network and video adapters fighting with each other, you may find that the built-in Plug and Play serial/COM ports will fight with add-in COM ports such as modems, and you will end up with a COM port set to some obscure logical device name like COM13 using nonstandard I/O addresses and an IRQ that conflicts with something else. If you are really unlucky at this high-tech roulette game, you won't notice anything is wrong until the operating system is done loading and has found all of the new hardware and claimed it is ready for use—only to discover when you need to run a specific program that it cannot find or use the nonstandard settings. To correct these abnormalities you need to know the basics of resource configuration, which built-in devices to reconfigure, and how all devices should be properly configured. In effect, you will find times when it is necessary to override Plug and Play's automatic settings. One example of this is demonstrated in "Let Windows Tell You About I/O Card Conflicts" [Hack #75]. In some cases, you may need to convince Plug and Play to question all its assumptions [Hack #18].

Unnatural Resources

In order to hack I/O settings that have run amok, you first have to know the main players and their device addresses, IRQ settings, and DMA channels. Every I/O device in your system has a physical address to which it responds and through which it passes data. The I/O address resources for Industry Standard Architecture (ISA) or legacy devices are well known (at least to your operating system and drivers), quite limited, and typically not tampered with or changed, but it is possible to improperly configure multiple devices with the same or overlapping addresses and cause conflicts that will render those devices useless.

PCI, PCI-X, AGP, IEEE-1394, and SATA devices also have physical hardware addresses, but they are built on a much larger (32- and 64-bit) and faster data bus than ISA (8- and 16-bit) devices were. Rarely will you ever see two Plug and Play devices fighting for the same I/O address, but it can happen.

Going beyond hardware I/O addresses, we find two other resources for hardware devices: Interrupt Request (IRQ) signals and Direct Memory Address (DMA) signals. These are also well known in the realm of legacy or ISA systems and have a minor role with PCI devices. Unlike I/O addresses, which are not plentiful but of which there are enough to go around, there are only sixteen IRQ signals and eight DMA signals, called "channels."

Of these, in a 16-bit ISA system and systems that have legacy devices but no ISA add-in slots, nine of the IRQ signals are reserved for system board and CPU functions: timers, memory, keyboard/mouse ports, numeric data processing, diskette drive, and commonly two disk drive interfaces. Some of the DMA signals are also reserved for system functions, but there is little chance of not having enough DMA signals.

This leaves a mere seven IRQ signals to be parceled out to several possible built-in or add-in I/O devices—serial/COM ports, parallel/LPT ports, sound, SCSI, network, and video adapters. At some point while expanding your system, you may run out of unique IRQ assignments for legacy devices (and some Plug and Play devices) and oddly enough find some devices must share an IRQ signal.

IRQ assignment problems are insignificant or nonexistent with PCI devices. The PCI bus is separate from the ISA bus and was designed with a lot more capabilities and possibilities, though some PCI devices do use virtual ISA IRQ assignments to maintain compatibility with DOS and DOS-based programs. It is the fact that PCI devices have to share some configurations with ISA (like a PCI-based Plug and Play modem that mimics being a COM port) to maintain compatibility with operating systems and applications that drives us to consider legacy and ISA issues and work around them.

Logically Speaking

Whether you're adding or changing a modem card, connecting a PDA, or trying to hook up that old Iomega Zip drive so you can recover some valuable files, you'll probably need to know something about the COM or LPT ports in your system to finish configuring the software so things work right. The configuration of the four COM ports and two LPT ports are well known because they were actually dictated in the design of the original IBM PC.

COM and LPT port numbering always seems a bit of a mystery because the COM port numbers do not follow specific pieces of hardware or settings; instead they follow a logical numbering scheme. If you only have one COM port in a system, regardless of its address or IRQ assignment, it becomes COM 1—logical because it's the first and only port. If you add a second COM port, provided it does not use the same address as the existing COM port, it may become COM 1 or be COM 2, depending on the address used. Similar logical assignments happen with LPT ports, and you even see a hint of this with disk drive letter assignments. (Between diskette drives A: and B:, the first hard drive is C:, and so on.)

No matter what the COM port's hardware address is, BIOS, DOS, Windows, and most programs expect that COM 1 will always use IRQ 4, and COM 2 will always use IRQ 3. Mix up the IRQ assignments and your software may have a problem communicating with the ports. You do not need to be as picky about LPT ports and their IRQ assignments in most cases, but all core system devices—clocks, timers, keyboard, mouse, and disk drive interfaces—have fixed, unchangeable IRQ settings.

To determine resource use and device conflicts under Windows, follow these steps:

1. Go to Start, select Control Panel, and then double-click Administrative Tools.

2. Under Administrative Tools, double-click Computer Management.

3. In the Computer Management console, select Device Manager. (You can also get here through a right-click on My Computer, selecting Properties, selecting the Hardware tab, and then clicking the Device Manager button.)

4. In the Device Manager, select View, then click Show Hidden Devices, select View again, and then click Resources by Type, as shown in Figure 2-3.

If you're using Linux, you can find out a lot about your system devices at the command prompt with a couple of simple commands. The first, lspci, lists PCI devices:

```
[root@rh9-lt root]# lspci
00:00.0 Host bridge: Intel Corp. 440BX/ZX/DX - 82443BX/ZX/DX Host bridge
    (rev 03)
00:01.0 PCI bridge: Intel Corp. 440BX/ZX/DX - 82443BX/ZX/DX AGP bridge
    (rev 03)
```

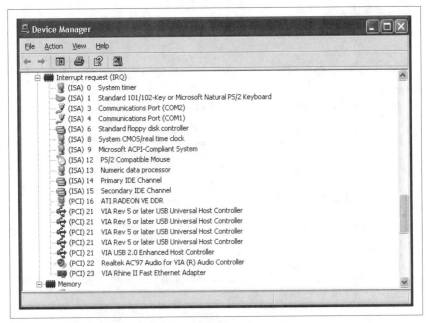

Figure 2-3. Device Manager console showing Resources by Type

```
00:02.0 CardBus bridge: Texas Instruments PCI1450 (rev 03)
00:02.1 CardBus bridge: Texas Instruments PCI1450 (rev 03)
00:03.0 Communication controller: Lucent Microelectronics WinModem 56k
   (rev 01)
00:06.0 Multimedia audio controller: Cirrus Logic CS 4614/22/24
[CrystalClear SoundFusion Audio Accelerator] (rev 01)
00:07.0 Bridge: Intel Corp. 82371AB/EB/MB PIIX4 ISA (rev 02)
00:07.1 IDE interface: Intel Corp. 82371AB/EB/MB PIIX4 IDE (rev 01)
00:07.2 USB Controller: Intel Corp. 82371AB/EB/MB PIIX4 USB (rev 01)
00:07.3 Bridge: Intel Corp. 82371AB/EB/MB PIIX4 ACPI (rev 03)
01:00.0 VGA compatible controller: Neomagic Corporation NM2360 [MagicMedia
256ZX]
05:00.0 Ethernet controller: Xircom Cardbus Ethernet 10/100 (rev 03)
```

To find out which resources are being used by what devices, change to the
/proc directory and inspect the *ioports* and *interrupts* files:

```
[root@rh9-lt root]# cd /proc
[root@rh9-lt proc]# cat ioports
0000-001f : dma1
0020-003f : pic1
0040-005f : timer
0060-006f : keyboard
0070-007f : rtc
0080-008f : dma page reg
00a0-00bf : pic2
```

```
00c0-00df : dma2
00f0-00ff : fpu
01f0-01f7 : ide0
03c0-03df : vga+
03f6-03f6 : ide0
03f8-03ff : serial(auto)
0cf8-0cff : PCI conf1
4000-401f : Intel Corp. 82371AB/EB/MB PIIX4 USB
  4000-401f : usb-uhci
4400-44ff : Lucent Microelectronics WinModem 56k
4500-4507 : Lucent Microelectronics WinModem 56k
4800-48ff : PCI CardBus #02
4c00-4cff : PCI CardBus #02
5000-50ff : PCI CardBus #05
  5000-507f : PCI device 115d:0003
    5000-507f : xircom_cb
5400-54ff : PCI CardBus #05
d000-dfff : PCI Bus #01
ef00-ef3f : Intel Corp. 82371AB/EB/MB PIIX4 ACPI
efa0-efbf : Intel Corp. 82371AB/EB/MB PIIX4 ACPI
fcf0-fcff : Intel Corp. 82371AB/EB/MB PIIX4 IDE
  fcf0-fcf7 : ide0
[root@rh9-1t proc]# cat interrupts
          CPU0
   0:    7292143        XT-PIC  timer
   1:        705        XT-PIC  keyboard
   2:          0        XT-PIC  cascade
   8:          1        XT-PIC  rtc
  11:       9534        XT-PIC  usb-uhci, Texas Instruments PCI1450, Texas
Instruments PCI1450 (#2), eth0
  12:      32040        XT-PIC  PS/2 Mouse
  14:     650116        XT-PIC  ide0
 NMI:          0
 ERR:         80
```

Configure Serial Ports

HACK #13

Starting with a clean, industry-standard serial port configuration can save hours of headaches when you're ready to add more devices.

If you currently or eventually will have to connect your PDA, a modem, a GPS unit, an uninterruptible power supply to protect your PC, or something else to a COM port, leave the COM port(s) enabled with a known configuration. If you know for sure how your ports are configured, it makes using them much easier.

There are several ways to tell if you have one or more COM ports on your system:

- Look at the back (sometimes the front for some COMPAQ and HP systems) of your PC to see if there is a connector with nine small male pins in two rows—one of five pins, the other of four pins, surrounded by a trapezoidal or D-shaped metal shell—or a connector with 25 male pins in two rows of 13 and 12, respectively. These are known as *DB-9 male* and *DB-25 male* connectors, respectively. Only serial ports have this style of male connectors.

The presence of these connectors does not tell you specifically that there are COM port electronics wired between the connectors and your system board—these may be *fillers* for the addition of COM ports to a system that does not have them.

The presence of these connectors also does not tell you if they are connected to an add-in card plugged into an ISA or PCI slot or directly to COM port electronics on the system board. Only a physical inspection of the inside of your PC can tell you for sure if the connectors go any-place and where they go.

- Look into the BIOS setup program for references to serial/COM ports in the I/O port menu sections. If setup refers to COM ports and the system contains the 9- or 25-pin external connectors, chances are you do have COM ports.

  It is possible your BIOS could report the existence of COM ports although you have no physical connectors for them, indicating that you are missing some cables to connect to the system board or the manufacturer never intended the ports to be used.

  If you have the connectors but do not see any references to COM ports in your BIOS, then it's likely the COM ports are provided by an add-in card.

- In Windows go to the Device Manager to see if any COM ports are present. This will not tell you how the COM ports are provided, by system board or add-in card, but will tell you if a port exists and provide details about its configuration.

- Use a system information or diagnostic program like SiSoft's Sandra (*http://www.sisoftware.net*), Windows Device Manager **[Hack #12]**, or a similar program to detect and reveal the port information. These programs will not tell you how the COM ports are provided—by system board or add-in card—but will tell you if a port exists and provide details about its configuration.

If you've determined that you have COM port connectors and the ports are configured in the BIOS, you'll want to set their configuration to known values so that other Plug and Play devices don't try to use their resources later on. The proper address and IRQ settings for COM ports are listed in Table 2-1.

Table 2-1. Standard COM port addresses and IRQs

Port number	Address	IRQ
COM 1	3F8	4
COM 2	2F8	3
COM 3	3E8	4
COM 4	2E8	3

Figure 2-4 shows the BIOS screens for typical Plug and Play COM ports. Auto is not the setting you want if you are concerned about establishing and maintaining a proper, known PC configuration.

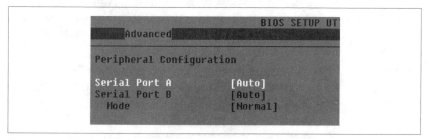

Figure 2-4. Default Plug and Play serial port configuration settings

You might add other COM ports to the system configuration in the future, so you want the built-in or first serial ports in the system to be set properly for COM1 and COM2, as shown in Figure 2-5. In this example, "Serial Port A" and "Serial Port B" refer to the labeling of the physical plugs at the back of the system board. Your system board labels and settings may differ slightly. To avoid a headache in the future, change your serial port settings to those shown.

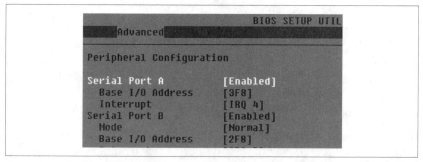

Figure 2-5. The desirable settings for the COM1 and COM 2 ports on the system board

The Mode parameter typically refers to whether or not this serial interface should use a true serial I/O port or consider an available Infrared receiver/

transmitter as this specific COM port. Infrared (IR) ports are rare on desktop and server systems but are quite common on circa 1995–2000 laptops. This setting should be set to Normal for most of us, unless you have a built-in IR device acting as a COM port and intend to use it. If you never intend to use your COM ports, disable or remove them entirely to leave the resources free for other devices that may need them.

Configure Parallel Ports

Set up your parallel ports in ways that accommodate your peripherals and your other expansion needs.

Although LPT ports are seldom used for much of anything (even printers, since most now use USB) these days, the occasion may arise when you need to use the port to hook up an old external disk drive to recover some important files or an old scanner to capture a document or photo, or to connect two PCs with a special transfer cable to migrate data from an old PC to a new one. Knowing the basics of your LPT ports will make these tasks easier.

Before you can use an LPT port, you need to have one, so you need to find out if you do. There are specific ways to tell if you have one or more LPT ports on your system:

- Look at the back of your PC to see if there is a connector with 25 female pin holes in two rows of 13 and 12, respectively, surrounded by a trapezoidal or D-shaped metal shell. This connector is known as a *DB-25 female*.

  Unfortunately, other types of interfaces use the same connector style—typically older SCSI ports and, rarely seen in the general PC population, connections for special test equipment.

  The presence of these connectors does not tell you specifically that there are LPT port electronics wired between the connectors and your system board—these may be fillers for the addition of an LPT port later on.

  The presence of these connectors also does not tell you if they are connected to an add-in card plugged into an ISA or PCI slot or directly to LPT port electronics on the system board. Only a physical inspection of the inside of your PC can tell you for sure if the connectors go anyplace and where they go.

- Look into the BIOS setup program for references to parallel ports in the I/O port menu sections. If setup refers to LPT ports and the system contains the 25-pin external connectors, chances are you do have LPT ports.

It is possible your BIOS could refer to LPT ports although you have no physical connectors for them, indicating that you are missing some cables to connect to the system board or the manufacturer never intended the ports to be used.

If you have the connectors but do not see any references to LPT ports in your BIOS, then it's likely the LPT ports are provided by an add-in card or the connectors are not parallel/LPT ports at all but have some other use.

- In Windows, go to the Device Manager (My Computer→Properties →Hardware) to see if any LPT ports are present. This will not tell you how the LPT ports are provided—by system board or add-in card—but will tell you if a port exists and give information about its configuration.

- Use a system information or diagnostic program like SiSoft's Sandra- (*http://www.sisoftware.net*), Windows Device Manager [Hack #12], or a similar program to detect and reveal the port information. These programs will not tell you how the LPT ports are provided, by system board or add-in card, but will tell you if a port exists and information about its configuration.

If you've determined that you have LPT port connectors and the ports are configured in the BIOS, you'll want to set their configuration to known values so that other Plug and Play devices don't try to use their resources later on. The proper address and IRQ settings for LPT ports are listed in Table 2-2.

Table 2-2. LPT Port address and IRQ assignments

Port number	Address	IRQ
LPT 1	378	7
LPT 2	278	5

Figure 2-6 shows the BIOS screen for typical Plug and Play LPT ports. Auto is not the setting you want if you are concerned about establishing and maintaining a proper, known PC configuration.

Figure 2-6. Default settings for a Plug and Play parallel port

To avoid the unknown and potential confusion in the future you should manually set the Parallel Port configuration to known values rather than Auto mode. Figure 2-7 shows a manually configured parallel port using default LPT1 values—address 378 and IRQ7—plus two other settings of note—Mode and DMA.

```
Parallel Port          [Enabled]
  Mode                 [ECP]
  Base I/O Address     [378]
  Interrupt            [IRQ 7]
  DMA                  [3]
```

Figure 2-7. Parallel port settings after manual configuration

On any given system the parallel port may be capable of any of four modes of operation: the original Standard or Output-Only mode, Bi-Directional, Enhanced Parallel Port (EPP), or Enhanced Capability Port (ECP). Of these, Standard, Bi-Directional, EPP, and ECP are typically the only ones available as normal configurations for BIOS. The definitions and significance of each of these modes are as follows:

Standard or Output-Only

Just as indicated—the port is normally used to send data out to a printer and get no data back.

Bi-Directional

The port is capable of reading data back from a printer or other device on demand from a program intended to do so. This (or its variants, EPP and ECP) is the most common mode in use today.

EPP

A faster variant of Bi-Directional mode with some other device status capabilities—rarely, if ever, used. ECP fixes some issues with EPP mode and adds much higher data rates and the ability to do DMA data transfers.

ECP

An upgrade to EPP. Made the LPT port the cheapest and fastest I/O port available for such things as page scanners and external storage devices before USB hit the market.

With the availability of USB and IEEE-1394 (FireWire), ECP mode is not used much if at all. Most parallel printers, even those with programs that tell you ink or toner status, use Bi-Directional mode to free up the IRQ and DMA lines that would be used by ECP mode.

The instructions for the device you want to connect to your LPT port should indicate which mode the LPT port is required to be in for the device to work properly. Some devices do not work with EPP or ECP ports.

Configure Sound Cards
#15 Make your sound card sing amidst the variations of limited PC resources by finding and using alternative settings.

Sound cards were among the first optional devices to be added to the old ISA PCs. When Windows 3.x became available, and with gamers demanding a more immersive experience, demand rose for a richer audio environment than the mere beeps and boops offered by the PC speaker. Users needed sound to complete "the experience." Companies like Creative Labs and MediaVision thrust sound from PCs into users' ears.

To accomplish this meant borrowing from emerging technologies, creating a few new technologies, and stuffing all of this into what there was of a 16- and then 32-bit PC computing platform.

The default settings for PC sound cards became address 220, IRQ5, and DMA channel 1. While there was seldom a conflict with I/O addressing, sound cards could be reconfigured to use an IRQ other than 5 and a DMA channel other than 1 to avoid other devices that could be present in the system. The DMA channel was needed to avoid stutter and skipping of data streams.

The most common symptom of a misconfigured sound card is a stuttering or choppy effect to otherwise smoothly streaming sounds. If Plug and Play is not solving a conflict and the sound card supports alternative configurations, try changing the IRQ to 7, 10, 11, or 15, or the DMA channel to 3 or 5.

You can determine the settings of your present sound card configuration using Windows Device Manager [Hack #12] or a program like SiSoft Sandra, which will detect and report on all of the I/O devices present.

Be aware that a sound cards needs consistent, exclusive access to IRQ and DMA resources, so these resources cannot be shared with other devices. If you have an ISA-based sound card, look for the jumpers on the card, as in Figure 2-8, or use the configuration software provided to set the card for the generally accepted address (220), IRQ (5), and DMA channel (3 or 5). If you are using an ISA sound card and cannot configure it with nonconflicting settings, upgrade to a PCI-based card to avoid any ISA resource conflicts and gain better sound card performance and fidelity in the process.

Figure 2-8. Jumpers to configure sound card address, DMA and IRQ settings

Configure SCSI Host Adapters

#16   Accommodate SCSI host adapters with nonconflicting configurations.

A SCSI interface is one of the best ways to add lots of devices—hard drives, CD-ROM or DVD drives, cartridge or tape drives, even some of the high-end graphics scanners—to your PC without using up a lot of resources. Very fast SCSI adapters and hard drives are used in servers, and most high-capacity server-grade backup tape systems use the SCSI interface because SCSI is simply faster and allows for more drive configurations like RAID.

Because of the performance offered by SCSI host adapters, you should have at least a PCI card. ISA cards are simply incapable of supporting the speeds required by today's SCSI drives.

Most SCSI adapters are readily identified and their configurations determined and reported by Windows Device Manager and readily available PC system information programs.

> Some of you may still be using 16-bit ISA SCSI adapters. As with the sound card, if you cannot configure the system to provide the host adapter with exclusive uninterrupted access to IRQ and DMA resources, an upgrade to a PCI-based adapter is your only solution, and you'll get a huge performance boost as well.

A SCSI host adapter may contain User BIOS, so adding a SCSI host adapter to your system might require you to enable scanning the User BIOS Region of memory [Hack #4].

IEEE-1394

As a means of connecting external devices, SCSI has been great for scanners and assorted storage devices, but it has not been forgiving or flexible in cable lengths nor as fast as newer technologies. Save SCSI for internal storage devices and high-performance server disk drive arrays, but upgrade your external peripherals—scanners, add-on and portable storage devices—to either USB 2.0 or IEEE-1394 (aka FireWire, aka i.Link). With USB or IEEE-1394, you also get the capability to add many more and different devices such as digital cameras, video recorders, printers, business card readers, SMART cards, and a variety of flash memory readers.

HACK #17 Configure Network Cards

Give your network card the resources it needs to get and keep your LAN and Internet traffic flowing smoothly.

Network cards are another enhancement to PCs that had to be squeezed in to the limits of old legacy I/O systems. Because networking usually requires a fast, steady stream of data, it is important that network interface cards have unique and exclusive use of address and IRQ resources. Symptoms of conflicts include the inability to obtain a network address or log on to a server, or poor data transfer performance.

The most successful implementations of early 8- and 16-bit network cards in practice used addresses 280 or 340 and IRQ5 (8-bit systems) or IRQ10 (16-

bit systems), depending on the presence or absence of a sound card using IRQ5.

Determining the presence, type, and configuration of older network cards is not well supported in most diagnostic and system information programs. Instead you may have to rely on reading the jumper settings or using a configuration program meant specifically for your network adapter.

> If you need Gigabit Ethernet (1000BaseT), you should use a motherboard that has it built in. If you install a 1000BaseT PCI card, it will likely saturate the PCI bus, leaving no bandwidth for other PCI cards. Onboard 1000BaseT uses a separate bus to talk to the CPU and memory.

Today, with PCI and Plug and Play, you seldom have to concern yourself with these issues. Nevertheless, knowing the commonly available configurations is useful should you ever have to configure the drivers and software for a LAN card to work in DOS, which often cannot use PCI net cards because the vendors may not provide DOS drivers for them.

> Although well published in IBM specifications, address 300 was "reserved" for use by IBM and prototype devices and recognized as such in many versions of BIOS. IBM even offered a plug-in card that used address 300 for others to develop new products around.
>
> Older ISA network cards may be set for address 300, which can cause problems for some older applications. Avoid using address 300 for anything.

HACK #18 Reeducate Plug and Play

Get Plug and Play back in sync with reality and Windows by forcing it to rethink what it knows about your PC and peripherals.

The Microsoft Windows Plug and Play BIOS extension generally knows when a new device is installed, as you can see in Microsoft Windows when a "New hardware found" dialog appears, but it doesn't know if you've changed the configuration of a device through its configuration/setup program or using Windows Device Manager.

It is possible, depending on the capabilities of the respective device drivers (usually for PCI network and SCSI cards), to reconfigure an I/O device through Device Manager. This reconfiguration is not dynamic: Windows won't really know about it until Plug and Play BIOS tells it things have changed. That only happens at bootup, and sometimes only if the BIOS is told to look for the change. Merely changing a device's internal configuration does not constitute a new or removed device in Plug and Play's "mind," and it never gets it without some help.

To tell Plug and Play that things have changed by adding or removing an I/O device, or by "soft" changes you made within Windows, you have to reboot your system, enter the BIOS setup, and then force Plug and Play to reassess the system configuration. This gets the BIOS to reconfigure the system properly, and informs the operating system of the changes.

Reeducating Plug and Play is done by a parameter most often named "Reset Configuration Data" or "Reset NVRAM" (non-volatile RAM). NVRAM is an area of memory on the system board that stores Plug and Play data. Make sure that Plug and Play OS is set to Yes (provided you have a Plug and Play–compliant operating system, such as Windows), set the Reset value to Yes, and then restart your PC. The BIOS will reevaluate the system configuration, store any new data, and make it available to the operating system (see Figure 2-9).

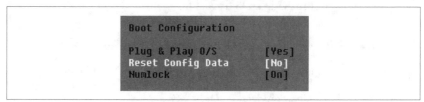

Figure 2-9. Resetting the configuration data forces Plug and Play to roll the dice again to reset device configurations based on new settings

## CHAPTER THREE

CPU Hacks
Hacks 19–29

"How fast can I make it run?" is likely the first question from any PC hacker. In the good old days of the original IBM PC, the answer was a breathtaking 8 MHz, up from 4.77 MHz—but only if you replaced the system's processor, an Intel i8088 CPU, with an NEC V20 chip. (Intel eventually beefed up the i8088 to run at 8 MHz.)

The PC has gone through numerous and tremendous performance improvements, starting with the CPU. At one time, 12 and 16 MHz were the top speeds; then 25 and 33 MHz; then 50 and 66 MHz; then 100, 150, 200, 266, 500 MHz, 1 GHz, and 2 GHz. After 24 years of technological advances, now 3 GHz, nearly 630 times faster than the first PCs, is an everyday, ho-hum, state-of-the-art PC standard.

At every step of CPU performance improvement, the system I/O bus and peripherals have had to catch up. We want the Internet to flash before us, its content challenging the CPU to keep up with the network. There was a time when application programs strained to crunch numbers and print documents; we are now waiting for applications to take advantage of what desktop super-computing capabilities have to offer. Once AMD got the rights to manufacture an Intel i80286 CPU, the horses, cows, pigs, and rocket-fuel powered CPUs were out of the barn, seldom to be corralled again. The functions of the x86 chip were well known and easily replicated: the race was on. The winners are millions of PC users around the globe.

The basic question may be, "Why do I want my CPU, or the entire system, to run faster anyway?" Numerous justifications and solid reasons exist for hacking your system for better performance, including:

- Because applications are slow with the present system
- Because you can get additional performance for little or no expense—a free or cheap upgrade
- Because you can—it's the nature of techies and geeks

The most critical elements in jacking up your CPU speed are also the limiting factors as to how fast it can get: the top speed of the CPU and design of the supporting circuits on the system board. In 1980, the year the PC was born, the IBM PC system board and peripherals could not easily be made to go faster, nor did the components support the challenge. The IBM PC/XT saw some improvement, but the methods of clocking the CPU and the peripherals were so tightly tied together that it took major circuit hacking to speed things up.

Circuit board technology as well as CPU and I/O bus clocking schemes removed many barriers to increased speed, made motherboard makers more likely to support whatever CPU could be plugged into the slot, and made life better for us hackers. If a CPU could be sped up, it gave us more computing power for our dollar. The trick was, has been, and always will be determining which CPUs can or cannot be *overclocked* (made to run faster than the rated speed).

CPU hacking is not without risk. With speed increases (and occasionally the need to increase the voltage fed to the CPU to accommodate higher speeds), electronic components such as CPUs, chipsets, and memory can get warmer. Some of the downsides to CPU hacking are:

CPU failure
> It is possible to push voltage changes too far. Attempts to get the CPU to run faster raise the risk of "smoking" the CPU. Risking an $80–300 CPU for "just one more notch" of performance increase is not good economics.

CPU temperature rise
> This can be a fatal condition if not addressed with better heat dissipation and ventilation; you will need to ensure adequate cooling for your CPU.

Higher power-supply current drain
> Faster CPUs consume more power, which means a higher capacity power supply is needed.

CPU unreliability
> If higher temperatures don't cause a CPU to flake out right away, the design and construction of the CPU itself simply may not be able to keep up with higher speeds or voltages for long periods of time; erratic operation or data loss may results in many cases.

System board, chipset, memory, and peripheral issues
> The CPU may run well at higher speeds, but other system components may not operate reliably or at all if the main clock speed is increased; again, erratic operation or data loss may result.

To reduce the risks of CPU hacking, follow these tips:

- NEVER operate the CPU without a properly attached heat sink—not even for a moment.

- ALWAYS provide adequate or "overkill" ventilation across the CPU's heat sink.

- Use a test drive, a drive that does not contain critical data, or back up the drive before overclocking. Expect that you may lose the operating system or datafiles during your testing.

- If you have an electronic thermometer with a probe, hold the probe tip on the heat sink for 3–5 minutes and check the temperature. Any component that has a surface temperature over 120 degrees is at risk: slow the system down or install additional heat sinks for these devices.

- **BEWARE!** It is not uncommon for the surface of an overheated component to exceed 120 degrees—hot enough to burn skin!

- If the system boots up improperly, operates erratically, or does not keep running for the length of time it takes to run a full set of system benchmark tests (10–30 minutes), you've gone too far in overclocking.

The Great CPU Performance Race

Since the first PC clone, there has been a simple drive to be faster, better, and even cheaper than the competition. This certainly holds true among the PC makers and, at the core of all PCs, the CPU makers.

The CPU speed race did not get exciting until there were three contenders in the race—AMD, Cyrix, and Intel—and the field grew after the relatively short life of the Intel i80386, the world's first 32-bit microprocessor. After those advances, the introduction of the Intel i80486, the promise of a vastly improved Microsoft operating system (Windows 95), and the revelations of the Internet put PC use into the consumer mainstream. The CPU contenders—AMD, Cyrix (now Via), and Intel—battled among themselves, while hackers enjoyed system boards that accommodated any one of these CPU products and provided switches or jumpers to adjust clock speeds to crank them up.

As we explore CPU hacks, we need to know which CPU is in the system now, whether the CPU is hackable, whether the CPU will survive the hack and how, and, of course, what tools (physical or in software) are required to perform the hacks.

Get More Power

HACK #19

Give your souped-up CPU the power it needs by upgrading to a new power supply.

Before you change out your system board, upgrade to a new CPU, or start jacking up the speed of your CPU and get lulled into a false comfort zone with your new blazing-fast turbocharged PC, make sure it's got the stamina to keep running smoothly. Many PCs have meager 200- to 250-watt power supplies, as shown in Figure 3-1, which are no match for the 300-watt capacity recommended by AMD for their CPUs. You'll need the extra juice to feed not only the CPU but the video card, RAM, disk drives, and other devices.

Figure 3-1. Power supply ratings are usually clearly labeled

Check the label on your power supply for its capacity rating in watts. 200, 225, 230, and 250 watts are common but usually insufficient for the needs of power users.

If you have an OEM system (such as those from Dell, Gateway, and others), it may not be possible to upgrade the power supply due to a unique physical design or specific electrical connections that are not industry-standard AT, ATX, or mini-ATX styles. Since most of us are not hacking name-brand OEM systems, we enjoy many options for customizing the system including changing the power supply.

One standard source for cool, quiet, high-performance PC power supplies is PC Power and Cooling (*http://www.pcpowercooling.com*). Their top-of-the-line supply can deliver a whopping 510 watts of power, which is more than adequate for any CPU and multiple disk drives.

Replacing the power supply is one of the easiest electromechanical tasks you can do with a PC. You'll need one of the following:

- #1 or #2 cross-point (Phillips) screwdriver
- T-15 TORX point driver
- 1/4" hex nutdriver

1. Turn off the PC and disconnect the power cord, as shown in Figure 3-2.
2. Disconnect power connectors from the individual disk drives and the system board, as shown in Figures 3-3 and 3-4.

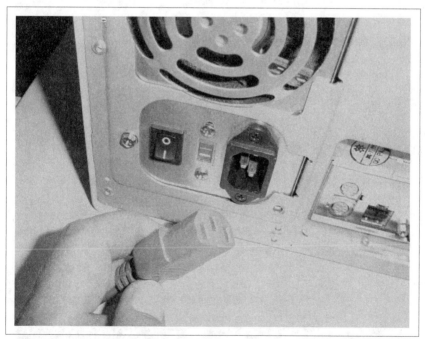

Figure 3-2. Disconnecting the AC power cable

Figure 3-3. Disconnecting the drive power connectors

Figure 3-4. Disconnecting the system board power connector

Figure 3-5. Removing the power supply screws

3. Remove the screws holding the power supply to the chassis, as shown in Figure 3-5.

4. Remove the power supply from the chassis, as shown in Figure 3-6.

5. Install the new power supply in the chassis and secure it with screws.

6. Connect the power cables to the system board and disk drives.

7. Reapply power to the system, boot up, and test away.

> Some chassis have additional brackets, air deflectors, or cables that may interfere with simple disconnection and removal of the power supply. Attend to these details before trying to remove the power supply from the system chassis.

Save the original supply as a backup replacement for your new supply or to use when building another system. If you have a defective power supply and feel like hacking into it, you can salvage the 12-volt DC-operated fan and use it to provide additional chassis cooling.

Figure 3-6. Removing the power supply from the chassis

Be aware that modern PC power supplies may contain residual high voltages for a few seconds or minutes after power has been removed, even under load. The internal fan is typically run from low 12-volt DC and can be removed safely by unplugging its power connector or cutting the wires near the power supply circuit board.

If you must dispose of a power supply, using a computer-parts recycler should be your first choice, as they may separate the chassis metal from the electronic components and then further separate respective components.

Your dead power supply is no more or less toxic than any other household appliance you might simply toss in the trash, but local regulations may dictate that electronics be disposed of separately from normal trash, or at additional expense.

Identify Your CPU

#20 Find out which CPU is in the system.

You can determine which CPU you have in your PC with any number of freeware and Shareware utilities, such as SiSoft Sandra (*http://www. sisoftware.net*) or AIDA32 (*http://www.aida32.hu*), or CPU information provided by Windows Me, XP, or 2003. To see which CPU you have in Windows Me, XP, or Windows Server 2003, right-click the My Computer icon and select Properties. The CPU information will be displayed at the lower right corner of the Properties dialog, as shown in Figure 3-7.

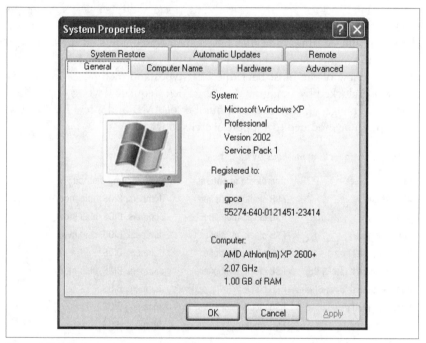

Figure 3-7. My Computer System Properties often displays CPU identity

Versions of Windows prior to Me could not accurately display the identity of the CPU because CPU identity information was not standardized until after Windows 98 and no attempt was made by Microsoft to update the CPU detection capabilities of their older operating systems. Users of these operating systems are better off using SiSoft Sandra or AIDA32 to identify their CPUs.

Which CPUs Are Hackable?

HACK #21

Know which CPUs can be hacked or overclocked.

With this brief look at the evolution of CPUs, you'll quickly see who makes the most hackable CPU. Armed with positive CPU identification and knowing what you want to accomplish in terms of performance, you'll be able to determine if your present CPU can be hacked or if you need a new CPU to gain better performance.

AMD CPUs are typically deemed more hackable than Intel CPUs as there are usually more system boards for AMD CPUs that provide the option to adjust the base clock speed **[Hack #25]** and clock multiplier **[Hacks #27 and #28]** Intel has typically locked down their CPUs to function at only one or a few clock multiplier settings, and they have usually rated and sold most of their CPUs at the highest speed they can be reliably be run. Table 3-1 provides a quick overview of the most hackable CPU types and methods. Most CPUs can be overclocked by changing the base clock frequency, while some allow multiplier changes. In the case of a number of AMD and a few Intel CPUs, the chip can be modified to support overclocking.

Table 3-1. Overclocking methods by CPU type

CPU	Overclocking options	Overclocking method
AMD Athlon	FSB clock, multiplier	Jumpers, BIOS, chip mod
AMD Duron	FSB clock, multiplier	Jumpers, BIOS, chip mod
Intel Celeron	FSB clock, multiplier	Jumpers, BIOS, chip mod
Intel Pentium I	FSB clock, multiplier	Jumpers, BIOS
Intel Pentium II (pre-8/98)	FSB clock, multiplier	Jumpers, BIOS, chip mod
Intel Pentium II (post-8/98)	FSB clock	Jumpers, BIOS
Intel Pentium III	FSB clock	Jumpers, BIOS
Intel Pentium 4	FSB clock	Jumpers, BIOS

The most significant limiting factors in overclocking potential are the features of the system board. As the Front Side Bus (FSB) speed is increased, the PCI and AGP bus speeds are also increased. So if the clock settings alter the FSB and PCI/AGP speeds in proportion to each other, you may reach the speed limit of the system components before you reach the limits of your CPU. If your system board features provide a variety of FSB speeds with separate PCI/AGP speed options, you can likely increase the CPU speed by 100% and still maintain reliable PCI/AGP bus speeds. The available clock setting options vary from system board to system board, even across boards from the same manufacturer.

According to *http://www.sysopt.com*, one of the most popular CPU analysis and overclocking sites, which collect data from dozens of real-world users who thrive on overclocking, the most overclockable CPUs are:

- AMD Thunderbird
- Pentium III Coppermine
- Pentium 4
- AMD Duron

Perhaps Intel saw the light in trying to recapture hobbyist market share and decided not to limit the overclockability of the Pentium III and 4 CPUs, a departure from their earlier restrictions on some Pentium II and Celerons chips. Do not let the lack of being able to change the multiplier values for Intel CPUs fool you into thinking they cannot run faster than rated speeds; most do run faster and quite well. While considering CPUs, you have to consider the most popular system boards for overclocking. According to *http://www.sysopt.com*, the top four overclockable system boards are:

- Asus Tek
- Abit
- MicroStar
- Epox

Intel CPUs

Relatively few Intel CPUs can be hacked because it's not in Intel's best interest to sell lower performance chips that can be made to perform like their higher performance versions. Some Intel CPUs perform better under overclocking conditions than others. Table 3-2 lists the most hackable CPUs based on end-user reports from *http://www.sysopt.com*.

Table 3-2. Hackable Intel CPUs

Processor	Published speed	Achieved speed	Percent increase
Pentium 4	3.1 GHz	5.0 GHz	+ 163%
Pentium 4	2.7 GHz	3.4 GHz	+ 25%
Celeron II	2.0 GHz	2.9 GHz	+ 45%
Pentium III Tualatin	450 MHz	1.2 GHz	+ 166%
Pentium II	400 MHz	2.6 GHz	+ 550%

While these performance gains are impressive, the claims by users who have achieved these speeds were not accompanied by how-to tips. Intel CPUs can be two to five times more expensive than comparable AMD CPUs, and hacking these CPUs and the system boards that support them is not well documented.

AMD CPUs

AMD CPUs are generally more overclockable than Intel's, with more parameter flexibility in the BIOS, for three reasons:

- The manufacturers of boards that use AMD processors and related chipsets tend to use the hackable Award BIOS.
- Available "white box" system boards are more hackable.
- The flexibility of AMD processors accepts higher clock speeds and various clock-multiplier values.

Intel carries the majority of the CPU *and* the system board market with reputable OEMs whose products generally use restricted versions of Phoenix BIOS. By contrast, AMD reaches out to a different market that includes AMD for CPUs, Via for supporting chipsets, and Phoenix's Award BIOS division with significant parameter flexibility.

Tweaking AMD CPUs yields impressive results, as seen in the data from *http://www.sysopt.com* in Table 3-3, feeding the myth that many slower CPU chips are really higher speed devices that failed high-speed tests, were marked as slower speed devices, and were undersold.

Table 3-3. Most hackable AMD CPUs and performance increases

Processor	Published speed	Achieved speed	Percent increase
Athlon MP	1.8 GHz	2.7 GHz	+ 50%
Athlon Thunderbird	1.7 GHz	2.4 GHz	+ 41%
Athlon Thunderbird	1.5 GHz	2.3 GHz	+ 53%
Athlon MP	1.5 GHz	2.1 GHz	+ 40%
Athlon MP	500 MHz	1.8 GHz	+ 260%

As with disclaimers for just about everything else, "your mileage may vary"—and it will—because the various combinations of CPU, chipset, BIOS, and system board design all yield different results. The distribution of overclockable CPUs for retail or online is not predictable; the plant where the chips are made may have had an excess of fast chips and a backlog of orders for slower ones and simply relabeled and shipped the faster CPUs to meet business needs or some monthly shipment quota.

Which System Boards Are Hackable?

Read the box and online reviews to determine if your system board might accommodate hacking the system and CPU clock speeds.

Determining if a system board is hackable—that is, whether it supports overclocking of the CPU—is not obvious. Here are some clues to the hackability of a specific board.

- Most boards for do-it-yourself system builders, also known as "white box" or generic products, support customizable CPU clock values.

- Check the technical specs for support for a range of CPU types and speeds, such as those indicating "AMD Athlon Thunderbird through Athlon XP CPUs," or "1.8-3.3 GHz" speeds. Motherboards thus labeled often provide the ability to change system speed settings.

- An Award BIOS is usually a good bet. Most Award BIOS versions implemented by system board vendors provide some parameters to control CPU and bus speeds.

- Look for a system board that includes jumpers or switches with obvious marking as to CPU clock frequencies and CPU clock-multiplier settings.

- If the motherboard instruction manual mentions selectable CPU clock settings, multiplier values, and/or different Front Side Bus (FSB) frequencies, it's somewhat hackable.

Check the usual sources for information about the hackability of various system board products:

- Ask another "PC junkie" for recommendations.

- Search Google for "overclock" and your motherboard model.

- Browse through overclockers.com, motherboards.org, sysopt.com, tweaktown.com, ocia.net, anandtech.com, pcguide.com, and similar web sites for reviews and "case studies" of overclocking experiments and successes.

As you review various system boards, look for examples of and references to additional cooling with larger heat sinks and fans, especially the space around the CPU socket to accommodate a large heat sink. Many articles will also indicate if a larger power supply is required or recommended to run the board, an overclocked CPU, and any additional fans you may be adding to the system.

HACK #23 Determine Your CPU Speed

Benchmarking programs can tell your present system speed and if you've made any improvements.

If you expect 2.4 GHz performance from your 2.4 GHz CPU, you should find out if you're getting it. If not, find out what's holding your system back with the Benchmarking Modules in a utility such as SiSoft Sandra, which allows you to identify and compare performance of your CPU, memory, disk drive, and video adapter.

Once you've run a benchmark test on your system, you have a reference to compare with when you check the results of your CPU hacks. Figure 3-8 shows the CPU performance results from an AMD Athlon XP 2600+ Barton series before overclocking. You may also wish to note the temperature before and after CPU hacking because excessive heat is the enemy of the delicate structure inside the CPU chip.

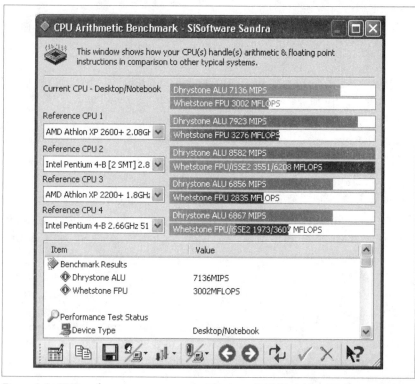

Figure 3-8. CPU performance measurements for a stock AMD Athlon XP Barton 2600+

Overclocking the CPU, as well as trying a handful of RAM speed tweaks covered in Chapter 4, is considered risky business by any standards. Certainly CPU-intensive work like graphics rendering, spreadsheets, and database sorting that involve a lot of math will benefit from a boost in just the CPU speed. Figure 3-9 shows the performance increase of this particular test system after increasing the CPU clock speed a mere 11.4%, from 1.91 GHz to 2.13 GHz. Raw CPU performance measured in millions of instructions per second (MIPS) and million-floating-point-(math)-operations-per-second (MFLOPS) reveals a proportional 11.4% increase.

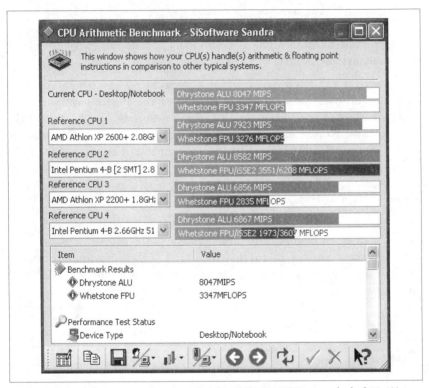

Figure 3-9. Performance measurements for the AMD XP 2600+ overclocked 11.4% to 2.13 GHz

Your total system performance is also affected by the speed, design, and operation of the chipset on the system board that binds all of the components together, the memory used, disk drive specifications, and disk drive interface cabling. Once you run benchmark tests against the system's state before overclocking, you will also learn what the Front Side Bus (FSB) speed is.

Within the realm of the CPU-chipset-memory combination, several different clock speeds are involved. The FSB is the interface between CPU and memory. The FSB is typically either 100 or 133 MHz in systems one to two years old, increasing to 200, 266, 333, 400, 533 MHz (and beyond) in newer systems. It is important that the speed of the RAM installed on the system be compatible with the FSB speed—unless your system board provides separate clocking for FSB and memory—or the system will be unstable because the slower RAM will not be able to reliably transfer data.

The FSB speed is typically the base speed of the CPU clock. The true CPU clock speed is a product of the FSB speed and an internal CPU clock-multiplier value; for example, 100 MHz (FSB) × 12 (CPU multiplier) makes a 1.2 GHz system. This tells us that we'd also like to be able to change the multiplier value to increase CPU performance.

The processor's PCI and AGP I/O ports connect to the CPU's FSB through what is known as the *Northbridge* portion of the system's chipset. Data moves between the Northbridge and FSB at FSB speeds. The PCI bus on the outside of the Northbridge usually communicates at only 33 MHz, and the AGP bus at 66MHz (AGP is clocked by separate multipliers to achieve 2–8X speeds). Slower speed I/O devices—ISA, USB, and IDE devices—connect to the CPU through the Northbridge PCI bus through a portion of the chipset known as the *Southbridge*.

In most cases, the FSB or base speed also affects the speed of the PCI, AGP, Level 2 cache, and Southbridge interfaces unless the chipset provides separate multiplier value control for these interfaces. This is important to note as overclocking FSB speed can cause failure or erratic behavior of the PCI and AGP buses.

HACK #24 Keep It Cool

Better to overcool than undercool. A CPU survives best with adequate cooling to keep it stable.

Hackability of the CPU and system board is not the only consideration for a CPU speed tweak. As the CPU goes faster, the internal temperature rises, stressing the incredibly small wires and component structures inside. With excessive heat comes random lockups of the system and possibly catastrophic failures, with some spectacular but short-lived fireworks as the CPU melts down. To counteract excessive heat requires significant cooling capability attached to the CPU chip, so you will see a lot of heat-sink and cooling fan gimmicks and gadgets for sale with CPUs. Check the documentation that comes with the CPU chips, and you will find recommendations and warnings about ensuring proper CPU-to-heat-sink contact and adequate ventilation. Figure 3-10 shows an example of a specially milled heavy-duty supercooling heat sink from an HP server with an integrated fan. HP engineers lay claim to inventing this style of cooling device, and it either works very well or just *looks* cool as heck! This design has been cloned by many aftermarket vendors.

Figure 3-10. This bolt-down heavy-duty heat sink from an HP server keeps the CPU quite cool

 Never run your CPU without a heat sink, especially the ultra-hot AMD processors!

Anyone who has run an AMD Athlon or Duron CPU—any version at any speed, overclocked or not—will tell you that the chip *must* be fitted with a decent heat sink and fan before any power is turned on, or the CPU will almost certainly fail. Figure 3-11 shows two CPU chips that have suffered catastrophic thermal failure when operated without a heat sink. Try as you might, you cannot put the "magic smoke" back in the chip and have it work again.

 Avoid inhaling the smoke or fumes from a "flamed-out" chip. When the internal elements of a CPU or other semiconductor melt or burn, they give off very foul-smelling and possibly toxic fumes. If a CPU does burn up, ventilate the area well to clear the air and be wary of nausea, dizziness, or other ill effects of toxic contamination.

Figure 3-11. Fried CPUs with evidence of explosive damage along the near edges of the cover over the CPU

The stock heat sink that comes with your CPU is adequate for operating the CPU at its rated speed, but overclocking and voltage adjustments can raise CPU temperature dramatically. In most cases of moderate (10–20%) clock or voltage (5–10%) increase, a slightly bigger heat sink and better ventilation will suffice to keep the chip temperature within safe operating range. In the rare cases when you can kick the CPU speed up by 25–200% or more, you need to provide some serious heat removal.

Current CPU types provide internal temperature sensors that can be read by the system BIOS and by some utility programs like SiSoft Sandra. Reading the temperature of your system running normally will give you a baseline operating temperature to compare with as you overclock. You must avoid reaching or exceeding the thermal limits of your CPU.

Although the maximum idle temperature on many AMD CPUs can be as high as 95 degrees Centigrade, the actual running temperature is 30–40 degrees C. Many BIOS versions provide CPU temperature alarms at 60, 65, and 70 degrees C. Your heat sink and ventilation should keep the CPU's running temperature well below 60 degrees C, and you should overclock your CPU no more than 25%.

The secret to heat removal is to have a large mass of material with low thermal resistance to conduct heat away from the chip into the surrounding cooler air. Alternatively, you can attach a device with a circulating coolant that draws the excess heat away quickly and dumps away from the system components, like the radiator in your car or home air conditioner does.

Aluminum is the ideal metal for most heat sinks. It has low thermal resistance, so it can accept and dissipate thermal energy very efficiently. It is inexpensive and easily manufactured into a variety of shapes that provide fast thermal dissipation and contact with almost any surface that needs cooling. Copper, also used in some heat sinks, is more expensive but is the material of choice for water-cooled devices.

In addition to using a highly thermal-conductive material, that material must be as tightly attached to the CPU as possible. It is not adequate to merely place the material next to the CPU: the bond must be as close to being a part of the CPU as possible. The bond is usually made with a *very* thin layer of thermally conductive grease or epoxy adhesive specifically for heat-sink bonding.

The layer must be *very* thin because the compound or adhesive is intended to improve the metal-to-metal contact by filling in minute imperfections in both surfaces to provide optimal contact and thermal transfer. If the layer can be made thin enough, it will only cover the imperfections and leave metal-to-metal contact at the high spots common to both surfaces.

An often neglected attribute of using a thin layer of thermal compound is that it eliminates air bubbles between the surfaces that may trap a small amount of moisture. Moisture trapped between a hot device and its heat sink does not constitute water cooling; instead it could be a small water bomb waiting to go off. See Step 11 in the instructions that follow.

If the temperature of the moisture bubble exceeds 100 degrees Celsius or 212 degrees Fahrenheit (the boiling point of water)—and it can with a souped-up CPU—the water will expand to 2,700 times its volume as steam and demand to go someplace. That will likely be in the direction of destroying the CPU chip or at least weakening the overall thermal bond, causing the CPU to overheat and self-destruct.

If you've removed a heat sink from a CPU (best done with either a slight twisting motion to separate heat sink and CPU or *very* light prying between the two), beware that some are glued on with high-temp epoxy and cannot be removed without destroying the CPU. You've probably experienced this thermal grease or heat-sink compound—a tenacious white material that looks and feels like toothpaste but stains like red wine in the middle of a new white carpet. Thermal compound is typically a mixture of aluminum oxide for thermal conduction and a silicon paste to hold the aluminum oxide together (see Figure 3-12).

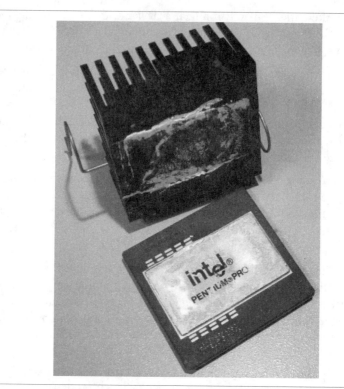

Figure 3-12. Thermal compound fills the gaps between heat sink and CPU

Two new compound mixtures have emerged: one containing aluminum oxide in a fine ceramic form, the other silver and silver oxide. According to product documentation at *http://www.articsilver.com*, the typical aluminum-oxide-based white paste provides the lowest thermal conductivity and the least CPU temperature drop (2–7 degrees), the ceramic compound is next in the order of effectiveness (2–10 degree drop), and the silver-based compound the most efficient, providing a 3–12 degree drop in CPU temperature. The effectiveness is also represented in the cost of the compound—between $4 and $9 per tube. Unless you see your CPU temperature rising towards its maximum limits, the typical aluminum oxide, and certainly the ceramic paste, are more than adequate for the task.

 For a time, Intel prebonded heat sinks to some versions of their Pentium I CPUs using thermal epoxy, making it impossible to separate the two if you wanted to add a larger heat sink.

To speed production processes and make applying thermal bonding cleaner, many vendors have chosen to use thermal pads, as shown in Figure 3-13.

Thermal pads are fine in lower-temperature applications, but, while they certainly fills gaps between surfaces, they do not give way to allow direct surface contact between high spots. If you separate a CPU and heat sink that were bonded with a thermal pad, it is acceptable to replace the pad with thermal paste instead, unless the warranty on your CPU requires the use of the supplied thermal pad and heat sink.

Figure 3-13. Two forms of thermal pads used on CPU heat sinks

No matter which compound you choose, the technique for properly applying thermal compound to obtain optimal thermal bonding between a cooling device and a CPU involves a few very simple items and steps.

What you will need (see Figure 3-14):

- Thermal compound
- A clean, dry cloth, something as lint-free as possible
- Isopropyl (rubbing) alcohol
- A vinyl glove or piece of plastic wrap
- A straightedge, such as a single-edged razor blade or used plastic card
- An antistatic pad or chip storage bag to pad the CPU pins and reduce the chance of static damage

Figure 3-14. Basic items needed to bond CPU and heat sink

Use these items to install your heat sink as follows:

1. Remove the CPU from its socket and set it pins-down on the antistatic material.

2. Maintain cleanliness! Apply a few drops of isopropyl alcohol to the clean cloth and wipe the contact surface area of your heat sink and the top cap of the CPU core. Alcohol will remove most oils and help evaporate moisture from the surfaces.

3. Apply a small bead/drop of thermal compound to the area of the heat sink that will contact the CPU, as shown in Figure 3-15.

4. Protecting your fingers with the vinyl glove or plastic wrap, smear the compound around and into the surface of the heat sink, as shown in Figure 3-16. This will help fill imperfections in the metal surface.

5. Using a clean, dry portion of the cloth, wipe the excess thermal compound off the surface of the heat sink, as shown in Figure 3-17. If the compound is especially thick and hard to wipe off, scrape the excess off with the straightedge and then wipe clean. You should not expect to remove all evidence of the compound, but leave minute amounts on the surface. Do not use alcohol to clean the surface.

Figure 3-15. Apply thermal compound sparingly

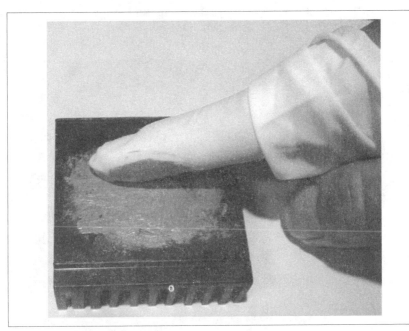

Figure 3-16. Rubbing thermal compound into the heat sink surface

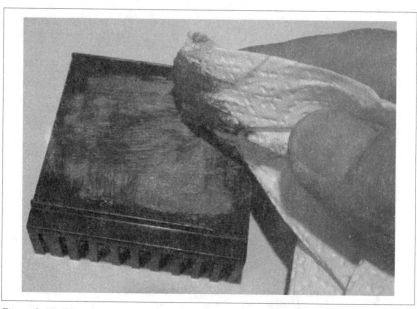

Figure 3-17. Wiping excess compound from heat-sink surface

6. Apply a small bead of thermal compound to a corner of the CPU's metal die/cap, as you did in Step 1.

7. Using the straightedge, distribute the compound evenly across the surface of the top of the CPU as shown in Figure 3-18.

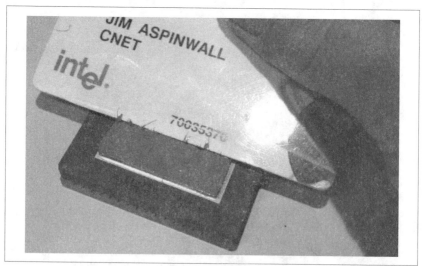

Figure 3-18. Spreading thermal compound on the CPU

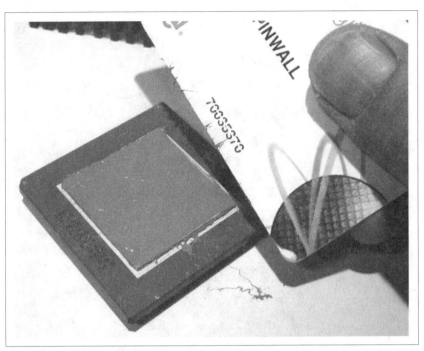

Figure 3-19. CPU with thermal compound ready for installation

8. Remove as much excess as possible but leave a thin layer of compound, as shown in Figure 3-19.

9. Install the CPU in its socket on your system board. Be careful not to disturb the thermal compound.

10. Align and place the heat sink as squarely and accurately in its final placement above the CPU as possible.

11. Apply a slight downward pressure evenly on the heat sink, then twist the heat sink to the left and right of its final placement position and back to its final centered position, as in Figure 3-20. This action will press out excess compound and fill in any gaps, reducing any bubbles and the surface-to-surface distance between the heat sink and CPU.

12. Secure the heat sink in place with its bracket (usually clipping in the back-end bracket slots and then the side with the "handle"), plug in the fan if your heat sink is equipped with one, and begin to enjoy your cooler CPU.

Figure 3-20. Slight pressure and twisting bonds the heat sink to the CPU

Follow the directions carefully for heat-sink fastening. The mechanics and fastening system for your heat sink, CPU, and system-board socket may be different than the one shown.

Control CPU Clock Speed from the BIOS

HACK
#25

Increase your CPU speed with parameters controlled by your BIOS.

After you've determined your present CPU speed [Hack #23] and temperature, and provided an adequate heat sink to draw away excess heat [Hack #24], you can dig into the system BIOS to see if and where it provides control over CPU clock speed and multiplier settings. (In lieu of settings in BIOS, you may find these controlled by jumpers on the system board.)

Some system boards give you everything you need to adjust clock speed from within the BIOS setup. Figure 3-21 shows very basic CPU speed control available in the Award BIOS of an ECS system board for an AMD Athlon CPU.

Starting with a system with an AMD Athlon XP that clocks at 1.9 GHz, with the original or default speed setting based on a 166 MHz CPU clock and an

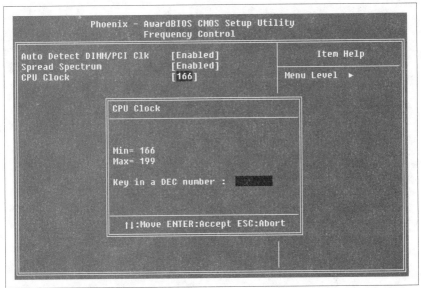

Figure 3-21. This Award BIOS setup program provides only CPU clock control with a default of 166 MHz

internal CPU clock multiplier value of 11.5 ($166 \times 11.5 = 1.91$ GHz), adjust the base clock speed up incrementally until the system fails to boot up or function reliably. Changing the base CPU clock speed to 185 MHz with the same fixed multiplier value (11.5), the CPU makes it up to 2.13 GHz (11.4% faster), runs reliably with no hacking other than this speed setting, and delivers a measured 11.40% performance increase per Sandra benchmarks [Hack #23].

Changing the CPU clock speed also affects the operating speed of other system components, most notably the Front Side Bus (FSB) that interfaces with the system's chipset and memory. If an overclock attempt fails, check the speed of your RAM and consider the limitations of the system board design and chipset.

If you start out with 333 MHz DDR RAM it may be limited to a mere 10–20% overclock rate and heat up considerably. Changing to 400 MHz RAM may allow you to further increase the CPU or FSB speed.

As shown in Figure 3-22, the CPU clock can be adjusted in 1 MHz increments up to 199 MHz. A setting of 185 MHz with a CPU multiplier of 11.5 causes the CPU to clock at 2.13 GHz.

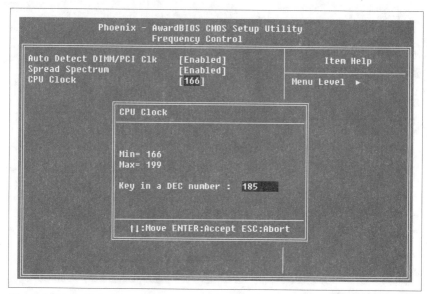

Figure 3-22. CPU clock settings in 1 MHz increments with 185 MHz chosen in the process of overclocking in small steps

When adjusting the CPU speed, you must be aware of one other clock value that may increase or decrease as the main CPU/FSB clock is adjusted, that of the PCI bus clock. System boards use various divider and multiplier logic circuits to keep the PCI and memory bus in sync with CPU operations. Like the CPU, ramping up these clock speeds too high (too low never seems to be a problem) can cause the system to function unreliably. The default FSB speeds for popular CPUs are shown in Table 3-4.

Table 3-4. FSB speeds for various common CPUs

FSB speed	CPUs
66 MHz	Intel Celeron
	Pentium I
100 MHz	AMD Thunderbird (early versions)
	Intel Pentium II (early versions)
	Intel Celeron
	Intel Pentium III (early versions)
133 MHz	AMD Thunderbird (C versions)
	Intel Pentium II (later versions)
	Intel Celeron
	Intel Pentium III

Table 3-4. FSB speeds for various common CPUs (continued)

FSB speed	CPUs
200 MHz	AMD Athlon XP (early versions)
266 MHz	AMD Athlon XP (mid-versions)
333 MHz	AMD Athlon XP (mid-versions)
400 MHz	AMD Athlon XP (late versions)
	Intel Pentium 4 1.3–2.6 GHz
	Intel Celeron 1.7–2.8 GHz
533 MHz	Intel Pentium 4 2.26 GHz and higher (Northwood and Prescott)
800 MHz (200 MHz × 4)	Intel Pentium 4 (with Hyper-Threading Technology) 2.4 GHz and higher

Both AMD and Intel update CPU versions and capabilities within major and minor product revisions. Table 3-4 is not intended to be a complete or exhaustive reference to every CPU or production version.

You can typically get away with allowing the default 33 MHz PCI bus speed to increase 10–20%, letting it run between 36 and 40 MHz, but this will depend on whether or not your peripheral cards (video, LAN, sound) can handle the higher speed.

I also tried overclocking an older Pentium III chip but ran into problems. The first sign of trouble when overclocking appeared in the P.O.S.T. phase. The Memory Test indicated that there were 524288 K of RAM (512 MB) when the system was running with the stable "124/31" overclocked settings. When I used the available 124/41 setting, the CPU still ran at 744 MHz, but the system became unstable once the operating system was loaded and running. Pushing the CPU even further with a selection of 133/33 allowed the system to run at 800MHz, but the memory test stopped testing at 360MB of RAM, as shown in Figure 3-23.

Failures in the P.O.S.T. typically indicate that the chipset, memory, or I/O bus cannot handle the higher speeds. It is recommended that you use clock settings that keep the PCI and AGP bus speeds within a few percent of their normal specifications.

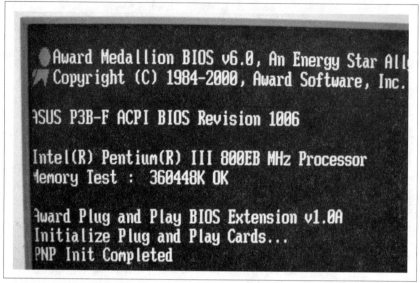

Figure 3-23. Memory test misses some RAM when overclocked

As Goes Voltage, So Goes Speed

Adjusting the power supply voltage to your CPU can make all the difference between an erratically performing speed-hack and a stable screaming demon.

Overclockers love to tweak every available parameter in attempts to squeeze every bit of performance out of their CPUs and system boards. Cranking up the speed is the most obvious way to get the CPU to run faster, but to get or keep it running at higher speeds you may have to jack up the CPU's power supply voltage a notch or two.

Today's CPUs run at extremely low voltages—in the range of 1.3 to 1.9 volts. As the CPU runs faster it gets warmer; as things get warmer their resistance increases, which causes loss of voltage and limits the available current to keep the device powered adequately. At these low voltages, it does not take much resistance to have a significant impact on voltage drop and increased heat generation.

Also, when the CPU runs faster the data signals tend to get a bit weaker, so increasing the voltage gives the data signals a little extra edge in getting through to the other components.

Be very careful with this hack; if you give the CPU too much juice, the internal temperature will rise quickly until the CPU components burn out and quite possibly release all of the "magic smoke" (and real smoke), rendering it useless. Ensure you have an adequate heat sink properly bonded and securely fastened **[Hack #24]** atop the CPU!

This is where you really need to check the BIOS CPU temperature alarm settings, if provided, and make sure they are enabled, or monitor CPU temperature with Sandra or a similar utility.

CPU voltage control may be available within your BIOS setup program, jumpers, or switches on the system board. Voltage adjustments may be in increments of 0.025, 0.05, or 0.1 volts, depending on design.

The common procedure for CPU voltage hacking is, at the CPU's rated speed, first try the next higher voltage increment than the default for your CPU. For example:

1. If the default is 1.3v, step it up to 1.325v and turn the system power on. If the system starts, boots up an operating system, and runs flawlessly for several hours, no damage has been done so far.

2. If the system passes the voltage increase test, begin increasing clock speeds until the system fails or becomes erratic, then back down to the last stable speed setting.

Repeat these steps until you crank it up as high as it will go while still maintaining stability. This seesaw setting method should allow you to get the clock speed up a bit higher. For common CPUs, the voltage limits are:

- Slot A AMD Athlon Classic: Max of 1.9v
- Slot A and Socket A Athlon Thunderbirds: Max of 1.85v
- Socket A AMD Duron: Max of 1.85v
- Intel Pentium, early Pentium II: Max of 2.8–3.3v
- Pentium II, early Pentium III (<600 MHz), Celeron: Max of 2.0–2.12v
- Pentium III (>600MHz): Max of 1.6–1.69v
- Pentium 4: Max of 1.6–1.85v

Do not increase the CPU voltage greater than its published operating voltage unless you can afford the risk of damaging and having to replace the CPU—sometimes an additional 2–5% performance increase is not worth the $80–300 for a replacement CPU. At those prices you can buy a faster system board and CPU combination.

Set the CPU Multiplier

#27 Changing the CPU's clock multiplier values can dramatically boost its performance without affecting other components.

The general nature of this hack applies only to AMD CPUs, all of which support multiplier value changes. Intel CPUs, with the exception of many Celerons, do not usually provide a means to change or even allow changing the CPU speed multiplier. Your system board must support the ability to change the processor clock multiplier value (the number the FSB or main clock speed is multiplied by within the CPU to arrive at the true operating speed).

The ability to change the multiplier value has significant merit in overclocking a system. First, it affects only the CPU, so neither the FSB nor the I/O bus clock values change. Second, it allows greater flexibility in altering the CPU speed; a small change of the multiplier value yields big changes in CPU clocking.

For example, if you have determined that your system will not boot or is unstable with an FSB/main clock value greater than 110 and your current CPU multiplier is 13 (yielding 1430 MHz), changing the multiplier value to 15 could yield a functional CPU speed of 1650 MHz. If 1650 MHz is too fast for your CPU chip to run stably, back down the FSB speed to 105 MHz and see if the CPU will survive at the resulting 1575 MHz, a 21% improvement from 1.3 GHz. AMD processors typically use odd-number multiplier values because of the way the CPU's internal clock works, so don't be surprised if trying x12, x14, or x16 leaves your system temporarily dead. Simply reset the multiplier value to an odd number and try again.

> Though many system boards can self-recover from erroneous settings, a "dead" system may have to have its CMOS settings reset to factory defaults [Hack #3].

If you've tried changing the multiplier value and nothing happens or the value returns to default during P.O.S.T., then it is likely the multiplier value is locked in your CPU and you may be able to unlock your CPU multiplier [Hack #28].

Unlock Your CPU Multiplier

#28 Overclocked AMD processors benefit from this down-and-dirty hardware hack that allows you to change the CPU multiplier value.

The objective of this hack is to release the electronic "lock" that prevents you from changing an AMD CPU's clock multiplier value. This is done by connecting circuits on the top of the CPU chip itself. From the steps below, which identify whether or not the two circuits of interest are connected, you will know if your multiplier needs to be unlocked. Unlocking the multiplier involves some very serious, precision work on the CPU chip itself and is not for the faint-hearted, caffeine-addicted, easily excitable types. In other words, patience, steady hands, good eyes, and controlled breathing are desirable assets. This technique is also described for many (but not all) AMD Athlon CPUs at various hacking/overclocking and gaming enthusiasts' web sites like *http://www.tomshardware.com*, *http://www.sysopt.com*, and *http://www.tweaktown.com*.

You will need the following tools to execute this hack:

- An antistatic work mat or foam pad
- An antistatic wrist strap and grounding point
- A magnifying lens
- A #2 pencil or 0.5 mm mechanical pencil with HB2 lead
- Optionally, an automotive window defogger repair kit (silver paint)
- Optionally, a soldering iron with a miniature tip, and solder (I recommend eutectic or SN63/37 blend solder for better connections)
- Optionally, the XP Unlocking Kit from *http://www.highspeedpc.com*

You'll be working with the CPU removed from its socket, connection pins down, preferably sitting in antistatic foam or on an anti-static work surface. It's a good idea to wear an antistatic wrist strap, with the other end clipped to a safety/earth ground someplace nearby. Do not trust the chassis of your CPU to be grounded, because if you followed the advice from "Bypass the BIOS Password" **[Hack #2]**, the power cord will be disconnected and the chassis will have no connection to ground.

You can observe the area of the CPU we'll be working on, as shown in Figure 3-24, with the naked eye, but you will probably want to do the actual work looking through a magnifying glass. The points of contact you will be working on are about 0.5mm apart. (If you're not into the metric system, let's just say it's a really, really small distance!) For visual comparison, the pencil in the photograph is an average mechanical pencil with 0.5 mm lead.

Locate the group of gold-colored connection points, known as *pads*, labeled "L1" on top of the CPU body—that's where you're headed. Orient the chip so "L1" appears normal—left-to-right, right-side up facing you. There will be four or five sets of connection pads, most of them connected up-and-down. If all of the pads are connected—appearing as four or five vertical bars—the CPU's multiplier section is already unlocked, as is the case with

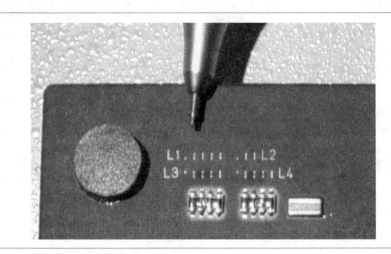

Figure 3-24. AMD L1 multiplier selection pins

the CPU shown in Figure 3-24, which came that way from AMD. If there are gaps between opposing pads top-to-bottom (like the two sets of dots in the middle two columns to the right of "L3" or "L4"), those are connections at "L1" that will have to be closed up. There should be *no* horizontal interconnections between the distinct vertical bars or across the dots left-to-right.

The first three items on the list of tools above are for your safety, comfort, and convenience, as well as the safety of the CPU. The remaining four items are choices for methods to "connect the dots"—drawing a small pencil line or placing a miniscule blob of silver paint or solder across the dots.

For experimentation, to see if this overclocking technique will work, start by using the pencil to connect the dots. The graphite of the pencil lead is suitably conductive to make a good temporary signal connection between the dots. Replace the CPU, heat sink, and fan; start up the system; and see if your overclock settings work OK. If the hack doesn't work, you can erase it, literally, by rubbing the lead off with a standard pencil eraser. If this modification works and you like it, you can erase the temporary connection, clean the area, and then solder or paint (using the silver repair paint) a more permanent connection blob in place.

Connect the dots to form a vertical bar. Connecting adjacent side-to-side dots or bridges can damage the CPU.

Check the Vents

#29

Properly venting your entire PC case will ensure longer component life for everything from your power supply to your disk drives.

Add it all up—a screaming 7,200 or 10,000 RPM hard drive, a lightning fast CPU, stunning RAM throughput, blinding video performance, and a modest few watts of sound power—and you realize that puny little fan inside the power supply is not going to be able to suck out the extra BTUs of heat generated by all these hopped-up devices.

The operative words here are "suck out." For some reason, PC chassis and power-supply engineers think that one little 2" fan stuffed into the corner of the power supply box is going to unload hundreds of BTUs of electronically induced heat and pick that heat out of all corners of the chassis. It's just not so. Even a newer PC with a fan and duct work placed above the CPU to remove significant amounts of heat from the PC chassis is not cooling the system as effectively as possible.

Generic PC design recommendations tell us we should evacuate or use a vacuum to pull hot air off the CPU and out of the PC chassis, but they do not tell us that to do so requires construction of air deflectors and ducting to create a maximum vacuum or negative pressure near the CPU heat sink. This is not practical for those of us who are building our own systems. (As well stocked and equipped as my shop is, I know I do not have plastic molding or sheet metal fabrication capabilities!) Those of us hacking prebuilt systems that have fancy ducting can benefit from this hack as well.

The basic physics of vacuum theory are pretty clear in that the pressure, or negative pressure in a vessel, especially a leaky one like a PC case, will not be even throughout. You can prove this quite easily at home with an average cardboard box, a pile of dust (sawdust works well) in one corner, and your typical household vacuum cleaner. Apply the nozzle end of the hose of the vacuum cleaner in any other corner but the one the dust is piled in, close up the box as best you can by folding over the flaps, and without moving the nozzle or the pile of dust around, see if you collect any, much less all of the dust from the other corner. It won't happen.

Leaving everything as it is, reverse the function of the hose: connect it to the outlet/pressure side of the vacuum cleaner and watch the sawdust spew out from every crack and crevice. Pressure wins over vacuum every time. The material leaves the holes in the chassis pretty much evenly and this is how pressurized air cooling works: one inlet and even distribution of the airflow all around. (Have you ever been in a building that vacuums air around to distribute cool or warm air for ventilation?) I have no idea what you're going to do with the mess you've just made, but the point should be obvious—pressurize your PC case!

> You will find that most server and network equipment chassis and enclosed rack systems use pressurization rather than convection and vacuum techniques to force-cool the contents.
>
> Assuming most server and network equipment rooms, and where you operate your PC, are relatively free of dust and debris, you should not have to worry about your PC filling up with every dust bunny, feather, and bug that happens to get near your chassis.

The little fan in the power supply is arranged to avoid blowing a lot of dust all over the components inside the supply, which happens anyway if all the air inside the PC leaves through the power supply: it heats up and fails faster. By luck and placement at the top of the chassis, a little convection flow will happen and some heat from the PC chassis will be drawn out, but not nearly enough. It's like trying to suck the air out of a balloon; as soon as one part of the balloon collapses you will never get all the air out.

Unfortunately, because of case design and all the cards and cables inside the PC, there are few places to mount a fan, inside or out, to be able to draw air in and blow it throughout the case. One of best places I've found is in between the plastic facia and the metal chassis, near where the PC speaker is typically mounted, or a grille area at the back of the chassis. I may rescue a 3–4" fan out of a failed power supply [Hack #19] (suitably disconnected from any power source and left to sit for a few minutes after removing power so there is no charge left on internal components) or buy a new 12v DC fan from a local electronics supplier, then attach male connector pins suitable to fit into an extra disk drive power connector, as shown in Figure 3-25.

Once the fan is ready to plug in, I find a suitable screw hole or two in the front or rear of the chassis (Figure 3-26), blowing inward through the copious holes that were supposed to draw air in for the power supply, mount the fan, and there it is—a cheap chassis pressurization system.

Just like the old "suction" method, pressurizing the chassis does have the effect of "inhaling" the dirt and dust bunnies that happen to float by your fan intake and pushing them around every component in the system. Adding a piece of thin foam-rubber padding as a filter to the intake side of the fan helps, but you have to remember to clean or change it occasionally to ensure ample airflow. While you're changing the filter, you can clean the dust off the components inside the case with a can of compressed air or a

Figure 3-25. Fans with Amp pins attached for connection to disk drive power connectors

Figure 3-26. Additional fan installed to move air into PC chassis from grille work and empty slots at the rear

small vacuum-cleaner nozzle to avoid building up an unwanted layer of insulation. PC components do not like being snuggled into a blanket of dust bunnies because the layer of dust holds in the heat we are trying to get rid of.

My experience has been that so much air moves so fast with a new fan that the dust bunnies do not have a chance to take up residence and instead get blown out with the warm exhausted air.

Besides that, what are you doing operating your PC in a dusty location anyway?

Memory Hacks
Hacks 30–39

A fast CPU has a voracious appetite for instructions and data. Instructions and data come to the CPU (through two or more layers of caching) from the main RAM on the system board. Optimizing the timing and performance of the memory systems can keep your hungry CPU sated.

Before you get concerned with memory performance, you may have an issue or three with the amount of RAM your hardware or operating system can support. Even if you can't kick your memory's performance up a notch or two, you can learn how to make the most of what you have by taming your operating system.

HACK #30 Install More RAM
Achieve top system performance with more RAM.

Having a significant amount of RAM in your PC provides enormous benefits, most notably that the operating system, drivers, programs, and data don't need to swap out to your hard drive to keep things running smoothly and you will have more memory for disk caching to speed up disk read and write operations. More RAM is also obviously important for loading applications and data, especially large ones like spreadsheets, databases, graphics, and video.

While the minimum RAM requirement for Windows XP is a meager 64 MB and Microsoft recommends 128 MB, 512 MB of RAM is the bare minimum for what most of us consider a fast Windows XP system. Long gone are the days of Windows 98 and Me, when 128 MB was the most memory that the majority of systems needed. Running an unhacked Windows XP configuration with only 512 MB of RAM does not leave a lot of room for programs, data, and disk caching. With 1 GB, the VCache [Hack #32] gets all of the RAM it can handle, leaving much more RAM for your use.

Depending on the chipset and design of your system board, performance may be enhanced if you install as few RAM modules as possible—changing out two 128 MB DIMMs (Dual Inline Memory Modules) for a single 256 MB DIMM, two 256 MB DIMMs for a single 512 MB DIMM, and so on. Fewer modules means less addressing and data-signal delays as the chipset switches between modules.

If the chipset in your system supports Dual-Channel Double-Data-Rate (DDR) RAM modules, as the Intel 865G and 865PE and 875P chipsets do, memory performance can be enhanced by using matched pairs of modules, which allow the chipset to split the RAM signal bandwidth across two memory modules. Your system board documentation should tell you which chipset it uses and the type of memory it supports.

> If you cannot determine which chipset your system board uses by looking at the chips on the board or from the manual, look up your system or system board model number using Google or *http://www.motherboards.org.*

Before adding more RAM, check your chipset against "Install the RAM Your Operating System Needs" **[Hack #32]** to see if more RAM is fully cacheable in your system. Beware that the more you fill up your RAM with programs and data, the longer it will take to swap any one of the larger memory hogs to the swapfile.

Recognize Memory Limitations
#31
Sometimes your system board and BIOS are your biggest limitations when it comes to adding more RAM—either a BIOS upgrade or a new system board is the answer.

When is any amount of RAM too much? When your system's sockets, BIOS, or chipset cannot address more than 256 MB, 512 MB, 640 MB, or more of RAM chips. System boards with three or four 72-pin SIMM (Single Inline Memory Module) sockets ordinarily will not accommodate more than four 32 MB ($4 \times 32 = 128$ MB) or four 64 MB ($4 \times 64 = 256$ MB) sticks of RAM.

So stuff as much RAM in the system as you have available, and determine from startup if the system recognizes it or not. If you install more RAM than the system can handle, save the RAM for another system that can use the same type of RAM.

Your old 486, Pentium I, or Pentium II vintage system may present you with a chipset or BIOS limitation that does not support as much RAM as you can physically install. Check the manual for your system board or look it up on the Web to see how much RAM the board will support. These limitations may be imposed by chipset design assumptions that no one would ever get their hands on that much RAM, much less have an operating system or program that could use it. If the chipset on your system board is capable of handling more memory, the limitation may be in your BIOS.

If you think that a BIOS upgrade might help accommodate more RAM, first scour the Internet for tips and advice to see if anyone else has successfully applied large amounts of RAM to the system board you have. You may be able to locate information on your specific board through a search of Google or Usenet newsgroups through Google Groups. Other resources to check are the chipset makers to determine the amount of RAM your chipset will support. This requires downloading and reading a lot of esoteric product specification data, but the documents may be informative reading even if they reveal limitations you were hoping to exceed.

If you determine that a BIOS update might help, check with your system board vendor or the folks at Unicore [Hack #9] to see if an upgrade is available for your system board.

Why put a limitation on the amount of RAM in any system? First, the 8088 CPU could only address a megabyte of memory space. Second, the first PC came with only 16K of RAM, and DOS and the few programs or BASIC programming tools available would fit quite nicely into a mere 64K of RAM. Third, RAM was expensive. Fourth, if no operating systems or applications needed more capability, there was no economic or practical reason to create a more expensive system than people would buy.

Another consideration was physics. Hardware and chip manufacturers could barely get a PC to function at 12–16 MHz in 1984–1985, nevermind the 3 GHz they can today. Memory and data components had to be designed to work at higher speeds. Getting more data bits to more memory chips meant signal lines had to be longer (and as a result noisier), making for tremendous reliability concerns.

Subsequent to the early PC days (when PCs ran at 4.77 MHz, "turbo" models ran at a whopping 8 MHz, and 286 systems started out with 8 MHz CPU clock speeds and eventually reached the blazing 16–20 MHz barriers), computer industry biggies like Lotus, IBM, and Microsoft began to understand the need for applications and data to consume more RAM than 640 KB. So, they concocted *Extended Memory* for the 16-bit i80286 CPU chips that could address 64 MB of RAM, even though many systems supported or had only 16.

The i80286-class processors had a known bug in them that limited the use of Extended Memory, so in the mid-1980s Lotus, Intel, and Microsoft created the Lotus-Intel-Microsoft (LIMS) *Expanded Memory Specification* (EMS) or LIMS-EMS Version 3.2, which readily made use of 8 MB of RAM regardless of the type of CPU in use, and this got us around the 286 bug. In 1987, Version 4.0 of the LIMS-EMS specification was released, which supported the use of 32 MB of RAM. Because LIMS-EMS worked with any CPU, it was the preferred method of adding and using additional RAM, until the i80386-class CPUs and Windows 3.0 arrived. These systems virtually eliminated the need for LIMS-EMS because the CPU could address and use all of the Extended Memory (above one megabyte) that was available. If a program still needed LIMS-EMS memory, it could be emulated with the EMM386 device driver.

These were the baby and giant steps in technology development that have driven or limited certain aspects of PC development and capabilities—captive to a seesaw effect of hardware or software limitations and the attempts to overcome one or the other. As these developments crept forward, hardware, BIOS, operating system, and software developers had to jockey around whichever technology looked the most promising.

The best way to know for sure what the RAM limitations are for your system board is to check the manual or manufacturer's web site. The documentation should indicate any special limitations on amount of RAM per socket or a requirement to install RAM in pairs. If you do encounter a limitation in the amount of RAM your system board supports, try these possible solutions:

- Rather than one module (SIMM or DIMM) with a lot of RAM on it installed in one slot, try two, three, or four smaller modules in each slot. If this works, the limitation is that the chipset and board design have a limited addressing range per RAM slot.

- Try a different type of module—switch from single- to dual-sided or dual- to single-sided. The limitation this addresses is module addressing/interleave incompatibility with the system board or chipset.

- Try two modules instead of one. If this works, the limitation is in addressing range per slot or a system board design that requires a pair of SIMMs/DIMMs to accommodate interleaving memory addresses across two devices.

- Try different or faster RAM. It could be that the memory you have is either not living up to its rated speed specification. The RAM could be too slow for or incompatible with the system board or chipset. Also, your modules could be defective.

- Check your system board manufacturer's web site or *http://www. unicore.com* for a BIOS upgrade that supports more memory.

Install the RAM Your Operating System Needs

Understand how your operating system and applications use RAM to solve memory dilemmas.

With today's operating systems and applications, the more RAM you can feed them, the better. Yes, Windows 95 only required 4 MB of RAM while Microsoft recommended 8, but trying to run Windows 95 on a system with less than 32 MB of RAM is definitely frustrating. The memory requirements for all versions of Windows are listed in Table 4-1.

Table 4-1. Windows operating system memory requirements and recommendations

Operating system	Minimum amount of memory required	Amount of memory Microsoft recommends	Practical recommendation
Windows 95	4 MB	8 MB	32 MB
Windows NT	64 MB	128 MB	128–256 MB
Windows 98/98SE	16 MB	24 MB	32–64 MB
Windows Me	32 MB	> 32 MB	64–128 MB
Windows XP	64 MB	128 MB	256–512 MB
Windows 2000	128 MB	256 MB	256–512 MB
Windows 2003	128 MB	256 MB	512–1,024 MB

Windows 98 was rumored to go into a memory-addressing performance frenzy with over 128 MB of installed RAM, but after much research this appears to be myth rather than truth. There is, however, a certain truth out there that may have implicated Windows by coincidence.

I've been exposed to several different system board chipsets as well as a variety of CPU choices from AMD, Cyrix, and Intel. It is evident from the sampling of chipset data in Table 4-2 that mass use of these chipsets in PC hardware was coincident with the era of Windows 9x (1995–2000). Keep in mind that these caching limitations in hardware affect Linux and other operating systems as much as they do Windows.

A RAM caching limitation is known to exist within the L2 cache features of some Intel chipsets and early Pentium II CPUs. The L2 cache of pre-dA1 production stepping level Pentium II CPUs is limited to caching up to 512 MB of memory. The Pentium II is not the only culprit in RAM limitations.

Table 4-2. Chipset cacheability limits

Vendor	Chipset	Supported CPU	Cacheable limit
ALi	Aladdin III	P54C	256 MB
AMD	640	P54C, P55C	768 MB
Intel	430 FX	P54C	128 MB
	430HX	Pentium	512 MB
	430LX	P5	192 MB
	430VX, 430TX	Pentium	64, 128, 256 MB
	440EX	Pentium II, Celeron	256 MB
	440 FX	Pentium Pro, later	4 GB
	815, 815e	P II, P III, Celeron	512 MB
OPTi	Python, Cobra	P5, P54C	128 MB
	Viper	P54C, P55C	512 MB
SiS	501–503	P5, P54C	128 MB
VIA	VP, VP2, VPX	P54C, P55C	512 MB

Cacheability significantly impacts overall system performance. Caching RAM significantly speeds up processing. If the L2 cache cannot, for example, accommodate more than 64 MB of RAM, that leaves any RAM in excess of 64 MB uncached, which means read and write performance is slower for a considerable amount of system memory (but faster than swapping to disk).

With the coincidence between Windows and various chipsets, it is quite possible that chipset and CPU limitations are to blame for the ill-placed rumors of Windows's memory-handling concerns. But I won't let Microsoft completely off the hook yet. According to Microsoft's Knowledge Base article 304943, Windows 98 and Me are specifically not designed to handle more than 1 GB of RAM. Above that amount, Windows may not boot completely, or it can crash. As we'll see in "Tame the Windows 95 and 98 Cache" [Hack #33], there is also another memory handling issue in Windows.

Certainly "huge" sums of RAM are possible with Windows 9x or Me (up to 1 GB), but unless your applications require it or you work with large data-files, more RAM may not be possible, practical, or efficient for some PCs. In the good old days, 16 MB of RAM was considered a lot and was very expensive—as costly as 64 or 128 MB memory components are today.

The trick is to balance overall system performance with the ability to get your work done. If you have a caching-impaired system that runs acceptably with 64 or 128 MB of RAM but you cannot work with your applications, you may have to sacrifice a bit of system performance because of the caching limitations by adding more RAM to get the job done. In any case, when your applications and data need more RAM than you have installed, Windows will swap out certain portions of itself, programs, and data to the swapfile, but performance will be so degraded that you probably won't be able to tolerate the sluggish behavior.

Large amounts of RAM are typically necessary only for processing graphic-intense programs like video games or drawing/rendering programs, as well as spreadsheet and database programs that process a lot of data. For these kinds of programs, adding more RAM (to 512–1,024 MB) has advantages in productivity, despite the overhead processing time the CPU consumes to address the "excess" RAM if it cannot be cached. More common activities like browsing the Web, reading or sending email, editing a chapter of a book, or figuring out your taxes are not as demanding of RAM and CPU time and will do just as well or better with an amount of RAM that is within the limits of your system's chipset cache and Windows.

The old, basic PC and DOS only needed to address a megabyte of RAM, and 384 KB of that was occupied by I/O device addressing between 640 and 1,024 KB without the addition of LIMS-EMS memory-enhancement software, such as Microsoft's EMM386 or the former Quarterdeck's QEMM driver software. In this regard, you were considered an avant-garde PC user if you had 8–32 MB of RAM and had "hacked" QEMM into your system to allow you to run Windows 3.x or 9.x and assorted applications more efficiently, or even Quarterdeck's DesqView or DesqView/X or IBM's OS/2 to enjoy a higher level of protected multitasking.

Windows NT, 2000, XP, and 2003, and even Windows Me, are significantly different from the legacy DOS+Windows configurations. Windows Me started up with DOS but quickly dismissed 16-bit DOS, loading in 32-bit Windows instead—to give the consumer a taste that DOS was indeed on the way out. Just as corporations skipped over Windows Me and stuck with 98 for the longest time, most consumers never saw anything like Windows NT or 2000 until Windows XP appeared, combining the significantly more stable components of a proven Windows 2000 OS with glitzy graphics taken from 98/Me and enhanced to the next level.

With Windows NT, 2000, XP, and 2003, the old DOS ways and limitations were banished from PCs forever—replaced with a graphical operating system that took over the motherboard and all system resources from the moment the BIOS finished testing the hardware and located a suitable boot-up device and the operating system. Perhaps the most important thing about Windows NT through 2003 is that we don't have to worry about different types of memory—DOS RAM, Extended Memory, Expanded Memory, etc. These operating systems see, address, and use all the memory that is available to them as one large chunk; there are no separate DOS and Windows portions of RAM to be concerned with.

The important message here is to provide an adequate amount of RAM based on your needs and system capacity. DOS alone is fine with 640 KB. For DOS+LIMS-EMS, with or without a memory manager like QEMM, with or without Windows 3.x–9x, 32–64 MB up to 128 MB of RAM is a real treat for select applications but not too practical or applicable for present-day computing applications.

Foraying into Windows based on Microsoft's "New Technology" (as "NT" stands for), you have a long way to go to exceed their memory limitations—4 GB today—though you may still be chipset-limited on memory efficiency. NT—whether in the form of Windows 2000, Windows XP, or Windows Server 2003—handles 4 GB just fine; your applications may never use all of it, but Windows will put it to use. These operating systems completely control memory addressing from bootup through shutdown—no meager 16-bit DOS limitations involved, ever. All of the RAM in the PC is available to the operating system to parcel out for operating system needs or applications. With many applications consuming 16–32 megabytes of memory to simply load and run, this is an important capability.

NT-based systems will make efficient and effective use of as much RAM as you can supply—but you will do fine with 512 MB. If you have an application need for more than 1 GB of RAM, be sure to pick a system board that will handle more than a gigabyte. The majority of system boards in prebuilt, off-the-shelf PCs or available to do-it-yourself geeks handle a generous 1–2 GB of RAM just fine.

If you've been limping along on 64–128 MB of RAM with Windows XP, splurge a little and kick the amount of RAM up a few notches to 256 or 512 MB and you will be amazed at the performance difference. Your system will boot and run significantly faster because the operating system has enough RAM for itself and several applications without ever having to swap inactive or low-priority memory contents off to the hard drive. Remember that RAM is orders of magnitude faster than a disk drive, so the more you can use RAM instead of the swapfile the better.

To judge the "right" amount of RAM and the impact of having more, consider that Windows XP itself needs a bare minimum of 64 MB of RAM to boot up and run. Beyond that you can start adding up the memory requirements of various applications by looking at the list of processes in Windows Task Manager.

A typical Microsoft Office application and document like this chapter will consume 32–64 MB, forcing a lot of memory content to the swapfile, so 128 MB of RAM barely keeps the operating system, your application, and data out of the swapfile. With 256 MB of RAM, most of the operating system and application should stay in RAM with room left over for virus protection, instant messenger applications, and other software programs. At 512 MB, there is more than enough room for the entire operating system, system cache, a typical office application, browser, IM programs, and virus protection with very little swapping of memory to the swapfile.

HACK #33 Tame the Windows 95 and 98 Cache

Stop Windows 95 from consuming all your RAM by fixing the VCACHE bug.

Microsoft does admit to a specific limitation of Windows 9x memory use in their Knowledge Base article 253912 (*http://support.microsoft.com/default. aspx?kbid=253912*). The article points to very real problems you may encounter if your Windows 95 or 98 system contains more than 512 MB of RAM. The article addresses a known problem with the VCACHE disk and disk caching driver, and the possibility that it may consume all available memory, up to 800 MB, leaving no memory for programs and data. There is a simple workaround for this—control the amount of memory VCACHE can use by changing its parameters following these steps:

1. Using Notepad, Edit, or another suitable text-only editor of your choice, open the *C:\WINDOWS\SYSTEM.INI* file.

2. Find the [VCache] section, which may have no contents under it. If a [VCache] section does not exist, create a new line entry for it just as it's written here, usually below the [386Enh] section.

3. Create or change the MinFileCache= and the MaxFileCache= lines with the desired new values, expressed in kilobytes.

4. If you want to create a 32 MB cache that does not grow larger than 40 MB, the lines should read:

```
[vcache]
MinFileCache=32000
MaxFileCache=40000
```

5. Save then close the modified *SYSTEM.INI* file and restart your PC.

Although VCACHE could consume more memory than it should, and supposedly will consume more than 512 MB, and Microsoft recommends setting the cache limit to 512000, they also claim they have not tested VCACHE settings larger than 40 MB, citing that unpredictable results or data loss may occur with values larger than 40 MB.

HACK #34 Manage the Paging File

Windows can get confused about what memory is and how it uses it. Giving Windows some guidance will keep things running smoothly.

Ever encounter an "out of memory error"? Been advised by an on-screen dialog message to "close some applications to free up memory"? These errors are usually *not* about adding or removing memory, but about how the operating system uses the memory available. Windows and some applications can present any number of "out of memory" error messages, such as:

- "There is not enough memory available to run this program. Quit one or more programs, and then try again."

- "Insufficient memory to initialize windows. Quit one or more memory-resident programs or remove unnecessary utilities from your Config.sys and Autoexec.bat files, and restart your computer."

- "The system is dangerously low on resources. Would you like to terminate the following application..."

Microsoft Windows 3.x–95/98/Me manage many types of memory—mostly RAM, but within and beyond the obvious system RAM, other resources that store data while the operating system and applications do their things.

There are three causes for "out of memory" conditions under Windows 9.x: truly having too little RAM to support the operating system, having too little free disk space for the operating system to be able to swap memory contents to the swapfile on a hard drive, or forcing the swapfile size into too small and overcrowded small segments of memory called "system resources."

A solution to the first problem is of course to add more memory [Hack #32]. When you've reached that point, 64–128MB of RAM or more if applications need it, it's time to look elsewhere for what's keeping Windows from being happy [Hack #35] or examine the Windows swapfile

The paging file or swapfile is controlled by Windows. While users can configure how much disk space to allocate to this file, only Windows decides how and when it is used. Left on its own, Windows could create a swapfile that is larger than necessary, or you could manually configure an unreasonably large swapfile yourself and waste hundreds of megabytes of disk space.

If the hard drive has too little free space available for making a swapfile, Windows can indicate "out of memory," meaning it could not swap out enough RAM contents to disk to leave your applications or data and the operating system enough memory to work with.

If the swapfile size is left for Windows to decide, it will also suffer fragmentation and be broken up across many different regions of the disk drive, further reducing performance. Swapfile fragmentation will occur if there is no single area of free space large enough to contain the entire swapfile, or, if the swapfile starts out at one size, files are subsequently stored "around it," and then the swapfile has to grow into a separate area of free space.

> Defragmenting your hard drive every week, certainly every month, is an excellent way to improve both filesystem and swapfile performance. But see "Hacking the Hack" for instructions specific to Windows NT and later.

There are several rules of thumb that can be applied to configuring the size of the swapfile. In most cases, the swapfile size should be at least equal to the amount of RAM installed on the system—that is, if you have 32 MB of RAM, the swapfile should equal at least 32 MB of disk space and preferably 2–3 times more (64–96 MB). The debate rages at this point whether or not the size of the swapfile should be exactly equal to, 150%, or 200%, or more of the amount of RAM in the system. Depending on the amount of RAM installed, most of us use 150% as the maximum value to give Windows a little extra room, but not an excessive amount, to play with.

It is important to remember that each version of Windows has a minimum RAM requirement, as shown in Table 4-1. Your system should have enough RAM to accommodate Windows (the minimum requirement) plus your applications and data if you want to reduce swapfile use and manage its size.

Setting the swapfile size tells Windows how much disk space it can play with when it decides it's time to swap a program or data out the file. You want Windows using the hard drive sparingly, and when it does use it, you want it to use it as efficiently as possible. So how do you determine what "size" to make the swapfile?

> All swapfile setting recommendations come with an explicit or implied "rule of thumb" caveat. Most of the recommendations exist for two reasons: a desire or need to limit the amount of disk space the swapfile consumes and to try to contain or limit the fragmentation of the swapfile and other files on the same drive.
>
> There are as many people telling us not to set a specific swapfile size as there are telling us what values to use for setting the swapfile. Nowhere is it documented that manually setting the swapfile size does any harm, unless you try to set it too low.
>
> Windows will allow you to configure no swapfile but will "complain" at startup with a strong message telling you to create a swapfile. As a built-in "self-preservation" feature, even with a zero-byte or no swapfile setting, Windows will create a swapfile anyway.

If you have less than 128 MB of RAM, set the swapfile to be at least equal to, or up to 150% of, the amount of RAM. At less than 128 MB of RAM, Windows is going to swap out idle programs and data more than it would with 128 MB of RAM. Going to a 150% swapfile size gives Windows room to rattle around and enough space for applications to play in memory, and enough swapfile space to swap it all out if necessary.

If you have more than 128 MB of RAM, you have to start believing that you have more than enough RAM to keep the operating system (at least Windows 95-Me) and most of your applications happy, since you've met the minimum RAM requirement for the operating system plus additional RAM for applications. At 128, 256, or 512 MB of RAM, the swapfile size should be equal to no more than the amount of RAM—after all, even a portion of 128, 256, or 512 MB is a *lot* of disk space to waste and a lot of data to read and write on a disk drive if Windows has to swap out, which considerably slows the system performance but is better than running out of memory.

> Windows XP is very "smart" about memory use and the swapfile. If you set the swapfile size too small and then run multiple large applications and open multiple documents, Windows XP can take precedence, ignore your maximum swapfile size setting, and force a larger swapfile size to protect itself and your work when both RAM and swapfile use have "maxed out."

It is obviously far better to add more RAM than hit the ceiling of RAM+swapfile size or keep increasing the swapfile size to overcome having too little RAM. For systems with abundant amounts of RAM, certainly at the 512 MB to 1 GB level, setting the swapfile to no less than 50% of the amount of RAM typically provides good performance. However, if you frequently use multiple large applications or have multiple large datafiles open, the swapfile should equal the amount of RAM so Windows has adequate space to swap to. Table 4-3 gives recommendations for swapfile sizes.

Table 4-3. Recommended swapfile sizes based on amount of RAM

Total system RAM	Recommended swapfile size
16 MB	32 MB
32 MB	32–64 MB
64 MB	64–96 MB
128 MB	128 MB
256 MB	256 MB
512 MB	256–512 MB

Table 4-3. Recommended swapfile sizes based on amount of RAM (continued)

Total system RAM	Recommended swapfile size
768 MB	512–768 MB
1,024 MB (1 GB)	512–1,024 MB

To ensure the best performance of the swapfile and prevent the swapfile from changing size and becoming fragmented, set the minimum and maximum size of the file to the same values. For a recently defragmented PC, setting the swapfile size will create a new, unfragmented swapfile. If you set the minimum and maximum sizes to different values, the swapfile can become fragmented and only a disk defragmenter that can defragment the swapfile can put it back together for a short time.

To set the swapfile size, follow these specific instructions for your operating system:

1. Right-click the My Computer icon.
2. Select Properties and then follow the instructions below for your particular operating system.

Windows 95, 98, 98SE, Me

1. Select the Performance tab, then the Virtual Memory button.
2. The default setting is "Let Windows manage my virtual memory settings." Instead, select "Let me specify my own virtual memory settings."
3. Type in the size you want in both the Minimum and the Maximum edit boxes.
4. Click OK to close the dialogs but do not restart the system yet; there is one more change to make in the system configuration.
5. See "Force Windows 98 and Me to Swap Less" **[Hack #36]** for the next set of steps to follow before restarting your computer.

Windows NT, 2000, XP, 2003

1. Select the Advanced tab.
2. In the Performance section, click on the Settings button. The Performance Options dialog appears.
3. Under the Virtual memory section, click the Change button. The Virtual Memory dialog appears.
4. Select the "Custom size:" radio button.

5. Type in the minimum and maximum amount of disk space you want to allocate for the swapfile size.

6. Click OK to save the information and close the dialogs, but before you restart your PC, take a look at "Pin the Kernel in RAM" [Hack #37].

Hacking the Hack

Windows NT, 2000, XP, and Windows Server 2003 can't defragment the pagefile, because it is open for exclusive use while the system is up and running. Sysinternals PageDefrag (*http://www.sysinternals.com/ntw2k/freeware/pagedefrag.shtml*) gets around this problem by defragmenting your pagefile at the next reboot: it uses the same defragmentation mechanism that Windows uses, but it runs before the operating system has opened the pagefile for exclusive use.

HACK #35 Manage Windows System Resources

Windows System Resources have been misunderstood and maligned for years. There isn't much you can do about them but change your software.

Many "out of memory" errors, specifically "out of resources" or "low on resources" error messages, on Windows 95, 98, and Me have nothing to do with how much RAM is installed in the system but how well specific portions of it are managed. The specific portions of RAM I'm discussing here are the system resources. Why Microsoft allows Windows to issue the same "out of memory" error for low resources that it issues for actually having too little system memory to run a program is anyone's guess; they know better and so do we.

System resources are (poorly documented) bits of memory that Windows 95, 98, and Me play with internally. They comprise three fixed-size 64 KB blocks of RAM known as the GDI, User, and System resources, each used for a specific purpose within the operating system. The GDI (Graphical Device Interface) is used for communicating graphical device instructions and is not usually implicated in "out of memory" or "out of resources" error conditions. System resources are rarely implicated in these conditions, as Windows manages this block pretty well for itself. User resources, on the other hand, really are not under user control but used at the whim of applications that PC users use.

Each resource in Windows 95/98/Me is limited in size as well as in the number of processes or blocks of each range that can be used (16). Programs may request and use blocks of available resources on a temporary basis, primarily for moving small amounts of data between other applications or storing them for themselves. Windows will manage and keep track of resource use, but not if a resource is no longer needed by the program that requested it. If a program closes or crashes and fails to tell Windows that the resources it used can be relinquished back to other uses, Windows never knows the difference. If you restart one of these errant programs and close it again, or if it crashes and keeps the resources tied up, the problem gets worse, since a new block of data is consumed while the old one is never released.

If all of the system resource allocations are consumed, no other program can use them, and you could encounter a mysterious "out of memory" or "out of resources" error. Since Windows has no way to know if the program that used a resource allocation no longer needs it, the condition will not improve without a reboot.

Windows 95, 98, and 98SE (see also the upcoming section "How Systems Resource Use and Tracking Changed Under Windows Me") keep pretty tight tabs on the amount of resources that are available and in use. You can monitor system resources and, as a result, the behavior of your application programs with regard to resource use and cleaning them up by using Windows's System Resource Meter program, *RSRCMTR.EXE*. To use the System Resource Meter, first install it by following these steps:

1. Click Start, select Settings, and then select Control Panel.
2. Double-click Add/Remove Programs.
3. Select Windows Setup and then double-click System Tools.
4. Click System Resource Meter and then click OK twice.

Access the System Resource Meter tool by either of these methods:

1. Click Start and select Run.
2. Type in **rsrcmtr.exe** and then click OK.

Or:

1. Click Start, then select Programs.
2. Select Accessories, then System Tools, and then Resource Meter.

The first time you run the System Resource Meter, you will receive a dialog like that of Figure 4-1 alerting you to the fact that Resource Meter itself consumes some resources, just to let you qualify your results knowing each tool you use may impact the readings.

Resource Meter displays a bar graph and percentages of each respective resource used, as shown in Figure 4-2. The measurements are an aggregate reading of the amount of memory consumed by resource use and the number of resources allocated.

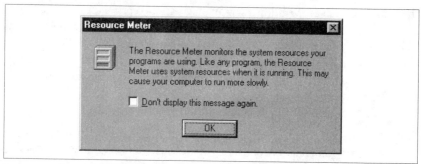

Figure 4-1. Resource Meter warns you that it too uses system resources

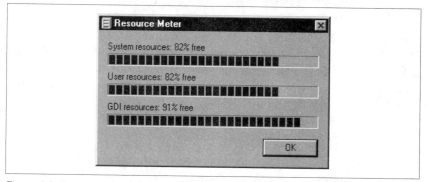

Figure 4-2. Resource Meter showing very little resource use

Many programs will monitor resources on their own and may indicate that insufficient memory exists to run if any of the measured resources gets below some internally defined percentage, even though the program may not need to use more resources than it takes to start the program and test for available memory. This condition causes a lot of support calls and fruitless efforts to add more memory.

> Unrecoverable or unreleased system resource abuse is one of the reasons Windows users feel the need to reboot so often, and rightfully so. Exiting some programs does not immediately or always release the resources they used—bad programming and the poor resource management of Windows are to blame. In cases where stubborn applications fail to release resources, restarting the system is the only way to get a "clean slate" of resources.

Some users watch the resource levels like hawks over new prey in hopes of participating in regulating the use of these resources and trying to keep as much of them available as possible. Manic users establish some self-imposed threshold levels on how much resource usage is too much, nearly panicking if a newly loaded program runs the bar up "too high" or if resource use doesn't drop immediately once a program is terminated.

Preying on this memory-monitoring tech anxiety are many utility software programmers who create RAM management programs such as RAM Idle, RAM Booster, MemTurbo, Mem Free, FreeMem, and the like. These programs try to intervene in the process of knowing which programs use the resources when they are run and try to clean up after them by forcing the resources free if a program terminates without doing its own housekeeping. Oh the wasted anxiety of it all when, in fact, there is very little a user can do to control specific resource usage, especially since such memory management programs also consume resources and CPU time and often conflict with Windows's own memory management functions. I really do not advocate the use of these programs for these reasons.

While the "sticky resource" problem is allowed by Windows it is almost certainly caused by improper application development. Instead of fighting resource issues with Windows 95/98/Me, you can avoid them by:

- Monitoring Resource Meter and experimenting with each application you use to determine its resource use and if it frees up resources when terminated. Any program that does not clean up when it exits is a program that should be avoided at all cost; if the people who created the program cannot manage memory use properly, you have to wonder what else they neglected. Look for an upgrade to the application and specifically for an upgrade that indicates it has solved its resource-hogging problems.

- Upgrading to a version of the program or a new operating system (like Windows 2000 or XP) that does not have issues with these legacy resources.

- Unfortunately, rebooting at least daily. This is the way to absolutely assure that resources are cleared after use and provide a fresh start for your applications.

How Systems Resource Use and Tracking Changed Under Windows Me

Knowing that System Resource management under Windows 9x was inadequate, when Microsoft created Windows Me, they broke the system resources mold, ground it up into tiny pieces, and burned it. The biggest problem with fixed-resource allocations was not so much the 64 KB limit but that only so many blocks of any size (up to 64 K) could be allocated. So, if more than 16 programs needed resources, the system immediately "ran out" of them. With Windows Me, Microsoft replaced the static 64 KB System and User Resources with dynamically allocated and managed schemes that allowed nearly all system RAM to be used as resources by unlimited numbers of programs.

Resources could be allocated to as many programs as needed them, and they could take up to the limit of available RAM memory, though no program probably ever put a dent in the many megabytes of RAM most Me systems had available.

Given Me's unlimited resources, you might think that a program would never produce an "out of memory" or "out of resources" error message and fail to run. Unfortunately, programs that kept track of Windows's resources did so unnecessarily (because they were designed for 95 and 98, where resources were limited) and did so with the only tool they had—the same data the Resource Meter used, which under Me is completely erroneous.

Resource Meter and similar measurements based resource limits on the percentage of memory used and allocated. Under Windows 95 and 98, a system running either 8 programs of 16 maximum or using 32 KB of the total 64 KB of resources indicated that 50% of resources were free. Under Windows Me, if just one program used 32 KB of resources, Windows allocated 32 KB, which is 100% of the available resources (allocated at that time), and Resource Meter would always indicate 100% use no matter what. A program that checks resource use would see 100% use, determine that no resources were available to it, and might kick out an error message instead of knowing it could have requested a resource allocation and gotten it.

And no, Microsoft did not update the Resource Meter program for Windows Me, nor did they openly publish this information for developers or users. Indeed, Microsoft did publish a paper about the change in resource allocation methods, but for some reason the paper quickly disappeared off their web site after enough attention was called to the matter, which is unfortunate because it explained a lot of things and would have allowed programmers to correct their software accordingly. Windows NT, 2000, XP, and Windows Server 2003 have unlimited resources using a completely different style of memory management from Windows 9x and Me, and these NT-based operating system do not have resource problems.

HACK #36 Force Windows 98 and Me to Swap Less

Tame Windows use of the swapfile and improve your system's performance in one simple parameter.

Windows 98 and Me can be configured to force the operating system to prefer operating in RAM, conserving swapfile use by not swapping memory to disk as much, and improving system performance. To do this, add a single line in the [386Enh] section of the *C:\WINDOWS\SYSTEM.INI* text. This hack is advantageous only if your computer exceeds the minimum RAM requirements for your operating system as listed in Table 4-1 by at least 2–3 times. This should give you more than enough RAM to hold the operating system and your applications.

> If you have only the minimum amount of RAM required up to the recommended amount, you may not have enough room for applications and data and may encounter an "out of memory" error **[Hack #34]**.

To perform this hack, follow these steps:

1. Using DOS EDIT, Windows Notepad, or another text-only editor, open the *C:\WINDOWS\SYSTEM.INI* file.

2. Scroll down until you find the [386Enh]. Move the cursor below that line and insert a new line that reads:

   ```
   [386Enh]
   ConservativeSwapFileUsage=1
   ```

3. Save and close the *SYSTEM.INI* file and then restart Windows.

Windows will now keep more of itself, applications, and data in memory and use the virtual memory swapfile less and more efficiently—a sure performance boost.

H A C K #37 Pin the Kernel in RAM

Force Windows NT operating systems to keep themselves in RAM for faster performance.

An excellent performance hack for Windows 2000, XP, and 2003 is a feature that lets you specify whether or not to allow Windows to swap the main portion of itself, the operating system kernel, and swappable drivers out to the swap/pagefile or not.

This hack is intended for systems with large amounts of RAM (512 MB or more) and involves editing the Windows registry or using a system tweaking program. If your system has 256 MB of RAM or less, consult "Install More RAM" **[Hack #30]** before taking advantage of this hack.

To use the registry editing method follow these steps:

1. Start the Registry Editor by opening the Start menu, then selecting Run.

2. Type in **regedit** and then click OK.

3. Navigate through the registry tree to the following subkey:

```
HKEY_LOCAL_MACHINE\SYSTEM\CurrentControlSet\Control\Session Manager\Memory
Management
```

4. Change the `DisablePagingExecutive` entry to 1. The complete registry information is:

```
Value Name: DisablePagingExecutive
Data Type: REG_DWORD
Data: 0 or 1 Default
```

5. Close regedit and reboot.

Setting the value of this entry to 1 forces the kernel and drivers to remain in physical memory. If it is set to 0, these items can be swapped from memory to disk as needed, obviously affecting performance because data transfers are slower to and from disk than memory.

If editing the registry is not your style, you can use a tweaking program called X-Setup or X-Setup Pro from X-Teq Systems (*http://www.xteq.com*) for setting this and many other gimmicks in Windows, as shown in Figure 4-3.

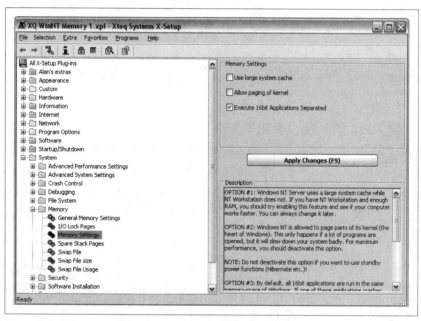

Figure 4-3. X-Setup provides access to many tweaks for Windows

To use X-Setup to configure this hack, follow these steps:

1. Go to Start and then select Control Panel.

2. Double-click the X-Teq Systems X-Setup icon.

3. Select the X-Setup Default UI from the welcome dialog.

4. Expand the System folder.

5. Expand the Memory folder.

6. Select Memory Settings.

7. In the Memory Settings region to the right, remove the check from the "Allow paging of kernel" checkbox.

8. Click the Apply Settings button, close the X-Setup program, and restart your system.

From this point forward, the operating system's kernel and swappable drivers will stay in RAM, and you should notice less swapping activity and slightly better performance over long-term use of the system.

> You probably will not see a performance improvement from this hack in a benchmarking program without also running other programs in the background to load up your RAM and keep the CPU busy.

Speed Up Your RAM

Get higher performance by optimizing the timing parameters for the faster memory in BIOS.

CPUs are not the only part of your system that can be overclocked. Memory timing settings have just as big an impact on RAM performance as the bus and CPU frequency. By hacking memory timing, you may be able to obtain as much as a 10–20% performance enhancement.

System board BIOS implementations may offer numerous settings to optimize your memory. These settings modify RAM functions that, while basic in nature, are often given widely different names.

> This hack is purely trial and error and is intended for those with a real sense of technical adventure. Hacking RAM speed settings can yield unpredictable results, such as the inability to boot, crashes, or data loss.

It is unlikely but possible that changing any of these parameters will damage your RAM. Some BIOS may provide an automatic fall-back setting recovery mode so you can restart without the hassle of wiping out the CMOS memory [Hack #2].

The first step to tweaking your memory is to turn off the Serial Presence Detect (SPD) function in your system's BIOS, as shown in Figure 4-4.

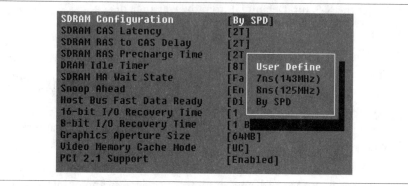

Figure 4-4. Memory timing controls in Award BIOS

The SPD function reads your RAM modules to determine what timing parameters to use; when it's off, you're in control of the clock speeds for your memory.

> Once you take control of your memory timing parameters there are myriad combinations of settings that may speed up, slow down, or crash your system. You should not work with critical data when hacking settings that could cause system crashes or data loss.

The following list shows several common memory hacking parameters, some of the names given to these parameters, and their functions. Where possible the normal, safe, or default values are listed. Please note that not all BIOS setup programs offer all of these settings, use the same names for them, or have the same default values, while some parameters are known universally by their technical or functional names.

Serial Presence Detect (SPD), Automatic Configuration (Auto)
    If you want to manually configure your memory timings, you will have to deactivate the automatic RAM speed detection function.

Bank Interleaving, Bank Interleave
    Typically set to 4. Addressing RAM through interleaving improves performance.

Burst Length, Block Transfers
    Typical values are 8, 4, or 2 data blocks transferred in one memory cycle. Performance should increase with a higher value.

Column Address Select (CAS), CAS Latency Time, CAS Timing Delay
    CAS specifies the number of clock cycles between a column of memory address being activated and the availability of data at the RAM's out-

put. A lower number is better, but if this setting is set for too few cycles output data will be unreliable and the system will become unstable. If set longer than necessary, performance will suffer.

Command Rate, Address Cycles

Command Rate specifies the number of clock cycles needed to access a memory chip to get to the specific address needed. This will take longer if you have a lot of memory modules in your system, making it desirable to use as few modules as possible for increased performance. A lower number is better, but a higher number may be necessary for your memory to work right, at the cost of slightly reduced performance.

Row Address (RAS) Precharge Time

Number of clock cycles needed to precharge the circuits so that the row address can be determined. Lower should be faster, but higher may be necessary to maintain stability.

RAS-to-CAS Delay, tRCD

Number of clock cycles between row address and column address. A smaller value can increase performance. However, if there are too few cycles, memory addressing errors will occur.

Row Active Time, tRAS, Active to Precharge Delay, Precharge Wait State, Row Active Delay, Row Precharge Delay

The time between addressing two different rows in a memory chip. Too little time will make addressing unreliable; too much will make performance suffer.

Memory Clock, DRAM Clock

The clock speed of the memory bus. With normal SDRAM, the rate is related to the front-side bus (FSB) clock. With DDR, the actual RAM speed is doubled.

The settings you are able to use are dependent on numerous factors: your BIOS default and changeable settings, system board chipset, RAM cacheability, CPU L1 and L2 cache sizes, system board design quality, memory module and chip manufacturer, memory speed, and type of memory used.

To test your hacks for performance gain or loss, you can use SiSoftware's Sandra diagnostic and benchmarking program, shown in Figure 4-5, available for download from *http://www.sisoftware.net*. Sandra provides system information, testing, and benchmarking of PC components. For testing memory, use the memory bandwidth and combined memory and cache benchmark tests.

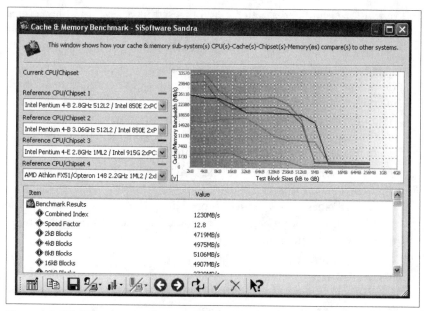

Figure 4-5. SiSoft Sandra provides a wealth of system benchmarking information

If you have an unhackable OEM system [Hack #9] or you have slow memory modules (PC100, DDR200) that are not reliable with faster timing settings, your only choice for improving performance through memory is if the BIOS supports SPD and you install faster RAM—PC133 instead of PC100 or DDR333 instead of DDR266. Hacking values for PC100 RAM may result in a mere 2–3% performance increase, while simply changing to PC133 RAM yields an expected 20–30% increase in performance with no hacking at all.

H A C K #39 Enable Memory Interleave for Via Chipsets

The Memory Interleave Enabler driver for Via chipsets optimizes memory settings for you.

Once in a while someone digs deep enough into an issue or exploits an opportunity and simply creates a single program or driver to take the guesswork out of fiddling with bits, bytes, microseconds, and clock rates.

Many Via chipset implementations do not have memory interleave enabled, which hinders performance. This feature is also not normally available in BIOS setup programs, and the only way to turn this feature on to gain a performance boost is to use a driver specifically written to enable it.

To find out if you have a Via chipset that could benefit from enabling memory interleave, visit *http://www.cpuid.com/cpuz.php* to download their CPU-Z program.

George Breese's Memory Interleave Enabler for Via chipsets (*http://www. georgebreese.com/sites/georgebreese_com/net/software/*) is a driver you install in Windows to do the work of turning on and tweaking the memory-interleave values for your chipset. Figure 4-6 shows SiSoftware's Sandra Memory Bandwidth Benchmark before installing Memory Interleave Enabler.

Figure 4-6. Sandra memory benchmark before enabling memory interleave

After installing Memory Interleave Enabler, you will notice at least a slight improvement in memory performance, as indicated in Figure 4-7. Any performance improvement, no matter how you get it, can be good for the overall system.

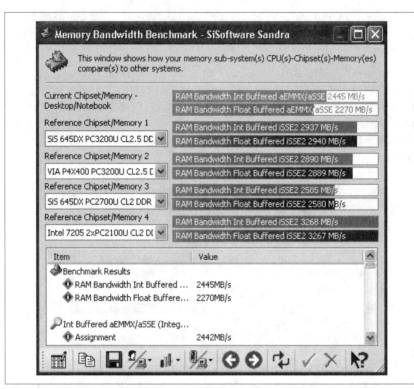

Figure 4-7. Sandra memory benchmark after enabling memory interleave

If you add up enough 0.5% improvements with subtle hacks, you'll be up to an additional 5–10% in no time. The documentation at George Breese's web site, *http://www.georgebreese.com/net/software/readmes/venabler_v015_readme.htm*, explains the details.

Disk Hacks
Hacks 40–57

No matter how fast your CPU or memory are, disk drives and peripherals are the biggest bottlenecks to system performance. After you spend all day tweaking and revving up your CPU and memory, you're rewarded with the same old sluggish disk drives, which undermine any other performance-improving hacks. In this chapter, we'll cover some easy and often free tune-ups to get your disks living up to your system's demands and your expectations of reliability by making informed partitioning choices and using the tools necessary to prepare a hard drive for file storage.

H A C K   #40   Partition and Format Wisely
Partition your drive for efficient file play.

Do you know how much of your hard disk space you're wasting? If you are using Windows 95, 98, 98SE, or ME (even 2000 or XP without NTFS), you could be wasting at least 10% and possibly up to 30% of your hard drive space due to suboptimal allocation unit sizes.

Disk partitions are logical regions of a disk drive containing a filesystem. Partitioning a hard disk is like subdividing parcels of land and dictating how those parcels will be further subdivided into lots or common areas. Partitioning establishes how big the parcel of land to be used will be. The filesystem within a partition contains files and directories that are organized in what we see as a hierarchical tree structure.

We use the filesystem and the tools and support for it within an operating system to put things into and take them out of the "parcels" (called *clusters*) of space allocated in the partition. If we put a small house in a large parcel (cluster) we have a lot of empty space. In terms of land, we could landscape or farm that space, but in terms of filesystems, we get only one "house" per cluster. One house may occupy many clusters, but nothing else can use that cluster, even if there is empty space within it.

The Different Partition Types

The different operating systems available for PCs provide support for various partition types and filesystems. There are five types of partitions you will encounter on x86 machines:

Primary

A primary partition is the first and often the only partition on a hard disk drive, occupying all available disk space. A primary partition is required for DOS and Windows 9x-Me, but Windows NT and later, as well as Linux, can boot from an extended partition. The primary partition can contain only one logical drive. You may have up to four primary partitions, or a maximum of three primary and one extended partition.

Extended

An extended partition can only exist if there is at least one primary partition. This partition may occupy the remainder of the drive's free space or only a portion of it; the remainder may contain either NTFS or non-DOS partitions. The extended partition may contain one or more logical drives.

Logical

Within an extended partition, at least one logical partition must be made if a DOS or Windows filesystem will access the space as a drive letter. If the extended partition is created but no logical partitions are created within it, any operating system may lay claim to the space or change the extended partition into a non-DOS partition.

NTFS

An NTFS partition is typically created and used by Windows NT, 2000, XP, or 2003. DOS and Windows 9x-Me utilities have no direct control over or access to NTFS partitions. Each NTFS partition may contain logical partitions and drives of their own.

Non-DOS

A non-DOS partition is any partition type not supported by DOS or Windows, which could be any of the different versions of Linux, FreeBSD, SunOS, or others. Those specific operating systems may allocate space and filesystem support through numerous other filesystem types.

The FDISK utility that comes with MS-DOS and Windows 95, 98, and Me refers to filesystems created by other operating systems (such as Linux or FreeBSD) as *non-DOS partitions*.

On most IBM, HP, Compaq, and Dell systems, the first partition may be a non-DOS rather than a primary partition, may have an MBR, and may be made Active, but instead of an operating system may contain a boot loader to access diagnostic, system setup, and recovery files. This partition may consume a few tens of megabytes to a few gigabytes, depending on what the vendor wants to store in it for later use.

The BIOS in these systems will present a boot loader option to press a specific key to access these features and boot from this partition, and if that key is not pressed within a preset amount of time the BIOS will set another partition (primary, NTFS, or other non-DOS partition) to Active to load the operating system. Alternatively, some systems require use of a recovery boot diskette or CD that provides access to the recovery files on the recovery partition.

Each partition type may be either the Active (bootable) partition or not. An Active partition is not automatically a system or bootable partition, but must be made into a system or bootable partition by whichever operating system you install.

The Active partition is the one the PC system BIOS looks for in order to find bootable files and an operating system. To be bootable, the Active partition must have a Master Boot Record and must contain the bootable operating system files to start. The remainder of the operating system's non-boot files may reside on another partition and logical drive. DOS and Windows 9x–Me will only boot from an Active and primary partition.

Third-party multiboot utilities like BootMagic, LILO, GRUB and System Commander change the Active partition to select which operating system will boot up.

The boot loader in Windows NT through Windows Server 2003 can boot DOS or other versions of Windows in the same Active partition.

Windows 2000 and Windows Server 2003 support two types of disk configurations—Basic and Dynamic—created with Windows Disk Management console. A Basic disk can use the partition tables supported by respective versions of Windows, MS-DOS, and Windows NT. A Basic disk, the typical type of partition you use, can hold primary partitions, extended partitions, or logical drives.

Basic volumes include partitions and logical drives and may contain volumes created using Windows NT 4.0 or earlier, such as volume sets, stripe sets, mirror sets, and stripe sets with parity. In Windows 2000, these volumes are called spanned volumes, striped volumes, mirrored volumes, and RAID-5 volumes, respectively.

Like a Basic volume, a Dynamic disk can hold simple volumes, spanned volumes, mirrored volumes, striped volumes, and RAID-5 volumes. However, with Dynamic storage, you can perform disk and volume management without having to restart the operating system.

In most cases, you will encounter only primary and extended partitions, or NTFS partitions with Basic disks.

The Different Filesystems

After you've partitioned a drive, you need to decide which filesystems will actually live on it. There are dozens of different filesystems you may encounter in the wild. Here are a few:

DOS FAT-12, FAT-16, FAT-32
DOS filesystems known as FAT-12, FAT-16, and FAT-32 (although no version of DOS supports FAT-32) have evolved from the early days (when only diskettes were available) to support increasingly larger hard drives. The "FAT" in the filesystem names stands for File Allocation Table, which is something every filesystem has in some form but that stuck as the exclusive name for DOS filesystems. The numeric designation refers to how many bits of information are available to identify the clusters where files are stored: 12 bits allows 4,096 clusters/files (including directories), 16 allows 65,536 clusters/files to be kept track of, and 32 bits allows up to 4.2 billion clusters/files to be kept track of in a single partition. The directory entry in a FAT filesystem keeps track of start and end clusters for each portion of a file that is stored, as well as the filesystem attributes—Read-Only, Archive status, Hidden, and System files. No file access security is provided for in a DOS/FAT file system.

NTFS
One or more NTFS partitions may exist on a hard drive, with or without Primary and Extended or Non-DOS partitions. NTFS is a *journaling filesystem*, meaning that it records information about filesystem activity to improve recoverability in the event of a system crash. NTFS uses two methods to keep track of directories and files: first, a Master

File Table (MFT) that "knows all" about the directories or folders and files on the disk and, second, the files themselves, which store information about the files. In fact, if a file is small enough, it is contained within the MFT itself rather than on a separate area of the disk. Directories in NTFS store information about the directory, not the files in them. The information about a file in an NTFS filesystem stores not only filename, location, and attributes, but also security information. The number of files and directories NTFS can store is almost limitless, unless the Master File Tables grow so large from keeping track of so many files that they consume all the free space on the drive.

ext, ext2, and ext3

The ext filesystems are used by Linux. ext supports drives and individual files as large as 2 GB. ext2 supports partitions as large as 4 Terabytes and files as large as 2 GB (Linux 2.2) and over 2 GB for Linux 2.4 and above. ext3 is a journaling filesystem compatible with ext2. A journaling filesystems makes a record of filesystem changes before they are made, which adds greater reliability to the file activity.

reiserfs

reiserfs is a journaling filesystem with exceptional granular security capabilities suitable for military applications, developed under DARPA (Defense Advanced Research Projects Agency) sponsorship. Significant information on reiserfs can be found at *http://www.namesys.com*.

jfs

jfs is a journaling filesystem for Linux servers developed by IBM. More information about jfs can be found at *http://oss.software.ibm.com/developerworks/opensource/jfs/*.

The FAT and NTFS filesystems track disk space use in predefined allocations of clusters. Clusters are made up of one or more 512-byte units of storage space. Under the FAT-16 filesystem, the maximum number of clusters is determined by a 16-bit numbering system and a predetermined maximum number of 512-byte sectors of space per cluster. These days, the only place you are likely to encounter FAT-16 partitions is on much older computers, flash memory cards, and embedded systems, but you can still create a FAT-16 filesystem if you need to access the space through an older (6.22 and earlier) version of DOS.

Under these design constraints and limitations, the largest possible disk partition in a FAT-16 filesystem may consist of 65,536 clusters of data. The maximum allowable cluster data size is 64 sectors per cluster, or 32,768 bytes. In total, the maximum size of a FAT-16 disk partition is approximately 2,048 megabytes (2 gigabytes). (The previous partition size limitation under early DOS versions using the FAT-12 filesystem was a meager 32 megabytes.) Table 5-1 lists the FAT-16 cluster sizes for various partition sizes. By the way, a cluster may contain only one file reference, so there is also a limitation on the total number of files a FAT filesystem can keep track of: 65,536 files for FAT-16.

Table 5-1. Cluster sizes for FAT-16 partitions

Partition size	FAT-16 cluster size
0–127 MB	2 KB = 2,048 Bytes (4 sectors)
128–255 MB	4 KB = 4,096 Bytes (8 sectors)
256–511 MB	8 KB = 8,192 Bytes (16 sectors)
512–1,023 MB	16 KB = 16,384 Bytes (32 sectors)
1,024–2,047 MB	32 KB = 32,768 Bytes (64 sectors)

> With a FAT filesystem it is possible under any filesystem to run out of disk space not because you've filled up your entire drive with files but because you've used up the number of file allocations the filesystem provides, so the more clusters you have, the higher the total number of files you can store.

The FAT-32 filesystem supported under Windows 95 OEM SR2, 98, 98SE, Me, NT (SP4 and later), 2000, and XP can accommodate disk drives up to 4 terabytes in size (32 GB under Windows 2000), with as many as 4 billion clusters/files with cluster sizes of 32 KB. For very small (512-byte) files this results in less than 2% file storage efficiency and a gross waste of space, indicating that partitioning your drive to use smaller cluster sizes is advisable for many of us. FAT-32 limits the maximum file size to 2 GB, which is adequate for most of us, but if you expect to work with larger files—large databases for example—you must use NTFS. Table 5-2 lists the cluster sizes for FAT-32 partitions.

Table 5-2. Cluster sizes for FAT-32 partitions

Partition size	FAT-32 cluster size
0-259 MB	512 bytes (1 sector)
260-511 MB	4 KB (8 sectors)
512-8,191 MB	8 KB (16 sectors)
8,192-16,383 MB	16 KB (32 sectors)
32,768 MB-2 Terabytes	32 KB (64 sectors)

The NTFS also allocates disk space in increments or units as little as 512 bytes—which, coincidentally, is the size of a single sector of disk space. Like the FAT filesystem, unless you select an allocation unit of 512 bytes when partitioning and formatting, sectors are usually combined to make up clusters, but NTFS has a large enough numeric range to keep track of a lot of clusters, so clusters can be as small as a single 512-byte sector or made up of multiple sectors. The maximum number of units—clusters or sectors—that NTFS can keep track of provides for maximum disk space capacities in the order of terabytes. The most space any file will waste is only some portion of the clusters—as is evident with FAT filesystems. As shown in Table 5-3, NTFS uses clusters to track file storage, but these clusters are much smaller than the clusters of FAT-16 or FAT-32 filesystems. It is possible to reformat NTFS partitions using XP's Disk Management console to use smaller or larger cluster sizes at your discretion.

Table 5-3. Cluster sizes for Windows NTFS partitions

Partition size	NTFS cluster size
0–512 MB	512 bytes (1 sector)
512–1,024 MB	1,024 bytes (2 sectors)
1,024–2,048 MB	2,048 bytes (4 sectors)
2,048–4,096 MB	4,096 bytes (8 sectors); 8,192 bytes and larger possible
4,096–8,192 MB	8,192 bytes (16 sectors)
8,192–16,384 MB	16,384 bytes (32 sectors)
16,384–32,768 MB	32,768 bytes (64 sectors)
> 32,768 MB	65,536 bytes (128 sectors)

In most cases, when you cannot predict the general size or types of files you will be saving, large or small, it is preferable for storage efficiency to use the smallest cluster size possible. By large files I mean those measured in tens or hundreds of megabytes, something that really chews up disk space that you want to access with as few repetitive disk operations as possible (such as huge database files that may be found on servers, or video files). Most of us, unless we collect a lot of audio and video files, have mostly small datafiles— far less than a megabyte—including all the text and graphics from web pages, email, and average documents and spreadsheets.

Depending on the disk-caching read-ahead method and amount of cache used within a specific disk drive, using a 1 KB cluster size under NTFS will require the equivalent of 1,000 discrete disk accesses to read or write a 1 megabyte file versus 250 accesses with a 4 KB cluster size, but the alternative is having your average 1–2 KB web page and little (50–256 byte) graphics files chewing up 2–4 KB more disk space than they need to. A measly 2–4 KB may not seem like much, but if you let Internet Explorer's Temporary

Internet File caching grow to 512 MB or larger, you're easily wasting 256 MB of disk space on a bunch of web files you may never see again anyway. Figure 5-1 illustrates the size of the datafile on an NTFS volume with 8,192-byte (16-sector) clusters (483 512-byte sectors or 30.1875 8,192-byte clusters) and the amount of disk space the file actually consumes (488 512-byte sectors or 30.5 8,192-byte clusters). This file ends up wasting 0.5 clusters or 4,096 bytes of disk space. If you add up a lot of datafiles wasting half a cluster or more—especially if the cluster sizes are 8, 16, 32, or 64 KB each—you end up with a lot of unusable disk space, also known as "slack" space, occupied by absolutely nothing of value.

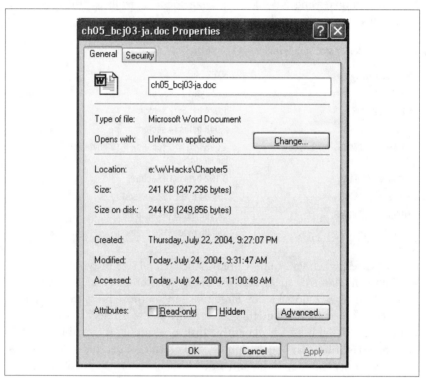

Figure 5-1. Windows File Properties reveals actual data size versus disk space used

It is important to note that the disk operations and performance seen by the operating system can be significantly different than what goes on inside the drive itself. The drive, of course, has to read or write all sectors containing data the operating system wants and will be doing all of the mechanical work to find each and every sector needed, be they contiguous (unfragmented files) or spread out in different places on the drive (fragmented files).

The operating system's file and directory scheme keeps track of files in the file tables (the directory of the Master File Table) and tells the drive where to get file fragments from. The drive only knows how to find tracks and sectors and doesn't know where specific files are. If the drive's firmware and caching scheme are smart, it will optimize file placement and file reads by itself. If the drive has a large internal cache, it will take in all or most of the operating system's commands, tell the OS it's "got it," and go off and do the work, releasing the OS to do other things. Someday perhaps we'll have operating-system-aware disk drives or specific disk drives that filesystems offload functions to so the OS can be an OS rather than a file manager, but for now the operating system and driver vendors are responsible for optimizing their file- and disk-handling functions.

> NTFS supports and can be configured to use on-the-fly file compression to save disk space on a drive-by-drive or file-by-file basis. NTFS will not compress files on a drive using a cluster size of 4 KB or less.

Determine Your Filesystem
#41 How do you tell what type of filesystem your disk is partitioned with?

In Windows, open My Computer, right-click on your hard drive icon, and then select Properties. You'll see a dialog similar to that shown in Figure 5-2. Within this dialog will be a designation of the hard drive's filesystem, in this case NTFS. With NTFS under Windows NT, 2000, or XP, we are assured of significantly more efficient use of available drive space than with FAT-16 or FAT-32 under DOS, Windows 3.x, 9x, or Me.

The mount command under Linux will also show you filesystem types, as in the example below, which shows an ext3 filesystem type:

```
[root@rh9-lt root]# mount
/dev/hda2 on / type ext3 (rw)
/dev/hda1 on /boot type ext3 (rw)
```

Create a New Partition with NT, 2000, XP, and
#42 **2003**
Use XP's Disk Management console to create a new partition in unused disk space.

You can create a new partition in unallocated or unused space on a disk drive with Windows XP or partitioning software like PartitionMagic. In this hack, we'll create a new 20 GB NTFS partition in unallocated disk space

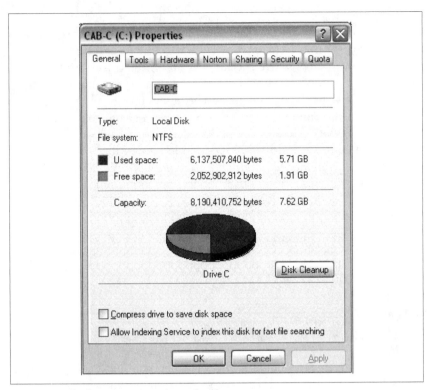

Figure 5-2. Windows Properties shows the filesystem type

using Windows XP's Disk Management tools. To do this, launch Control Panel, select Administrative Tools, then Computer Management, double-click Disk Management under Storage, and follow these steps:

1. Right-click on the area marked Unallocated. Select New Partition from the menu that appears (Figure 5-3).

2. When the New Partition wizard introduction dialog appears, click Next.

3. The New Partition wizard gives you the choice of making a new primary partition, or an extended partition, as in Figure 5-4. Create a primary partition, then click Next.

> A drive may contain up to four primary partitions, or three Primary partitions and an extended partition (which may contain logical drives, letting you overcome the four-drive limit that primary partitions impose). Primary partitions may be made bootable for Windows or other operating systems.

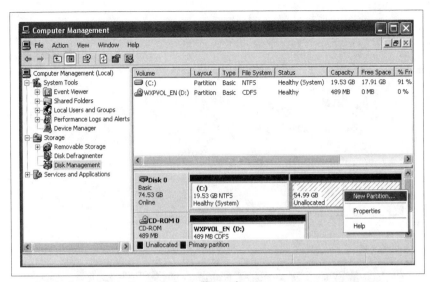

Figure 5-3. Create a new partition in unallocated space

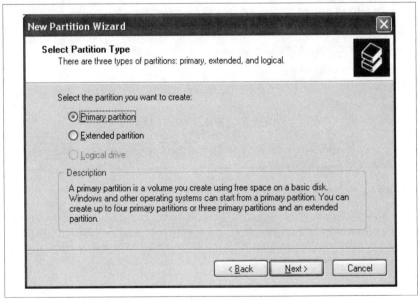

Figure 5-4. A new partition may be a Primary or Extended type

4. Next you can set the new partition (Figure 5-5) to the desired size (20 GB in this example).

5. The next option is to assign a drive letter to the new partition for when it is formatted. At this point, the next available drive letter is E:, as

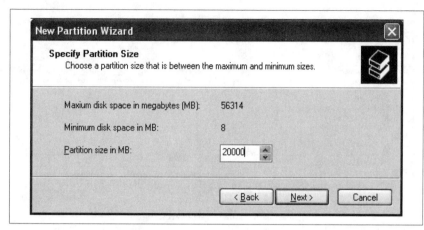

Figure 5-5. Setting the size for a new partition

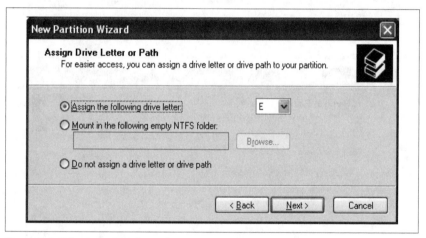

Figure 5-6. Selecting a drive letter for a new partition

shown in Figure 5-6, which is fine for now. Normally a second disk or partition would become drive D:, but if you already have a CD-ROM drive as D:, that letter will be claimed. You can come back to Disk Management and change this later.

6. The final step in this process is to format the new partition. Figure 5-7 shows the default values to be used. You can elect not to format the partition at this time, which is fine if you intend to install another operating system to boot off this partition, or decide to format it later, but we'll format it for NTFS now.

You may also choose between NTFS and FAT-32 for the partition type, select the allocation or cluster size, and give the new drive a label. When you are done with your selections and changes, click Next.

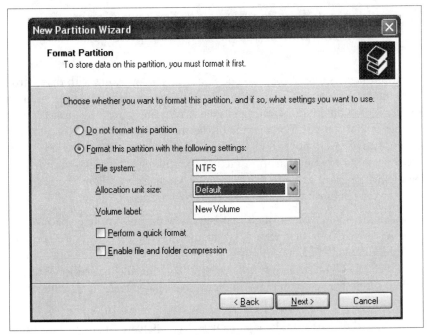

Figure 5-7. Selecting format options for a new partition

7. After you choose the formatting options, you'll get a summary dialog of the actions to be taken with the new partition. You can still back up to revise your selections or cancel at this point. Once you click Finish, the partitioning and formatting process starts, and in a few minutes you'll be ready to use the new space.

Partitioning During Windows Setup

By default, the Windows NT, 2000, XP, or Windows Server 2003 setup program will claim all of the space on a bare hard drive. This does not leave you any free space to dabble with different partitions or operating systems.

Instead of letting one operating system "own" the entire drive, change the amount of space for the operating system to a value large enough to hold all of the operating system files, your normal application programs, and as much data as you think you'll cram onto the drive—20 to 30 GB is usually adequate. To constrain the installation to a smaller space, wait until you get to the screen showing the unpartitioned space, select that space, and press C to create a partition. When prompted for the size of the drive, type in the amount of disk space you want the installation to use. The rest will be available to hold other primary or logical partitions.

Create a New Partition with PartitionMagic

#43 Create new partitions from free or existing partition space with PartitionMagic.

PartitionMagic is one of the most popular tools for working with disk partitions under Windows. It lets you create, delete, resize, merge, or prepare partitions for different operating systems. Working on a disk drive with a couple of existing partitions is one of the things PartitionMagic is great for because its wizards show you the state of existing partitions, let you borrow space from an existing partition (actually shrinking it to make room) for a new partition, and provide three levels of safeguards to help protect your existing data before any changes are made to your disk.

In this hack, I take you through making a new partition in free space on an existing drive. Your first step is to acquire a copy of PartitionMagic and install it on your PC. You can buy and download a copy online from Symantec's web site (*http://www.symantec.com*). Once installed, PartitionMagic is at your service to help you perform many disk-related tasks. To create a new partition, follow these steps:

1. From the PartitionMagic menu select "Create a new partition" (Figure 5-8).

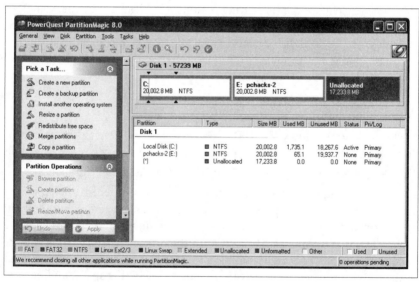

Figure 5-8. PartitionMagic's main dialog and menu

2. Select where you want the new partition to be created (Figure 5-9). This is where the value of a tool like PartitionMagic becomes impressive; the program can actually insert a partition before, after, or between two others. Inserting a partition causes two operations to happen: at least one of the partitions is moved and then the new partition is created. The typical choice is to create the new partition after any existing partitions.

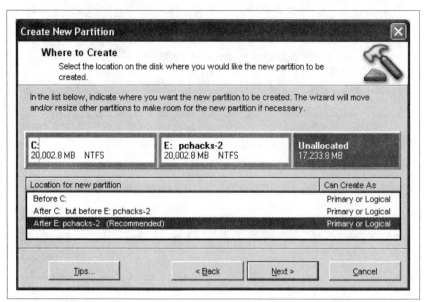

Figure 5-9. PartitionMagic lets you select which disk space to use for creating a new partition

3. If the partition you want to create will need more space than you have free to use, you can take space from another partition, as shown in Figure 5-10. In this case, there is ample free space (17 GB) to make a third partition and not have to take space away from another. If space is borrowed from another partition, then the existing partition is resized, optionally moved, and the new partition is created.

4. Next select the size and type for the new partition, as shown in Figure 5-11. The default settings, plus typing in a label for the new partition, are all that is necessary to get to the next step. If the drive letter seems out of sequence at this point, there are tools to change drive letters [Hack #52] to suit your preferences or sense of logical order.

5. Review the details of the drive partitions before and after the changes, as shown in Figure 5-12. Click Back to make any changes and Next to queue up their execution.

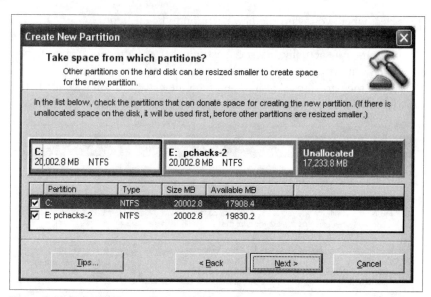

Figure 5-10. PartitionMagic offers to take space from one partition to make a new one

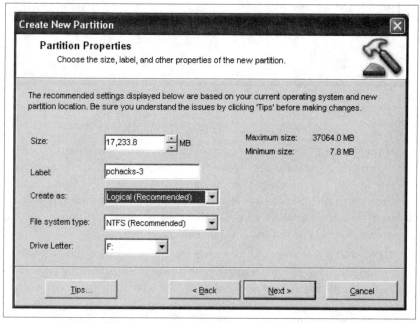

Figure 5-11. Selecting properties for a new partition

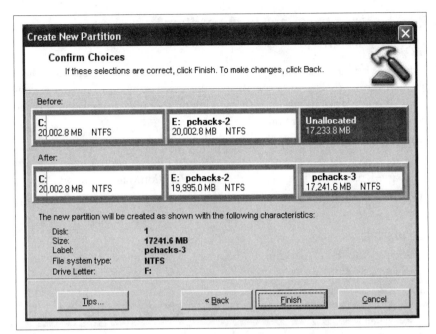

Figure 5-12. Confirming the new partition details before proceeding

6. Back at the main screen, you will see that the Apply button is available. Selecting it tells PartitionMagic to make the changes you've indicated. In a few minutes the process will be complete and you will have a new partition made to order, as you can see in Figure 5-13.

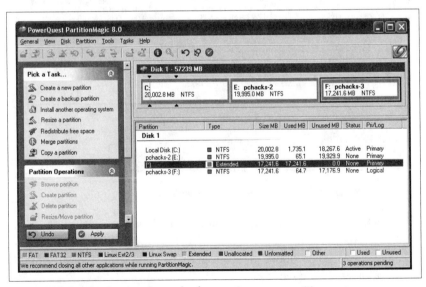

Figure 5-13. Report showing the result after creating a new partition

Merge Partitions with PartitionMagic

#44   Merge two partitions into one with PartitionMagic.

Whether you have two partitions or ten and need to make an adjustment to shrink or grow the size of a specific partition, or you want to move the contents of one partition into another by merging them, PartitionMagic has the power to do the work for you.

In this hack we'll take two of the partitions we had from the previous hack, "Create a New Partition with PartitionMagic" [Hack #43] and merge them into one larger partition. Starting at the main PartitionMagic window, follow these steps:

1. Select Merge partitions under Pick a Task... from the main menu at the upper left.

2. Select the first partition to be merged with another, as shown in Figure 5-14.

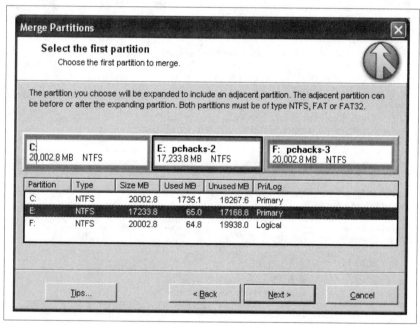

Figure 5-14. Selecting the first partition to merge with another

3. Select the second partition to be merged, as shown in Figure 5-15.

4. The contents of the second partition will be moved into a folder on the first or merged partition, so the program needs to know the name of this new folder, as you see in Figure 5-16.

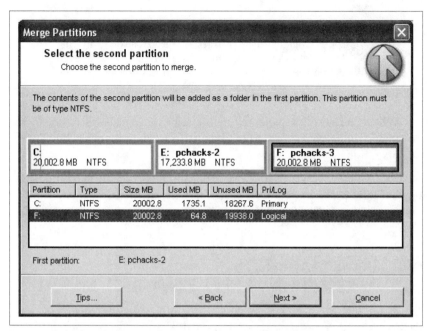

Figure 5-15. Selecting the second partition to merge with another

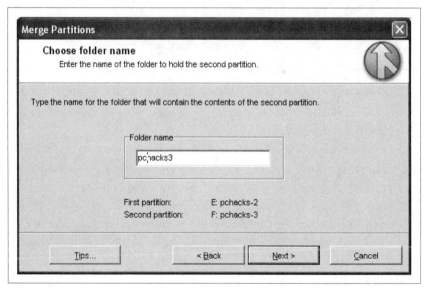

Figure 5-16. Selecting the folder to hold the second partition's data

> At this point, you're probably worried that Windows or
> some program will lose track of the data you're moving;
> however, PartitionMagic includes a tool called Drive Map-
> per that looks for and changes references to the old partition
> and folders to reflect the new drive and folder they moved to.

5. When you are done with the merge selections, you will return to the
   main window. Click the Apply button to let the program complete the
   operation.

In two hacks, the power of third-party partitioning software should be quite
obvious and prove to be much easier and less risky that making a lot of
backups, using FDISK or XP's Disk Management tools, and moving data
yourself.

HACK #45   Convert FAT to NTFS

Use NT/2000/XP/2003's CONVERT program to change a FAT partition to
NTFS.

CONVERT is a command-line program with one simple function: to change
a FAT partition to NTFS. Normally CONVERT applies user and system
security settings to all of the files in the partition, but the command-line
option /NoSecurity leaves the access rights to all files open to everyone, as if
the partition were an unsecured FAT partition.

To use CONVERT to make your C: drive NTFS:

1. Click Start, then Run. Type in CMD or open a Command Prompt window.

2. At the command prompt type:

   ```
   convert c:\ /fs:ntfs
   ```

3. If the partition has a volume label, you will be prompted to type it in.

4. Press Y to proceed. If this partition is also the system root, you will see a
   message telling you the partition will be converted at the next reboot.

5. Close all open programs and restart your PC. Convert will run
   CHKDSK to verify the contents of the partition and then begin the conversion. After conversion the system will restart with the new partition.

Hacking the Hack

Converting an NTFS partition to FAT-16 or FAT-32 is not something
Microsoft ever intended and does not support with FDISK, FORMAT, or
Disk Management tools. Rarely do you need to gain access to files in an
NTFS partition from a FAT-16 or FAT-32 OS, but it happens. To convert to

FAT from NTFS, you need to use a third-party utility like Symantec's PartitionMagic or V-Com's Partition Commander. Since NTFS partitions are normally secured by the operating system, you must run the drive you are converting under the operating system that supports NTFS, have privileged access to the drive, and have rights to access the partition.

If you simply need to read data in an NTFS partition from a FAT-only operating system you can use NTFSDOS, NTFSDOS Professional, or NTFS for Windows 98, available from *http://www.sysinternals.com*.

Create or Delete NTFS Partitions from the Recovery Console

#46

Create and delete NTFS partitions using the DISKPART from the Recovery Console.

Windows versions from NT to Windows Server 2003 know nothing about FDISK but provide their own partitioning tool, DISKPART, which is run from the Windows Recovery Console. DISKPART is a command-line utility used to add/create or delete NTFS partitions with some very simple commands.

1. Boot using your recovery diskettes or setup CD and select the Recovery Console option. Alternatively, you can boot with a DOS diskette that provides CD-ROM support and type:

   ```
   \i386\winnt32.exe /cmdcons
   ```

2. At the command prompt, issue the DISKPART command followed by the appropriate command.

   The following command lines delete a partition:

   ```
   diskpart /delete \Device\HardDisk0\Partition3
   diskpart /delete F:
   ```

   The following command line adds a 2,048 MB partition:

   ```
   diskpart /add \Device\HardDisk0 2048
   ```

3. Type **exit** to leave the Recovery Console and restart the system.

The command line for DISKPART supports only the /add and /delete commands:

/add

   Adds a new partition. Supports the optional parameter size, which specifies the partition size in megabytes.

/delete device_name | drive_name | partition

   Deletes a partition. device_name specifies the device on which to create or delete a partition. Use the MAP command from the Recovery Console command line to get a list of device names (for example, \Device\ HardDisk0). drive_name specifies the partition you want to delete by drive letter (for example, D:). partition specifies the partition you want to delete by name (for example, \Device\HardDisk0\Partition1).

HACK #47 Fix the Master Boot Record on FAT Partitions

Use FDISK to restore the ability to boot from your FAT-16 or FAT-32 hard drive.

FDISK is a DOS program that can actually help you out of some of those nasty "unable to locate operating system" and "no boot drive available" error conditions Windows 9x and DOS users encounter from time to time. The Master Boot Record can be corrupted by an improper shutdown, power glitch, or disk failure. Re-creating a new Master Boot Record at the first sector of the hard drive—which is what your system BIOS is looking for in order to turn over the startup operation to an operating system—is an easy fix.

> If your hard drive is managed by a drive overlay utility from OnTrack or a specific program provided by your drive manufacturer (as indicated by a Disk Manager or similar announcement message during bootup) or is set to boot with the GRUB or LILO boot managers, or into Linux, using this hack will destroy access to the drive.

To use FDISK's Master Boot Record restoration feature to get your main or additional drives back into bootable shape, follow these steps:

1. Boot with a DOS diskette, boot CD, or bootable USB FLASH drive or hard drive containing DOS and FDISK. A Windows 98 or Me startup diskette will do nicely.

2. At the command prompt type in either:

   FDISK /MBR

   or

   FDISK /CMBR x

3. Remove the disk or device you booted to DOS with and then restart the system to verify that you can boot from the hard drive.

FDISK /MBR re-creates the Master Boot Record, the first sector of the hard disk. This can be helpful to repair a damaged or corrupted bootable drive.

FDISK /CMBR x re-creates the boot sector of the first (x = 1), second (x = 2), third (x = 3), or fourth (x = 4) hard disk(s).

Fix the Master Boot Record on NTFS Partitions

HACK #48

Windows NT, 2000, XP, and Windows Server 2003 users having problems accessing or booting from an NTFS disk can use the FIXMBR program to rewrite a new Master Boot Record on the hard drive.

FIXMBR is available only through the Recovery Console feature of Windows NT, 2000, XP, or Windows Server 2003. To access the Recovery Console, you must boot up with recovery diskettes you made during installation of the OS or select the recovery options from the installation CD. FIXMBR has one function, just like DOS's `FDISK /MBR`: to write a new Master Boot Record on the disk drive.

> Do not use the DOS FDISK program to replace the Master Boot Record on an NTFS drive, as doing so can render the drive and data inaccessible.

To use FIXMBR follow these steps:

1. Boot using your Recovery diskettes or setup CD and select the Recovery Console option.

2. Log on to the drive/partition you wish to repair, typically *C:\WINNT* or *C:\WINDOWS*.

3. At the command prompt, issue the `MAP` command to determine the device name for the disk partition you want to "fix"—typically it will be *\Device\HardDisk0*.

4. At the command prompt, issue the `FIXMBR` command followed by the name of the disk partition to be "fixed." For example (press Enter after the command):

   ```
   fixmbr \Device\HardDisk0
   ```

5. Type **exit** to leave the Recovery Console and restart the system.

> Do not use this method to repair a primary active boot partition that uses GRUB or LILO boot managers **[Hack #50]**. Apply it only to the specific drive or partition containing an NTFS boot sector.

If you do not supply a device name, a new Master Boot Record will be written to the default boot device, which is typically what you want to do anyway.

If an invalid or nonstandard partition table signature is detected by FIXMBR, you will be asked if you want to continue with FIXMBR or not. How you proceed is determined by whether or not you are having problems accessing the drive. If you are not having problems accessing your drives, you should not continue.

> Writing a new Master Boot Record to your system partition could damage your partition tables and cause your partitions to become inaccessible

HACK #49 Fix the Partition Boot Sector on NTFS Partitions

Use FIXBOOT to restore the ability to boot from your NTFS hard drive.

Windows NT, 2000, XP, and 2003 users having problems accessing or booting from an NTFS disk can use the FIXBOOT program to rewrite a new Master Boot Record on the hard drive.

FIXBOOT is available only through the Recovery Console feature of Windows NT, 2000, XP, or Windows Server 2003. To access the Recovery Console, you must boot up with recovery diskettes you made during installation of the OS or select the recovery options from the installation CD. FIXBOOT has one function, similar to DOS's SYS: to write fresh boot information on the disk drive.

> Do not use this method to repair a primary active boot partition that uses GRUB or LILO boot managers [Hack #50]. Apply it only to the specific drive or partition containing an NTFS boot sector.

To use FIXBOOT, follow these steps:

1. Boot using your Recovery diskettes or setup CD and select the Recovery Console option.

2. Once booted, you will be prompted to log on to the drive/partition you wish to repair, typically indicated as 1 for *C:\WINNT*.

3. At the command prompt, issue the FIXBOOT command followed by the name of the disk partition to be "fixed." For example (press Enter after you've typed the command):

   ```
   fixboot C:
   ```

4. Type **exit** to leave the Recovery Console and restart the system.

If you do not supply a drive letter, FIXBOOT will write a new partition boot sector to the current partition you logged on to.

Fix GRUB or LILO Boot Problems

HACK #50

Use the SystemRescueCD to repair a blown GRUB or LILO boot.

Linux has advanced disk management and repair tools too. Of note is the SystemRescueCD from *http://www.sysresccd.com*. SystemRescueCD is offered as an ISO file that can be written to a CD-R to make a bootable rescue CD. The packages includes several essential tools for fixing Linux boot-up problems, including:

GNU Parted
　　Used for editing disk partitions under Linux.

QtParted
　　A Linux-based clone of PartitionMagic.

Partimage
　　A Linux-based clone of Ghost/Drive Image to create images of disks and partitions.

Sfdisk
　　A tool that lets you back up and restore a partition table.

It also includes a variety of filesystem tools that allow you to format, resize, and debug an existing partition of your hard disk supporting e2fs, reiserfs, xfs, jfs, ntfs, and DOS partition types.

With these tools on hand, you may never have to reinstall a Linux operating system again.

Format Your Disk

HACK #51

Lay down some awesome data tracks on diskettes, hard drives, Zip disks, or LS-120 cartridges with FORMAT.

Logical drives and drive letters are created by the process of formatting a partition so that it is ready to accept files. Formatting is done by either the DOS FORMAT program, within the Windows 9x–2003 setup processes, or within the Disk Management console in Windows NT–2003. FORMAT provides limited options: it either creates nonbootable disk space, creates a bootable disk, or it can quick-format (erase) a diskette. For hard drives, FORMAT will lay out either NTFS, FAT-16, or FAT-32 file structures, depending on the filesystem of the partition. For 3.5" diskettes, Zip, and LS-120 media, the filesystem will always be FAT-16.

> FORMAT also establishes a single partition for portable media such as diskettes, Zip (100 and 250), and LS-120 media because they have limited storage capacity well below 512 MB.

In the process, FORMAT also establishes the logical drives or drive lettering scheme we use to refer to our drives. Although the FORMAT program has more options applicable to various diskette capacities, it is also a very powerful utility when applied to hard drives.

To use all of the features of the FORMAT program, you need to be at a DOS or command prompt. Then follow these steps:

1. Boot with DOS or a startup diskette, boot CD, or bootable USB FLASH drive or hard drive containing the version of the operating system you wish to repair. A Windows 98 or Me startup diskette will do nicely.

2. At the command prompt, type in **FORMAT** followed by the parameters necessary to establish the type of format you want to create. To format a hard drive, the parameters would be:

    FORMAT C: /S

3. The program will advise you that formatting will overwrite all of the datafiles on the drive (which isn't a problem on a new drive) and ask you to confirm that you really want to format the drive. Press the Y key for Yes and then press the Enter key and allow the program to start.

4. Formatting a drive can take quite a bit of time depending on its size and the speed of the computer. At the end, you will be prompted to give the drive a name or label (optional), and you're done.

You have to format every partition you want to use for the operating system or data. FORMAT establishes the FAT filesystem and directory space. FORMAT is typically not used on NTFS partitions, which are instead formatted as part of the operating system setup process or with the Disk Management console within Windows (NT, 2000, XP, and 2003 only).

FORMAT provides the following command-line options:

```
FORMAT drive: [/V[:label]] [/Q] [/F:size] [/B | /S] [/C]
FORMAT drive: [/V[:label]] [/Q] [/T:tracks /N:sectors] [/B | /S] [/C]
FORMAT drive: [/V[:label]] [/Q] [/1] [/4] [/B | /S] [/C]
FORMAT drive: [/Q] [/1] [/4] [/8] [/B | /S] [/C]
```

The purposes of these options are as follows:

/V[:label]
    Specifies the volume label.

/Q
    Performs a quick format.

/F:size
    Specifies the size to format the disk to (such as 160, 180, 320, 360, 720, 1.2, 1.44, or 2.88).

/B
Allocates space on the formatted disk for system files.

/S
Copies system files to the formatted disk.

/T:*tracks*
Specifies the number of tracks per disk side.

/N:*sectors*
Specifies the number of sectors per track.

/1
Formats a single side of a floppy disk.

/4
Formats a 5.25-inch 360 K floppy disk in a high-density drive.

/8
Formats eight sectors per track.

/C
Tests clusters that are currently marked "bad."

FORMAT under Windows 2000 and XP offers some additional command-line options:

/FS:*filesystem*
Specifies the type of the filesystem (FAT, FAT32, or NTFS).

/C*(for NTFS only)*
Indicates that files created on the new volume will be compressed by default.

/X
Forces the volume to dismount first if necessary. All opened handles to the volume will no longer be valid.

/A:*size*
Overrides the default allocation unit size. The following default settings are strongly recommended for general use:

- NTFS supports 512, 1,024, 2,048, 4,096, and 8,192 bytes; 16 K, 32 K, and 64 K.

- FAT supports 512, 1,024, 2,048, 4,096, and 8,192 bytes; 16 K, 32 K, and 64 K (128 K or 256 K for sector size greater than 512 bytes).

- FAT-32 supports 512, 1,024, 2,048, 4,096, and 8,192 bytes; 16 K, 32 K, 64 K, (128 K or 256 K for sector size greater than 512 bytes).

Examples of common uses of FORMAT are:

`format a:`
> Erases all the contents of a disk. Commonly used on a diskette that has not been formatted or on a diskette you wish to erase.

`format a: /q`
> Quickly erases all the contents of a floppy diskette.

`format a: /s`
> Formats and makes a diskette bootable.

`format c:`
> Erases all the contents of your hard disk drive. Unless you wish to erase all of your computer's information, this command should not be used. It is also the command used to format a hard drive partition for data use, without being bootable.

`format d: /FS:NTFS /A:2048`
> Formats drive D: with the NTFS filesystem and forces the cluster size to 2 KB. You can accomplish the same thing in the Disk Management console of Windows 2000, XP, and 2003 systems.

Logical Drive Assignments Under DOS

While your system BIOS sees hard drives in the order they are attached to their interface cables and configured by jumpers, DOS dynamically assigns drive letters in a most unusual but quite logical order, alternating between physical/electronic order and partitions found. Drive letter assignments by default first follow physical and then logical/partition order.

For systems with only one partition, it's simple: DOS assigns drive letter C: to the first partition it finds on that drive. If there are more partitions it assigns them drive letter D:, E:, and so on.

For systems with two hard drives, if the first hard drive has only one partition that is assigned drive letter C:, then the first partition on the second hard drive is assigned drive letter D:, and if the second hard drive contains more partitions they are assigned drive letters E:, F:, and so on. Simple enough.

For systems with two hard drives, where the first hard drive has two or more partitions, grab a pencil and paper or head to the nearest white board to map out what happens, or you can refer to Table 5-4. The first partition on the first hard drive is assigned drive letter C:—again, simple enough. The first partition on the second hard drive is assigned drive letter D:—nothing complicated so far. If you have two or more partitions on the first hard drive, they are then assigned drive letters E:, F:, and so on until you run out of partitions or letters. Now that's interesting! If the second hard drive has two or more partitions, the drive letters for the second and all subsequent partitions are assigned in order *after* the last letter used for the partitions on the first hard drive.

Table 5-4. Logical drive assignments on multiple drives and partitions

Drive letter	One hard drive (any number of partitions)	Two hard drives, (two partitions each)	Two hard drives, (three partitions each)
C:	First partition	First partition of first hard drive	First partition of first hard drive
D:	Second partition	First partition of second hard drive	First partition of second hard drive
E:	Third partition	Second partition of first hard drive	Second partition of first hard drive
F:	Fourth partition	Second partition of second hard drive	Third partition of first hard drive
G:	Fifth partition	None	Second partition of second hard drive
H:	Sixth partition	None	Third partition of second hard drive

Under Windows NT/2000/XP you cannot change the drive letter of the Active boot or system partition, but you may change the drive letters for subsequent partitions within the Disk Management console [Hack #52].

Change Logical Drive Letters
#52

Rearrange your drive letters with the Disk Management console in Windows NT-2003.

Changing drive letter assignments is useful if you have added a second hard drive to a Windows NT/2000/XP/Windows Server 2003 system. Suppose you start out with a hard drive as drive C:. The CD-ROM drive is automatically assigned as drive D:. A second hard drive added to this configuration would become drive E:, which is not what you might expect if you think hard disk drives are supposed to flow in logical, alphabetical order. What we have learned to expect from the days of DOS is for the second hard drive to become D: and the CD-ROM drive to become drive E:. You can make your new NT-2003 systems appear more like old DOS systems with a few simple drive-letter changes.

It may be more convenient now (and for later on if you add more hard drives or partitions) to move the CD-ROM drive letter up to a value far out of the way from any anticipated hard drive assignments. You can do the same for other removable media, such as digital cameras and USB FLASH drives that come and go—connecting the devices and then assigning them permanent drive letters so they will always show up as the same drive letter when used.

> Reassign CD-ROM and DVD drive letters before installing or using any application or game that depends on the presence of a CD or DVD to run.
>
> Although many programs can search for their respective CDs and adapt to a drive letter change, a change in drive letter may cause some applications or games to fail.

Follow these steps to shift the hard drive and CD-ROM drive letters to a more intuitive and predictable order:

1. Access the Disk Management console from Start→Control Panel→Administrative Tools→Computer Management.

2. In the left pane of the Computer Management console, select Disk Management from the list.

3. Right-click on the drive whose letter assignment you want to change. In this case, start with your CD-ROM or DVD drive, D:, and then select Change Drive Letter and Paths...

4. Click on the Change button and change this to an "out of the way" drive letter like R: (for CD-ROM) or another unused letter, then click OK twice.

5. Right-click on the new hard drive and then select Change Drive Letter and Paths...

6. Click on the Change button and change this drive letter to D:, then click OK twice.

> If your PC connects to one or more network- or server-based disk drives that have drive letters mapped to them, be sure you do not assign local drive letters that are the same as pre-defined network drives.

Restore DOS Bootability

#53 Make your drive bootable to get a DOS or Windows 9x-Me drive back up and running quickly.

Just as the FDISK /MBR command [Hack #47] can rebuild the lost boot information from the beginning of a hard drive, a little command-prompt program named SYS.COM can help you take that bootability to where it needs to be—containing the operating system files to get the system started. If you've got a nonbootable drive for DOS or Windows 9x-Me that is missing either the IO.SYS, MSDOS.SYS, or COMMAND.COM DOS files, start your fix with **FDISK /MBR**. Boot from a startup diskette for the operating system you need to repair and then execute:

SYS C:

SYS copies the basic operating system files—IO.SYS, MSDOS.SYS, and COMMAND.COM—from the diskette to the drive letter designated: in this case, drive C:. Remove the diskette from the drive and restart the system from the hard drive.

Rescue a Blown 2000 or XP Installation

Corrupt installations of Windows 2000, XP, and 2003 can be fixed in minutes with their bootable setup disks.

Failed Windows 2000, XP, or Windows Server 2003 bootups—the ones that hang somewhere before or while loading Windows or produce a missing file error or blue screen—*might* be fixed in a few minutes using the Repair feature of their setup programs. Although FDISK /MBR and SYS C: can repair a blown boot record and replace the operating system files for DOS and Windows 9x–Me, you cannot use these commands to put the operating system boot files back onto an NT-based boot drive or for NTFS partitioned drives.

Because many prebuilt systems come with recovery CDs and a non-configurable version of the operating system, the following recovery process may not work for you.

Instead, recovery forces you to reinstall the entire operating system, causing loss of at least the links and Registry entries for applications, if not all data if the recovery process also reformats your hard drive. Yet another reason that backups are so important.

If you want a more personalized recovery that preserves your applications, data, and settings, use a full backup program like Stomp's Backup My PC or make a complete image of your drive with Symantec Ghost, Drive Image, or Acronis True Image.

Follow these instructions to repair a broken installation:

1. Start the system with the bootable setup diskettes or CD.
2. At the beginning of the installation process you are given three options:
   - Setup Windows now
   - Repair an existing installation
   - Quit setup (F3)

   Press the R key to continue.

3. At the next screen you have three options:
   - Repair the installation using the Recovery Console, press C
   - Repair the installation using the emergency repair process, press R
   - Quit setup (F3)

   Press the R key to continue.

4. At the next screen you have four options:
   - Manual Repair: To choose from a list of repair options, press M
   - Fast Repair: To perform all repair options, press F
   - Cancel this step and go back (press Esc)
   - Quit setup (F3)

   The Fast Repair covers all bases easily and is the selection you want, so press F to continue. If you choose the Manual Repair option you have three choices: inspect the startup environment (to see what might be wrong), verify Windows system files, or inspect the boot sector. There are two other options at this step: cancel and go back, or quit entirely.

5. At the next screen you have four options:
   - If you have an Emergency Repair disk press Enter
   - If you do not have an Emergency Repair disk, press L. Setup will attempt to locate the Windows installation for you
   - Cancel with Esc to go back one screen
   - Quit setup (F3)

Emergency Repair disks for NT and 2000 can only be created at the time you install the operating system. They contain just enough boot and system configuration files to restore a hard drive and the operating system to a bootable condition.

Although most of us skip the distraction of creating the recovery diskettes in the anxious moments of installation, it is something that should be done.

   Assuming that a set of Emergency Repair disks does not exist, press L to continue. If you have an Emergency Repair disk, place it into the diskette drive and press Enter.

6. If you chose L in the previous step, at the next screen you'll have one more chance to provide the Emergency Repair disk or let Windows try to find the existing installation. Either way, press Enter to continue.

From this point on, the repair process will try to establish the bootability of your drive and installation and restore files as needed. Admittedly a rather involved process compared to a simple FDISK /MBR and SYS C: for DOS and Windows 9x–ME systems, but it very often gets the job done. If this fails, you will have to reinstall the operating system.

Fix the Windows 95 File-Caching Bug

Implement this hack to fix the "Typical Role of This Computer" bug in Windows 95.

Windows 95/98/Me provide a bit of disk performance control through the "typical role" settings system parameter accessible through the Hard Disk tab of the My Computer/Properties dialog, shown in Figure 5-17. This setting does not control the amount of memory allocated for disk caching by VCACHE; instead it sets aside a specific amount of RAM to hold look-up references about most recently used files and folders.

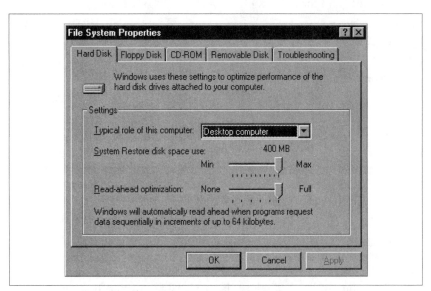

Figure 5-17. Disk performance controls in Windows 9x-Me

The number of folders and files tracked, and the amount of memory for storing the folder and file references, varies depending on the "typical role" setting, as listed in Table 5-5.

Table 5-5. "Typical role" and its caching allocations for Windows 95/98/Me

Role	Number of accessed folders cached	Number of accessed files cached	RAM used
Desktop	32	677	10 KB
Mobile/Docking	16	337	5 KB
Network Server	64	2,729	40 KB

The "typical role" settings for Windows 95 are incorrect according to Microsoft *(http://support.microsoft.com/default.aspx?scid=kb;en-us;138012).* The values for folders and files are reversed for Mobile and Network settings. Only the Desktop role is correct. If the Desktop setting seems right to you, leave the settings alone. If Mobile or Network settings appeal to you, then you need to correct or modify the values stored in the Windows Registry by following these steps:

1. Start the Windows Registry editor by selecting Start and then Run. Type in **REGEDIT** and then click OK.

2. In the left pane of the Registry Editor double-click HKEY_LOCAL_ MACHINE.

3. Double-click Software, then double-click Windows, then double-click CurrentVersion.

4. Click once on the FS_Templates listing.

5. Notice two data entries in the right pane, one named NameCache and the other PathCache. If the "typical role" for this computer is Network (more folder and file lookup caching), enter the values shown under Network. If it's Mobile (less memory used), enter the values shown under Mobile:

```
Network
NameCache    a9 0a 00 00
PathCache    40 00 00 00

Mobile
NameCache    51 01 00 00
PathCache    10 00 00 00
```

6. When you are finished, close the Registry Editor and then restart your computer for the new values to take effect.

> If later you select the Desktop role, these values will be changed correctly for that role, but if you select Mobile or Network again, the values will be changed to the improper settings you had before.

HACK
#56

Avoid the Delayed-Write-Caching Blues

This Windows performance enhancer could make you a real loser, of your data. Make this simple tweak and compute with peace of mind.

In an effort to give us another performance boost, Windows provides the ability to cache (store in memory for later use) data that is to be written to your hard drives, writing the data only when the system is less busy. This feature puts your data at risk for some short period of time and can result in data being lost if the system crashes or the power fails before the data is safely transferred from memory to the disk drive. Write-caching is not a bad thing unless you live where power fluctuates or fails frequently. Admittedly the time window affecting this risk is very short, a second or two at most, but you cannot control when a power glitch will happen in that second or two to cause data loss.

If your PC gets power from an uninterruptible power supply, especially one that can tell Windows that power is failing so it can do a proper shutdown, you probably don't need or want to use this hack.

Write-caching, or delayed writing, is enabled by default in all versions of Windows. We have to take deliberate steps to turn it off.

To remove the risks of delayed-write-caching for Windows 95/98/Me, follow these steps:

1. Go to Start, select Settings, select Control Panel, and double-click the System icon.

2. In the System Properties dialog select the Troubleshooting tab.

3. In the Troubleshooting tab dialog click the "File System..." button. The File System Properties dialog, shown in Figure 5-18, will appear.

4. To disable this risky feature, click on the box labeled "Disable write-behind caching for all drives" and then click OK.

5. Restart your system.

To disable delayed-write-caching under Windows 2000, XP, and 2003, follow these steps:

1. Double-click My Computer, right-click on the drive you want to change the settings for, and then select Properties.

2. In the Properties dialog, select the Hardware tab.

3. Highlight the listing for the disk you will make this change for and then click the Properties button.

4. In the Properties dialog for this drive, select the Policies tab.

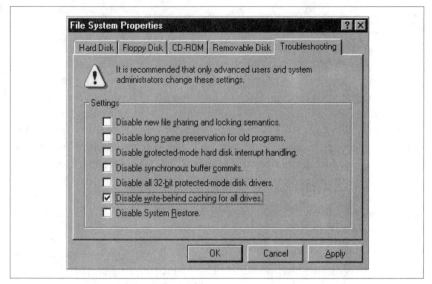

Figure 5-18. Troubleshooting holds the key to write-behind caching

5. In the Policies dialog (Figure 5-19), the "Enable write caching on the disk" checkbox is marked by default; click it to disable the feature.

6. Click OK to close all the dialogs, and then restart your system.

Write-caching does boost your performance, but it is best to use it only if you have a very stable system and are running your PC on an uninterruptible power supply with automatic shutdown of Windows enabled. It's a good idea to enable the Self-Monitoring, Analysis, and Reporting Technology (S.M.A.R.T.) capabilities in your BIOS [Hack #57].

 ## HACK #57 Detect Drive Failure Before It Happens

Monitor the condition of your disk drives for predictions of failure.

Roughly 60% of all disk drive failures are mechanical in nature—from spindle-bearing wear to read/write heads banging into delicate disk platters—and now technology built into the drives can report anticipated and specific failures to give you a chance to rectify the situation, hopefully before it is too late to retrieve your data.

In addition to monitoring a variety of parameters related to mechanical events (disk platter RPM, time to spin up, motor current, head seek failures, and sudden shock to the drive chassis), S.M.A.R.T. (Self-Monitoring, Analysis, and Reporting Technology) can report read and write retry attempts necessary due to defective areas on the disk or head failure or drive

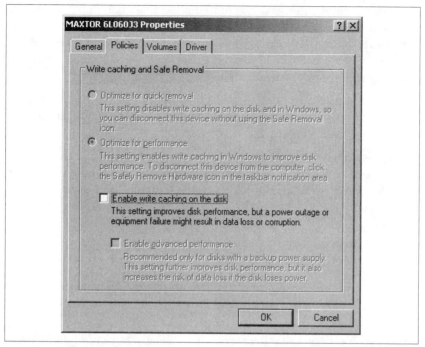

Figure 5-19. The write-caching controls for Windows 2000 and XP

temperature. Many S.M.A.R.T.-enabled drives can also report how many times they have been turned on and off and the number of hours the drive has been on.

If S.M.A.R.T. is enabled in your system BIOS, the BIOS will check and report any early or permanent signs of disk failure. You can also monitor your drive's condition with a S.M.A.R.T.-aware disk monitoring program.

To view all available S.M.A.R.T. information about your drive, try the free DiskCheck utility from *http://www.passmark.com/products/diskcheckup.htm*. DiskCheck is a nonresident utility that will show you exact drive information and all of the supported S.M.A.R.T. statuses from your drive. There's also Ariolic Software's ActiveSMART (*http://www.ariolic.com/activesmart/*) resident monitoring tool, which provides a wealth of detail on drive status and notification of potential failures. If you get a S.M.A.R.T. warning about a drive failing, back up your data immediately and replace the drive.

Hacking the Hack

A failing disk drive is no fun. A failed disk drive is even less so. In my work in various IT shops, I've encountered a lot of grieving "Have I lost all of my data?" looks from end users. It is indeed a sad time, but an opportunity to become a hero. If you can spend the time with various tools to attempt, and even better succeed, at saving someone else's work, you can feel like you actually accomplished something in the course of your day besides resetting some forgetful user's password or plugging their mouse back in.

A plethora of disk drive repair and data recovery tools are available to help you emulate that fictional superhero "Super DataMan." (OK, he doesn't really exist, I made him up...)

I've long since given up on the pedestrian Norton Utilities like Norton Disk Doctor because it does not do enough to spend the time running it, especially for those really cranky lost partitions, erratic mechanical problems inside the drive, and when S.M.A.R.T. says the drive is bad or going to be bad soon.

When it's time to recover partitions and data I unlock my arsenal of serious disk recovery tools, which are:

- Steve Gibson's SpinRite 6.0 (*http://www.spinrite.com*) for finding and fixing or moving bad data blocks on FAT, NTFS, Linux, Novell, Macintosh, and even TiVo volumes

- Ontrack's Easy Data Recovery (*http://www.ontrack.com*) for digging deep inside a drive and extracting recovered data to other media

- Symantec's GHOST (*http://www.symantec.com*) to "peel" data off a bad drive to a disk image for replacement onto another drive, or to extract individual datafiles with Ghost Explorer

- Kurt Garloff's dd_rescue (*http://www.garloff.de/kurt/linux/ddrescue/*) to image Linux partitions to other media for later recovery use (see *http://www.oreillynet.com/pub/wlg/5205* for an excellent write-up and tips)

If your own data recovery efforts fail, you can always resort to a data recovery service like Ontrack (*http://www.ontrack.com*) or ActionFront (*http://www.actionfront.com*).

Disk Drive Performance Hacks
Hacks 58–67

While filesystem choices can have an effect on storage efficiency and performance, the hacks in this chapter address a variety of topics on getting the best raw hardware performance possible from your system board and disk drives. As with most performance-related things, lower timing values and higher clock, rotation, and data transfer speeds yield the best results.

Disk performance is ultimately measured in bytes transferred per second, which can be metered with a variety of benchmarking programs, such as SiSoft Sandra (*http://www.sissoftware.net*). Such programs can also tell you what the capabilities of your system board and disk drives are so you can determine if the real performance is living up to specification.

The following list describes the capabilities of each type of disk drive interface you're likely to encounter. From this list and a benchmarking program, you can tell what type of changes you can make to improve overall disk performance. Each version of the ATA specification, maintained by the industry trade group T13 (*http://t13.org/*), covers one or more implementations of technology and performance. You will find a lot of uses of the term *ATA*—UltraATA, UltraDMA, ATA-33, etc.—on product packages and advertising material. These labels may be misleading, as they can cover a wide range of capabilities from ATA-3 to ATA-5 rather than relating to specific industry standards. Check the product package and documentation to find the actual ATA industry standard a product is designed for when making performance comparisons. The current specification is ATA-5, which covers 44–133 Mbps data transfer rates using DMA-4 and UDMA-5 I/O methods.

ATA
Uses Programmed I/O Mode 1 (PIO-1) for a maximum data transfer rate of 4 megabytes per second (MBps). PIO mode requires constant attention by the CPU to handle data transfers at the expense of other I/O transactions and program operations.

ATA-2 (aka ATA-16)
> Uses DMA-2 for a maximum data transfer rate of 16 MBps. DMA differs from PIO in that the CPU opens a direct memory-to-I/O device communications channel to let data flow freely without CPU intervention, so other I/O and program operations can continue at the same time.

ATA-3 (aka ATA-16)
> Uses DMA-2 for a maximum data transfer rate of 16 MBps; ATA-3 devices are ATA-2 devices with the addition of S.M.A.R.T. internal drive diagnostic technology to "predict" drive failures.

ATA/ATAPI-4 (aka ATA-33, DMA-33, or UDMA-33)
> Uses UDMA-2 for a maximum data transfer rate of 33 MBps.

ATA/ATAPI-5 (aka ATA-66, DMA-66, or UDMA-66)
> This is the first in a series of devices with significant DMA-mode performance increases. Uses UDMA-4 for a maximum data transfer rate of 44 or 66 MBps. Requires 80-wire cable [Hack #59] to achieve maximum throughput.

ATA/ATAPI-5 (aka ATA-100 or UDMA-100)
> This update to the ATA-5 specification increases the throughput capabilities to 100 Mbps using UDMA-5 I/O methods.

ATA/ATAPI-5 (aka ATA-133 or UDMA-133)
> This update to the ATA-5 specification increases the throughput capabilities to 133 Mbps using UDMA-5 I/O methods.

As you can see from the list, Direct Memory Access (DMA) is required to achieve the highest possible performance, but data transfer mode is not the only determining factor affecting overall drive performance.

Direct Memory Access DMA is a feature that allows an I/O device and memory to directly interact for faster data transfer without the CPU. DMA transfers occur in a burst or periodic timeframe, allowing control to be returned to the CPU to handle other program operations.

There are three other factors about the hard drive itself to consider, rotation speed, seek time, and on-disk cache [Hack #58].

HACK #58   Choose the Fastest Hard Drive

You will be amazed at the difference a millisecond or two makes in achieving hard-drive-speed nirvana by knowing and buying according to the specifications.

Did you know that the "high performance Brand X" hard drive inside your PC is probably not the highest performance version of the drive that "Brand

X" makes? PC manufacturers use the most current disk drive series available from their drive vendor, but typically only the most economical model of that series. Your PC maker buys a select version of the popular disk drive brands, so their "select" or so-called "OEM" components are not necessarily top of the line, even if you think your PC maker is the best in the world.

> OEM, or Original Equipment Manufacturer, has become a generic term for products branded or labeled by a "big name" company like Hewlett-Packard or Dell that are actually made by another company. For example, that beautiful charcoal gray or black monitor with the Dell logo on the front is not actually manufactured by Dell but by Sony, NEC, Nokia, or a no-name assembler of PC parts with a license and a big order to produce a lot of Dell-branded products.
>
> The big PC makers do not make disk drives; they make a special deal to get a lot of drives from either of three or four different drive makers and then put their name on them. The PC maker makes more profit if they can "OEM" a cheaper but adequately performing disk drive.
>
> If you are a do-it-yourself PC builder, you'll also hear the term "OEM" in reference to some of the components that you can buy directly from an online retailer like Newegg (*http://www.newegg.com*). OEM parts typically come with nothing more than some packaging and a minimal warranty. Compare this to retail boxed versions that include fancy packaging, a longer warranty, and some extras. For example, a retail CPU will usually include a heat-sink/fan unit, while an OEM CPU includes nothing except the anti-static packaging.

Often the same basic drive mechanics and electronics are used across different models of disk drives to minimize manufacturing complexities. Then drives are tested to see if they meet maximum, intermediate, or minimal performance specifications, reprogrammed, and then labeled and sold accordingly. This is similar to the practice of CPU and memory makers that sell the same components at different performance and price points to maximize profits from their manufacturing processes (providing many opportunities to overclock and hack more performance from lesser-rated parts).

Disk drive models from the same manufacturer, in the same model series, differ either by programmed-in or actual speed and access-time limitations, amount of on-drive data buffering, and even total available drive capacity. Western Digital (*http://www.wdc.com*) openly lists "High-Performance EIDE," "Mainstream EIDE," and "Value EIDE" drive families with essentially the same capacities but different performance specifications. When you go to buy a disk drive, be sure to check specific model numbers and the labeling on the packaging to be sure you are getting the performance you expect. Unfortunately there are no known ways to hack into disk drives, change their firmware or operating parameters, and gain similar performance improvements as you have seen with hacking CPU and memory speeds.

A top-of-the-line model might be available with the following specifications:

- Rotation speed (how fast the disk platter spins): 7,200 RPM
- Buffer size (the amount of on-disk cache memory): 8 MB
- Average latency (the average length of time it takes the drive electronics and mechanics to begin responding to a command to perform a function—seek, read, or write): 4.20 milliseconds
- Average read-seek time (the average time it takes the read/write heads to find a specific disk track and be able to read data from it): 8.9 milliseconds
- Average write-seek time (the average time it takes the read/write heads to find a specific disk track and be able to write to it): 10.9 milliseconds
- Track-to-track seek time (the length of time it takes the read/write heads to travel from one data track on the disk platter to an adjacent track): 2.0 milliseconds
- Full-stroke seek (the length of time it takes the read/write heads to travel from inside to outside of the disk surface): 21 milliseconds
- Buffer-to-disk transfer rate (how fast the data gets written to disk from the on-disk cache): 737 megabits per second

The same drive maker's value-line specifications read:

- Rotation speed: 5,400 RPM (25% slower)
- Buffer size: 2 MB (75% smaller)
- Average latency: 5.00 milliseconds (20% slower)
- Average read-seek time: 8.9 milliseconds
- Average write-seek time: 10.9 milliseconds
- Track-to-track seek time: 2.0 milliseconds
- Full-stroke seek: 21 milliseconds
- Buffer-to-disk transfer rate: 506 megabits per second (30% slower)

Even though the seek times are the same, and both drives support UDMA Mode 5 or ATA-100 I/O performance to the system interface, you can see from the rotation speed, buffer size, latency, and buffer-to-disk parameters that the value-line disk will be slower than the high-performance model.

Why would you want a slower drive in your system? Slower drives are a bit quieter. It's cheaper to make slower drives and reduce the amount of buffer memory; the lower cost of the drive means your total system can be more affordable—but wouldn't you like it to be faster ?

The performance of the disk drive makes a significant difference. The disk drive is the slowest critical component in your system. No matter how fast your CPU and RAM are, the system's biggest bottleneck is the disk drive. A faster drive can make a system with a slow CPU speed bootup and work faster than one with a higher CPU speed (even with the same amount of RAM). Look to the specs and buy the best, especially when shopping for a value-priced PC.

If it's time to upgrade the disk drive in your second PC, consider buying the best drive you can for your main PC and move its drive to the second PC or an external enclosure—no sense giving your old PC something better than your new one has!

Use an 80-Wire Cable

HACK #59

It's not free, but upgrading your hard drive cable could be a very economical boost to your disk drive's performance.

It's all about the data, and in this case how reliably the data makes it between your disk drive and the interface on your system board—and that depends on the quality of the short ribbon cable interconnecting the two. The original IDE drive and 40-pin cable specifications were not too picky about the length and type of cable used, did not require nor provide shielding from other signals nearby, and could not deliver higher data transfer rates.

Almost every PC built in the last 3–4 years comes with a newer style 80-wire cable attached to 40-pin connectors at each end. In an 80-wire cable, 40 of the wires do the same things they always did: handle data and control signals and provide common ground for the signals. The additional 40 wires provide extra protection for the very fast, sensitive data signals traveling through the other 40 wires. The result is the ability to have and fully take advantage of the performance benefits of the fastest UDMA-/ATA-100 and UDMA-/ATA-133 disk drives and interfaces that would otherwise be impaired by noisy signals on 40-wire cables.

You don't need to wait until you upgrade to a new PC or even a new disk drive to benefit from the new cable type. Most systems with UDMA-/ATA-66 disk drives and interfaces get a performance benefit from upgrading the interface cable from a 40-wire to an 80-wire cable because the new cable reduces performance-robbing noise for any disk drive, though not significantly enough to matter for ATA-33 and slower drives like CD-ROMs and much older disk drives (typically less than 500 megabytes as a general rule).

The 80-wire (Figure 6-1) enhanced IDE cable costs about $6 at most computer stores and is easily replaced in about 5 minutes. You'll probably notice the system booting up faster right away.

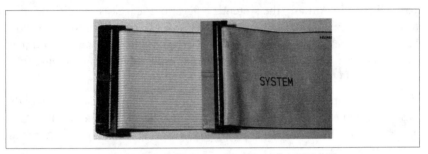

Figure 6-1. Comparing a 40-wire (left) and an 80-wire (right) IDE cable

HACK #60 Upgrade Your IDE Interface

Speed up your system with a turbocharged IDE interface.

If you are stuck with a slower ATA-33, ATA-66, or ATA-100 IDE interface on your system board and want to soup up the system with an ATA-133 drive, you can disable the built-in interface, install a new IDE interface board, connect your new super-fast drive with a shiny new 80-wire cable, and zoom ahead.

Promise Technology (*http://www.promise.com*) offers two replacement Ultra ATA adapters: the Ultra100 TX2 and the Ultra133 TX2. These interface cards and similar versions from other manufacturers like Belkin (*http://www.belkin.com*) are available through computer retailers for $50 and up.

The adapters can only enhance the performance of systems with a 66 MHz PCI bus, so the upgrade is not effective for users of Pentium I and some Pentium II system boards with only 33 MHz PCI speed.

To upgrade your present system with a faster EIDE add-in card, follow these steps:

1. Following the add-on card manufacturer's instructions, install the card and drivers.
2. Install your hard drive and connections for data and power.

3. Start up your PC and verify that the new drive interface and drive are identified and available for use.

4. If you are going to use your new drive for data only, partition and format the drive using your operating system's disk management tools or third-party utilities. If you are going to boot and run the operating system from the new drive, do the following:

   a. To preserve your current operating system, application programs, and data, use a disk-cloning program like Symantec's Ghost **[Hack #95]** to copy your old drive to the new drive.

   b. After cloning, shut down the system and remove your old drive unless you are going to use it as an extra data drive. If you remove the old drive, restart the system and access your system BIOS menu to select which drive you want the BIOS to boot the system from. If the old drive is to remain as a spare data drive, you can either erase all of the old data or reformat the drive.

Kick It Up a Notch with Serial ATA

Upgrading to Serial ATA will stomp all over UDMA-5's 133 MBps performance.

Disk drives using the new Serial ATA (SATA) data interface could deliver data throughput performance enhancements 12%, 125%, and even 350% higher than today's fastest UltraIDE-133 disk drives. We won't see these phenomenal (+125–350%) improvements as long as SATA interfaces on the system board continue to use the lagging PCI bus, but some motherboards with built-in SATA interfaces provide an alternative bus for higher performance. You can get that extra 12% boost today with Serial ATA-150 adapters, like Promise Technologies's SATA150 TX4 and SATA150 TX2Plus.

> Newer chipsets, such as the Intel 865PE, provide a separate data bus dedicated to faster storage devices. (For example, the 865PE provides a 150 MBps bus for Serial ATA.)

Serial ATA devices have spindle speeds and access times similar to the drives we're already used to—7,200 RPM and 8.5 milliseconds. As drive manufacturers adapt their faster 10,000 and 15,000 RPM SCSI or Fibre Channel drive products with 4.7 and 3.6 millisecond access times to SATA, we begin to see a true performance enhancement for storage on everyday desktop systems. Still, various performance tests would lead us to believe that we could already achieve a 20% performance boost in data reading by switching to SATA—an improvement worthy of serious consideration.

The best way to achieve a storage speed boost using SATA drives today is to use them in a RAID-1 through RAID-5 configuration, which SATA is ideal for. SATA drives can be hot-plugged (connected and disconnected), just like you may be used to with your USB camera or FLASH-drive/memory stick, under Windows XP (Windows 2000 does not support hot-plugging these devices and complains when you disconnect them), so swapping out a failed drive can be done without a lengthy system reset or power down.

For those who like to trick out their PC cases with lights and cool-looking cables, SATA's seven-wire data cable will help put an end to ribbon-cable-clutter. The connectors measure just 8 mm wide, and the cables can be up to a meter (39") long, allowing for more flexible drive placement than is possible with parallel ATA.

Keep SATA in mind, look for system boards with true SATA interfaces for eventually faster performance rather than limiting SATA with a sluggish PCI-based SATA interface board, and give your data a test-drive. To upgrade a non-SATA system to a SATA drive, you'll need to follow these steps:

1. Check your system board maker's web site to see if there are any issues with their BIOS and supporting SATA add-in cards (and get an upgrade if there is one to fix any SATA problems).

2. Obtain a PCI-to-SATA interface board, with any required driver software included (but always check the manufacturer's web site for updates).

3. Get a SATA cable.

4. Get a SATA power cable (to get power from the interface board) or an adapter to get power from a standard 4-pin-drive power connector.

5. With the PC power turned off, follow the instructions to install the interface board—but install the drivers first if required, then power off and install the board. Make sure Windows recognizes the new board with the Add New Hardware wizard when you start up again.

6. Shut down the system (power off) and install the new disk drive. Make sure Windows recognizes the new drive with the Add New Hardware wizard when you start up again.

7. For Windows 95/98/Me, partition and format the disk with FDISK and FORMAT in DOS. For Windows 2000 and XP, use the Disk Management tools in Control Panel/Administrative Tools/Computer Management.

Get the Fastest IDE Driver for Intel Chipsets

#62 The proper driver for your Intel is the key to top drive performance for free.

The Integrated Drive Electronics (IDE) interface ports that your hard drive and CD-ROM drive are connected to are basically standard across every PC system; they have to be for any operating system to recognize the ports and drives at startup. Once the operating system loads up, the IDE port can either languish in a low-performance state or be revved up to maximum potential with the right driver software.

If your system board uses an Intel chipset, there's a good chance that the bundled IDE driver is not the latest and greatest, so go to Intel's web site (*http://downloadfinder.intel.com*) and locate and download the IDE Bus Master driver that matches your chipset; in most cases one driver covers your system. If your system does not use an Intel chipset [Hack #63], the driver will not install, so you're safe from corrupting the system.

To identify if you have an Intel chipset and which one, go to *http://www. intel.com/support/chipsets/sb/cs-009245.htm* for tips on how to identify your chipset or get the Intel chipset identifier utility from *http://downloadfinder. intel.com/scripts-df/Product_Filter.asp?ProductID=861*. You can also determine if your operating system includes or needs Intel software by the charts at *http://www.intel.com/support/chipsets/inf/sb/CS-009270.htm*. The System Devices section in Windows Device Manager may also list Intel devices to help you narrow down what type of chipset you have.

> A system information utility such as SiSoft's Sandra, available at *http://www.sisoftware.net*, can provide a wealth of information about chipsets, system settings, and IDE drive modes.

Get the Fastest IDE Driver for Via Chipsets

#63 Optimize your hard drive parameters for their best performance.

System boards that use Via chipsets (*http://www.viatech.com*) come with drivers for the many features of these boards, but one small program, known as the IDETool by Via, is often missing. IDETool is not a device driver but works with the Via chipset driver. IDETool runs in Windows and lets you view and reconfigure the I/O performance capabilities of your hard drives and CD-ROM drives. If you are using a current AMD CPU your system probably has a Via chipset, and there are Via chipsets for some Intel CPUs as well. The System Devices section in Windows Device Manager may also list Via devices to help you narrow down what type of chipset you have.

A typical Windows and driver installation will not have recognized and enabled advanced features such as the fastest DMA or multiword DMA performance levels the IDE interface and drives are capable of. Finding Via's IDETool is not easy, and it is not provided with every version of Via chipset drivers, so you need to visit the following URLs to find it:

- *http://www.rettesoft.hu/ftpdir/DriversMK/via/Drv/IDE/open/IDE_ MPD3014/*

- *http://www.rettesoft.hu/ftpdir/DriversMK/via/Drv/IDE/open/IDE_ MPD3014/IDETOOL/*

- *http://www.tools.atrcomputers.com/drivers/Motherboards/GB-7VTXH/ Chipset/VIA/IDE/IDETOOL/*

IDETool installs as a small resident program, giving you access to and ensuring the performance settings you want when Windows is running. Figure 6-2 shows IDETool in operation, indicating all of the possible I/O modes and other parameters of the disk drive and the current operating mode.

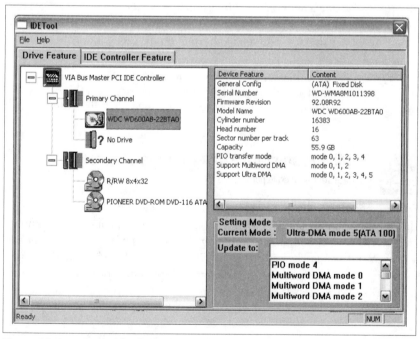

Figure 6-2. Via's IDETool unlocks drive performance

Speed It Up with RAID
#64

If one fast drive is good, then five working together is surely better.

Redundant Array of Inexpensive Disks (RAID) technology has been a significant lifesaver and performance boost for file servers. RAID can be set up in different configurations to provide systems with fault-tolerance or performance enhancements that are crucial to keeping data safe. It can be applied to personal desktop systems to provide significant disk drive performance enhancement.

RAID-0 (zero) is the most basic and highest performing RAID configuration. Portions of data normally stored on one disk drive are spread out across multiple drives, and those drives are accessed in parallel to deliver the data faster, because each drive does not have to access all of the data before it can be delivered. RAID-0 is unfortunately and by nature the least reliable in terms of data integrity, because a failure in any single drive renders all of the data useless.

In contrast to RAID-0, in a RAID-1 configuration all of the data is stored equally on two drives, in parallel. This slows the storage and reading performance but almost guarantees that the data remains intact even if one of the drives fails.

RAID-5 is somewhat a mix of RAID-0 and RAID-1, striping data across multiple drives but also adding error correction information across the drives, providing the advantages of parallel drives and a high degree of ability to recover data if one drive should fail.

Another hybrid implementation of RAID that is very affordable and intended for desktop system is RAID-0+1. The Promise Technology (*http://www.promise.com*) FastTrak TX4000 RAID controller card is specifically meant for desktop users with an appetite for high-performance disk systems. Performance enhancements of up to 30% are possible. Upgrading with top-performing disk drives and putting them into a RAID configuration just might knock the dust bunnies out of your keyboard.

The basic steps to install a RAID configuration on your PC are listed below. Be aware that the specific steps will be unique to the RAID controller (system board or add-in card type), your system BIOS, and RAID configuration software. After installation, the RAID configuration should appear to your operating system as a single-disk volume.

1. You need a RAID controller or RAID capabilities built into your system board. Promise Technologies is one of the most popular brands of add-in RAID controllers for IDE drives.

2. Have at least two identical disk drives on hand for RAID-0 and 1. Configuration of a simple RAID is a lot easier if the drives are identical: there will be no wasted space, and they should mirror each other and perform equally well. RAID 0+1 will require at least four disks.

3. If necessary, make a bootable DOS diskette with any necessary drivers or configuration program for your RAID controller. For BIOS-based RAID setups, familiarize yourself with the RAID setup screens and options in BIOS. It is likely you will have to connect the RAID drives to different IDE connections than the normal non-RAID IDE interfaces.

4. With the system powered down, install and connect the drives to the RAID controller interface connectors.

5. Start the system and either boot with the DOS diskette containing the RAID controller configuration program or get into the BIOS setup to access the RAID configuration screens.

6. Select the type of RAID you will be creating—typically 0, 1, or 0+1.

7. Partition the drives with the configuration program or BIOS screens. This process establishes how the RAID controller views and uses the drives.

8. When RAID controller configuration and disk partitioning is complete, you will either FORMAT the drives under DOS or start the installation of your operating system onto the new RAID system as the primary boot drive.

9. (RAID 1 and higher only) To test your configuration after installing your operating system, shut down and disconnect one of the RAID drives, then restart to verify that indeed the RAID system actually mirrors data to one of the drives.

HACK #65 Speed Up DOS with SMARTDRV

You can add a boost to disk performance with the DOS SmartDrive program.

Caching or reading data from a hard drive and storing it in RAM is one method to speed up disk drive performance. Most disk drives have at least some RAM dedicated to buffering data between the disk and the data cable, some disk drive interface cards and chips provide data caching, and even DOS and Windows provide disk caching. DOS's own SmartDrive program, SMARTDRV.EXE, provides a tremendous performance boost for DOS systems. (If you install SMARTDRV for a Windows 95-98 system, Windows unloads SMARTDRV at startup. With or without SMARTDRV for DOS, Windows provides its own disk caching driver, VCACHE, to speed up disk performance [Hack #66]. For Windows Me and later, the device drivers and VCACHE provide disk caching.)

Loading SMARTDRV in DOS before running any DOS program or manually installing Windows will speed up the process tremendously.

SmartDrive provides a number of options for you to configure it, but as often as not, the simplest invocation is the best—it just works. SMARTDRV's command line can look pretty convoluted with all these options, as shown and listed below, but the final examples shown are more than adequate for most of us:

```
SMARTDRV [/X] [[drive[+|-]]...] [/U] [/C | /R] [/F | /N] [/L] [/V | /Q | /S]
[InitCacheSize [WinCacheSize]] [/E:ElementSize] [/B:BufferSize]
```

The available parameters for SmartDrive are:

/X
Disable write-behind caching for all drives.

drive
Sets caching options on specific drive(s). Takes the form of a single letter followed immediately by + or -. The specified drive(s) will have write-caching disabled unless you add +.

/U
Doesn't load the CD-ROM caching module.

/C
Writes all information currently in write-cache to hard disk.

/R
Clears the cache and restarts SmartDrive.

/F
Writes cached data before the command prompt returns (default).

/N
Doesn't write cached data before the command prompt returns.

/L
Prevents SmartDrive from loading itself into upper memory.

/V
Displays SmartDrive status messages when loading.

/Q
Does not display status information.

/S
Display status of read cache, write cache, and buffering for all drives.

InitCacheSize
Specifies XMS memory (KB) for the cache.

WinCacheSize

   Specifies XMS memory (KB) for the cache with Windows. If this option
   is not specified, SMARTDRV will default the WinCacheSize to the
   amount of extended memory available.

/E:ElementSize

   Specifies how many bytes of information to move at one time.

/B:Buffersize

   Specifies the size of the read-ahead buffer.

> To use *SMARTDRV.EXE*, you must have *HIMEM.SYS*
> loaded in your *CONFIG.SYS* file. To do this, add the line
> `DEVICE=\PATH\TO\HIMEM.SYS`, as in `DEVICE=C:\DOS\HIMEM.SYS`.

To implement SmartDrive, follow this example:

1. Open your *C:\AUTOEXEC.BAT* file using Windows Notepad, the DOS
   Edit program, or another plain-text editor program.

2. Insert either of the following lines near the top of the *AUTOEXEC.BAT*
   file, before the CD driver, MSCDEX, is loaded:

   ```
   c:\dos\smartdrv.exe /x
   ```

   which loads SMARTDRV, caches everything, using all available memory as needed, and writes data immediately to disk, or:

   ```
   c:\dos\smartdrv.exe C+ 1024 512
   ```

   which loads SMARTDRV, caches everything, and uses a megabyte of
   RAM for DOS but only 512 KB of RAM under Windows; data written
   to drive C: is cached/delayed for faster performance.

3. Save the newly edited *C:\AUTOEXEC.BAT* file and then restart your
   system. Alternatively, you can launch SMARTDRV from the DOS
   prompt with the desired arguments.

HACK #66 Speed Up Windows with VCACHE

If you absolutely must stick with Windows 9x or Me the least you can do is
give your system this free performance-boosting tweak to your Windows disk
cache.

The Windows operating system creates and maintains its own read-ahead
disk-caching service to help speed things up, but Windows itself does not
give you any direct control over VCACHE. Instead, you have to dig into the
C:\WINDOWS\SYSTEM.INI file with a text editor to set the caching service
to your liking.

When setting a value for disk caching, you have to balance the amount of RAM to be used for programs and data with the RAM set aside for disk caching. If a lot of RAM is assigned to disk caching, that leaves less for programs and data and Windows will use the swapfile more, which will slow things down. If you assign too little RAM for disk caching, disk operations may be a bit slower but Windows may use the swapfile less, thus keeping performance up a bit.

There is also another balancing act going on here: do you let Windows waste time looking in the cache for data that is not there, which can happen if the cache is too large, or give it less space to look through so it can get directly to the disk drive as quickly as possible? The best approach is to have just enough memory allocated for some caching benefit and not so much that we cheat our programs and Windows.

Fortunately most disk drives have between 256 KB and 8 MB of cache dedicated to data caching to and from the disk drive interface. So, as long as the IDE, SCSI, or SATA interface can keep up, the disk drive will not be a significant data bottleneck (beyond being hundreds of times slower than CPU and I/O bus speeds). With that in mind, you should not have to assign a lot of RAM to Windows disk caching.

> Windows 98 has a known problem with VCACHE consuming all or nearly all available memory on systems with more than 512 MB of RAM, causing out-of-memory errors or crashes. Setting the parameters for VCACHE manually is the official fix for this problem.

To keep Windows from stealing too much RAM for VCACHE, you can add two lines to the *SYSTEM.INI* file to nail the disk caching down, following these steps:

1. Using Notepad or DOS EDIT, open the *C:\WINDOWS\SYSTEM.INI* file, locate the section labeled [vcache], and insert two new lines:

   ```
   [vcache]
   minfilecache=256
   maxfilecache=256
   ```

2. Save the file, close the editor, and then restart Windows for the changes to take effect.

I chose to give the cache only 256 KB of RAM because I've found that more is not always better. If you have a lot of RAM in your system, you may certainly use 512 or 1,024 KB, but you may not see a significant performance boost because of all of the overhead of Windows and drivers between the disk and the CPU.

Microsoft recommends that VCACHE not be set over 40 MB (40,000), which is a significantly high amount of RAM to leave for possible disk caching.

At most, matching the amount of cache on your hard drive—256 KB to 8 MB—may be the best balance between RAM consumption and drive performance.

HACK #67 Linux's Drive Performance Booster

HDPARM is to Linux what the Intel Bus Master and Via IDETool driver-performance enhancements are to Microsoft Windows. Don't forget to include this gem in your next Linux system build.

To be on the safe side, your new Linux installation starts up with the least common denominator of disk drive performance capabilities—typically DMA-33—robbing you of 50–150% of your potential performance. Once Linux is installed, you are free and encouraged to start tweaking the configuration of your disk drive and its interface to squeeze the most of them.

Setting HDPARM parameters too aggressively—that is, in excess of the disk controller or drive capabilities—can lead to data loss.

It is best to test HDPARM settings on a fresh installation of the operating system before committing any applications or programs to the drive and prepare to back down on the settings and reinstall the OS if the drive is unstable or the HDPARM tests show erratic results or fail.

The tool needed, HDPARM, is included with the operating system (or available from your package manager). It can be adjusted manually and then put into a startup script to make your chosen settings effective every time the system starts up.

HDPARM is a command-line utility that provides powerful control over your hard drive parameters (HD PARaMeters). It can also tell you a lot about your disk drive. Everything you do with HDPARM, until you make a script for it, will be done at the command line.

You must be logged in as root to run HDPARM. You can also use the sudo command to run the command as root if you have sufficient privileges.

Assume */dev/hda* is the designation for your hard drive. (This is the default for the first IDE drive; a SATA drive may appear as */dev/hde* if your motherboard also has IDE interfaces.) Run the following command:

```
hdparm -i /dev/hda
```

You should get some info like the following:

```
/dev/hda:
Model=QUANTUM FIREBALLlct, FwRev=APL.1234, SerialNo=1234567
Config={ HardSect NotMFM HdSw>15uSec Fixed DTR>10Mbs }
RawCHS=16383/16/63, TrkSize=32256, SectSize=21298, ECCbytes=4
BuffType=DualPortCache, BuffSize=418kB, MaxMultSect=8, MultSect=off
CurCHS=16383/16/63, CurSects=-66060037, LBA=yes, LBAsects=39876478
IORDY=on/off, tPIO={min:120,w/IORDY:120}, tDMA={min:120,rec:120}
PIO modes: pio0 pio1 pio2 pio3 pio4
DMA modes: mdma0 mdma1 mdma2 udma0 udma1 udma2 udma3 udma4 *udma5
AdvancedPM=no
Drive Supports : ATA/ATAPI-5 T13 1321D revision 1 : ATA-1 ATA-2
ATA-3 ATA-4 ATA-5
```

This tremendous amount of data provided tells you:

MaxMultSect
    The maximum number of sectors your hard disk can read at a time.

MultSect
    The current number of sectors being read at a time.

PIO *modes and* DMA *modes*
    The modes supported by your hard drive. The one marked with an asterisk (*) is the one currently set.

AdvancedPM
    Indicates whether or not your hard drive supports Advanced Power Management.

Another command:

```
hdparm /dev/hda
```

reveals the following information:

```
/dev/hda:
multcount    = 0 (on)
I/O support  = 0 (16-bit)
unmaskirq    = 0 (off)
using_dma    = 0 (off)
keepsettings = 0 (off)
nowerr       = 0 (off)
readonly     = 0 (off)
readahead    = 8 (on)
geometry     = 2482/255/63, sectors = 39876480, start = 0
```

The items of interest are:

multcount
> The number of sectors being read at a time.

I/O support
> The operating mode of your hard disk (16/32/32sync).

using_dma
> Whether or not the drive is using the DMA feature. This may be on by default if your version of Linux properly detects and supports your chipset and drive's DMA capabilities.

keepsettings
> Whether the settings are kept after the drive resets (usually caused by errors).

readonly
> Whether the drive is read-only. Normally set to 1 only for CD-ROMs.

readahead
> How many sectors ahead will be read when you access the hard drive.

The HDPARM program provides two performance-testing features that are crucial to letting you know whether or not you're making improvements as you tweak along. The command:

hdparm -Tt /dev/hda1

will show results such as the following before enhancing the performance:

```
/dev/hda1:
Timing buffer-cache reads: 128 MB in 5.97 seconds = 21.43 MB/sec
Timing buffered disk reads: 64 MB in 17.97 seconds = 3.56 MB/sec
```

and then results like these after enhancing the performance:

```
Timing buffer-cache reads: 128 MB in 0.91 seconds =140.66 MB/sec
Timing buffered disk reads: 64 MB in 3.78 seconds = 16.93 MB/sec
```

The goal of this hack is to see the time in seconds decrease and the MB/sec to increase. You can do that by using a variety of parameters, invoked one at a time, then rerunning the performance tests to see if things are improving or not.

Mistakes during the setup process may damage your filesystem and all of its data, so it's best to do this after a fresh install of Linux or right after you've done a full backup.

Begin by setting the operating mode of the interface between the system and the disk drive using one of the following parameters:

```
hdparm -c0 /dev/hda   #sets operating mode to 16-bits
hdparm -c1 /dev/hda   #sets operating mode to 32-bits
hdparm -c3 /dev/hda   #sets operating mode to 32-bits synchronized
```

Mode 1 (-c1) is used most often for best performance. Mode 3 (-c3) only is needed for some chipsets.

Next set the data transfer parameters, which you can determine from the output of the "-I" command shown earlier (in that case 8 is the maximum supported):

```
hdparm -m8 /dev/hda
```

Next try activating DMA mode for your system interface:

```
hdparm -d1
```

Then set the drive mode (a value of X32 is most common; UDMA-5 is X69):

```
hdparm -X32 /dev/hda
```

or:

```
hdparm -X69 /dev/hda
```

Finally, try setting the read-ahead value, which is typically set to the same value as multcount from earlier, or 8:

```
hdparm -a8 /dev/hda
```

If any or all of these settings make incremental improvements in performance, remember them and create a script that sets them all sequentially or includes them all in one line. I prefer sequential lines to ensure the drive accepts each command separately and I do not lose a setting if another fails to take. From all of this, you might typically be using the following parameters:

```
hdparm -c1
hdparm -m8 /dev/hda
hdparm -d1
hdparm -X34 /dev/hda
hdparm -a8 /dev/hda
```

Another single-command example that may work best for your system is:

```
hdparm -X66 -d1 -u1 -m16 -c3 /dev/hda
```

Save either to a file and make the file a script to place in the directory for the runlevel at which you normally use Linux. For example:

1. Using a text editor, create then save the script as */etc/init.d/hdparm.local*.

2. Configure it to start in runlevel 5 with the following command:

   ```
   ln -s /etc/init.d/hdparm.local /etc/rc5.d/S20hdparm.local
   ```

3. The rc5.d part of the parameter string indicates runlevel 5, which is the normal operating mode for most Linux systems. To find out your default runlevel, examine */etc/inittab* for the inittdefault entry, as in:

   ```
   id:5:initdefault:
   ```

The next step is to keep an eye on dmesg and/or */var/log/syslog*. In some cases, an error will cause the settings to be reset. So that's where the -k (keep) flag comes in. If you're 100% positive that these settings won't corrupt your data, you can add -k to the script.

## CHAPTER SEVEN

Video Hacks
Hacks 68–74

Except for the CPU and memory, the video card handles more data more often than any other component in your PC. It's possible for a 1024×768 display with a color depth of 32 bits (4 bytes) refreshed 60 times per second to move tens of megabytes per second—if the entire screen refreshed with new data at each screen refresh interval. This is a *lot* of data, and it does not include the processing and rendering the video card's CPU has to handle to generate a constantly dynamic display. Enhancing video performance is most important to graphic designers and gamers, but it can also make Windows less sluggish and clunky for the rest of us.

Overall video performance is affected not only by the speed, quality, and features of the video adapter card (which in some cases you may overclock just as you can your CPU and system RAM) but also by which I/O interface your video adapter uses—ISA, PCI, or AGP (including video adapters built onto the system board).

The ISA and PCI buses can be used for just about every type of I/O device there is, from modems to network to video adapters. A lot of activity is going on within these buses. The 16-bit (2-byte wide) ISA bus runs at 16 MHz, yielding a maximum throughput of 32 megabytes per second (MBps). The 32-bit (4-byte wide) PCI bus runs at 33 MHz, yielding maximum throughput of 133 MBps.

The AGP bus is dedicated specifically to graphics—a straight pipe from the PC's CPU to the display—and it's *fast*! The 64-bit-wide (8-byte) AGP bus runs at 66 MHz, providing 266 MBps throughput; AGP 2x's throughput is 533 MBps; AGP 4x's is 1.1 GBps (gigabytes per second); and AGP 8x yields 2.1 GBps throughput, all of it dedicated to graphics. By all means, if you are still using an ISA bus video adapter, it is time to upgrade to at least a PCI adapter, if not a new system board and AGP video.

The hacks in this chapter are all about getting and maintaining the highest video throughput numbers you can, which will affect both 2D normal desktop appearance as well as 3D graphics. Data bus throughput numbers are important because the data has to get from the CPU to the video adapter somehow—the faster the better. In rare cases, overclocking may achieve a 50% increase in video performance, but a 10–20% increase is typical.

The real measure of video performance lies in the results of various benchmark tests, such as the free FutureMark (*http://www.futuremark.com*) 3DMark test suite. This is the most popular among those who will do nearly anything to boost graphics performance: gamers.

Within 3DMark and similar tests are measurements of several graphics performance qualities. Specifically, the number of *pixels* (picture elements) processed per second is evaluated for 2D performance testing, and the number of *texels* (texture elements) processed per second (measured in millions of texels) is evaluated for 3D performance testing. The higher the texel and pixel test results are, the better.

Pixels are the individual dots of light you see on your computer screen, made up of a combination of the three colors used by your video display (red, green, and blue). The data that creates the appearance of each pixel consists of a pixel address (in row and column) and how intense each color is to be. The color depth, or resolution, you can obtain depends on how much data is used to define the brightness of the colors, from 8 bits (256 colors) to 32/24 bits (16.8 million colors—8 of the 32 bits are used for a transparency layer called the *alpha channel*) and even higher. High pixel data transfer performance is important for overall text and graphics display speed and appearance. Texels are pixels that are given special attributes that help produce a three-dimensional appearance of depth and are treated differently in video data processing to provide this effect; thus it is important to have high texel performance to avoid clunky and rough-looking 3D.

Full-motion video benchmark tests are used to evaluate the video frame rate—our current standard is 24 frames per second—as we see in big-screen movies. Normal broadcast and cable television images refresh the screen twice at 60 times per second, yielding a picture that is completely refreshed at 30 screens or frames per second. In video gaming, the mantra is "Frame rate is everything." The closer our PC's video performance gets to live TV, the better (and better yet if it can exceed TV).

Get off the PCI Bus

#68 Upgrading to an AGP-based video adapter is the ultimate video boost.

If your PC lacks an AGP port, you are stuck with PCI. You may find a PCI video adapter (see Figure 7-1) with more video RAM and higher performance than the card you have now, but that's about as far as you can go with PCI. If you have an AGP bus connector on your system board, by all means get down to the computer store and pick up a late model nVidia GeForce or ATI Radeon card to get that well-deserved, long-awaited performance boost. An AGP video adapter can perform 15 times faster than a PCI adapter. It may not improve your game skills, but you'll better enjoy the playing you do.

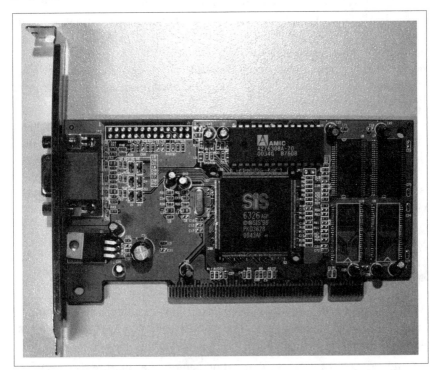

Figure 7-1. A typical PCI-bus VGA adapter

Before you simply grab the latest AGP card and plug it into your system, you need to know which level of AGP performance and what voltage your system board's AGP I/O slot supports. Specifically, will the slot support something better than the original AGP 1x cards? Will it take an AGP 2x, 4x, or 8x card? AGP 8x cards are not backwards compatible, so an AGP 8x card will not run in an AGP 1x, 2x, or 4x slot; the slower slots do not have the proper clocking or voltage to run an 8x card. Plugging an AGP 2x card into a 1x slot will not give you the 2x performance increase you may be expecting; the slot does not provide the higher clock speed for 2x, and similarly a 4x card will not run as fast as it can in a 2x slot.

HACK #69   Upgrade from Built-in Video

Untie yourself from that low-performance built-in adapter by upgrading to an after-market AGP video adapter.

If your system has a built-in video adapter, there is the possibility that some of your main memory is shared over to the video system. This is not a good thing, since system memory is much slower and functions differently than video RAM. The RAM on your video card is typically dual-ported, meaning that it can be written to (by the PC) and read from (by the video processor) at the same time, saving critical timing cycles. When system RAM, which must be written to and read from in separate timing cycles, is used for video, its contents must be moved into video RAM and processed before it can be used for display.

If you have an AGP slot available and can disable the on-board video, get a late model AGP-based video card like the one pictured in Figure 7-2 to take the place of the built-in video system. Be sure that it's compatible with your system's AGP slot. Check your motherboard documentation for the supported AGP modes [Hack #68] and compare it against the specifications of the video card.

HACK #70   Don't Expect Much from AGP Aperture Size

Setting the AGP aperture size is not a performance boost, but it will let your AGP adapter work to its maximum rendering and display capabilities.

AGP aperture size is a value in BIOS setup, shown in Figure 7-3, that establishes a range of memory-addressing space that may be used for video texturing. It does not:

- Immediately set aside the amount of memory the aperture size is set for.
- Need to be set proportionate to the amount of system RAM.
- Have a direct correlation to video performance.

Additionally, it may be set lower than the amount of RAM on your video card.

When your operating system initializes for an AGP video card, it maps the aperture to a collection of 4 KB pages of main memory. This memory may

Figure 7-2. A second-generation AGP-bus video adapter

System BIOS Cacheable	Enabled
Video BIOS Cacheable	Enabled
Video RAM Cacheable	Disabled
AGP Aperture Size	64M
AGP-4X Mode	Enabled
AGP Driving Control	Auto

Figure 7-3. BIOS setup parameters for AGP aperture size

never be used as you work with your PC, some of it may be used from time to time, or all of it may be used, depending on how graphic-intensive your applications are. These memory blocks are not one big chunk of system memory carved out all at once, nor are they all in one section of memory. Instead, they are fragments, but AGP requires its memory to be addressed as a continuous block—and this block is the AGP aperture, a range of memory above that of the physical system memory used to give AGP its required continuous addressing block to work with. Generally, the AGP aperture may use only half as much system memory as the aperture size is set for and may never use any or all of that amount.

Performance tests run by a number of independent sites (*http://www. tweak3d.net/articles/aperture-size/*, *http://www.cybercpu.net/howto/basic/ AGP_aperture_2/*, and *http://www.adriansrojakpot.com/Speed_Demonz/ New_BIOS_Guide/AGP_Aperture_Size.htm*) indicate the proper setting to be either 64 or 128 MB. The 3DMark tests I ran showed no performance difference between the two settings, so I leave the AGP aperture set at 64 MB.

> Video performance can be inhibited by the wrong aperture size. Setting the AGP aperture size below 32 MB or above 128 MB has been found to cause system crashes for some experimenters. It is suspected that the video driver requires a minimal aperture size to work in and some cannot handle the larger aperture size, probably due to deficient programming.

HACK #71   Choose the Correct AGP Mode

Tell your system BIOS to throttle up the AGP bus for the best video data throughput.

Most recent video cards support AGP 4x and 8x, but not all system boards do. AGP 1x and 2x run off 3.3 volts, while AGP 4x and 8x use 1.5v power. AGP 4x and 8x cards are keyed so they will not plug into a 1x- or 2x-only slot.

Maximum performance is obtained by using the highest AGP clocking value your system and video card will support. In other words, if you have an AGP 8X card and you have a BIOS parameter that sets the AGP mode (2X, 4X, 8X) that is set to 4X, your AGP card will not be running at its best performance. This parameter may be automatically set by your BIOS (you see only a display of the automatically determined parameter), or you may be able to override the setting to a lower or higher value than appropriate. If your system BIOS defaults to a 1X setting but you have a 2X video card, by all means set the value to 2X. If your system BIOS defaults to a 4X setting but you have an 8X video card, set the value to 8X.

The AGP Mode setting can be found in your BIOS settings (see Table 1-1 in "Recover a BIOS That Won't Boot" [Hack #3]), usually under Advanced Settings or Advanced Chipset Features.

HACK #72   Overclock Your nVidia Adapter

Specifically designed for video adapters that use the nVidia chipset, nVidia's Detonator driver or the RivaTuner utility give you control over your video clock speeds.

The first thing you need to make your nVidia chipset overclockable is a small bit of Windows Registry hacking, which is made simple by downloading a file named *geforce_overclock.reg* within *geforce_overclock.zip* (link and content subject to change) from *http://www.softpedia.com/public/cat/12/1/ 12-1-31.shtml*. To merge the Registry entries in this file into the Registry:

1. Download and unzip *geforce_overclock.zip*.

2. Locate and double-click the *reg* file within the zip file to merge it into the Registry.

3. Click OK and reboot. First part accomplished.

> If you want to manually apply this Registry hack (or if you can't find the download), launch *regedit.exe* (click Start→Run and then type **regedit** and press Enter), navigate to (or create) the key HKEY_LOCAL_MACHINE\Software\NVIDIA Corporation\Global\NVTweak, and add a DWORD value named CoolBits and set its value to 3.

With the *geforce_overclock* Registry modification applied, if you already have the nVidia Detonator driver and utility software, you're all set to begin the overclocking by following these steps:

1. Right-click the desktop and select Properties.

2. In the display properties dialog, select the Settings tab

3. Select the Advanced button.

4. Select the tab with the name of your card, and you will be taken to a dialog with an option named Clock Frequencies, similar to the one in Figure 7-4.

5. You can now control the frequency of the nVidia's card memory and core speed independently.

> nVidia and other video card manufacturers warn that overclocking your video card's CPU or memory can damage it. While no one is specific about the damage overclocking causes, you can expect excessive heat build within the chips that can cause catastrophic failure of the components.
>
> If you overclock your video card, you should invest in and apply a larger heat sink to the video CPU and provide additional cooling across the entire card to help maintain lower overall temperatures and reliability.

If your nVidia Riva-based card doesn't use the Detonator driver, set you can still ramp up your adapter with the RivaTuner utility shown in Figure 7-5, from *http://www.guru3d.com/rivatuner/*. RivaTuner is a simple but effective way to speed up your video.

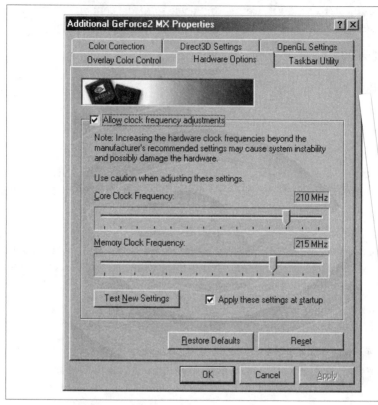

Figure 7-4. Accessing the nVidia overclock settings

While most of the current tweaks, Detonator drivers, and overclocking utilities indicate they are for nVidia's GeForce and Quadro products, as you see here, they work fine on the Riva and Riva TNT products dating back to 1998 also, giving new life to an older but still capable video card.

Overclocking the CPU or "core" speed of your video card yields overall pe[...] formance and frame-rate improvements proportionate to how much yo[...] increase the video card CPU speed—a 10% increase in CPU clock yields a[...] 8–12% performance increase. In my test case, a Riva TNT-based video car[...] running a default 90 MHz displayed an average of 12–13 frames per secon[...] (fps) before running the core clock up to 100 MHz. As mentioned earlier i[...] this chapter, frames per second is but one measure of performance. Fps is [...] great benchmark for full-motion video and gaming action, but the overal[...] quality of textures can still suffer at high frame rates, so your card needs t[...] have high performance in rendering texture elements and smooth texture[...]

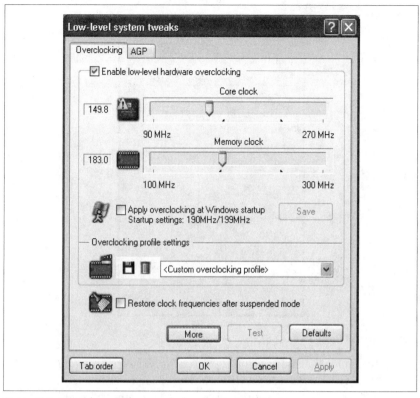

Figure 7-5. Set and save video overclock values in RivaTuner

transitions. In addition, some video presentations are set at a specific frame rate, and no amount of overclocking will improve them. I experimented with an old Diamond Viper 770 card using a Riva TNT chipset and found the frame rate already maxed out at normal speed, and it did not change with higher clock speeds, but other performance measurements and the appearance of benchmarking video tests with 3DMark2001 showed calculated improvements of 8–10% and significant appearance-by-eye improvement after increasing the clock rate by 30%.

HACK #73 Overclock Your ATI Radeon

Perhaps the simplest and safest way to determine and set the highest speeds for your ATI adapters.

The easiest and safest way I found to kick up your ATI video adapter and get a performance increase is with a nicely written, easy-to-use program called ATITool, shown in Figure 7-6.

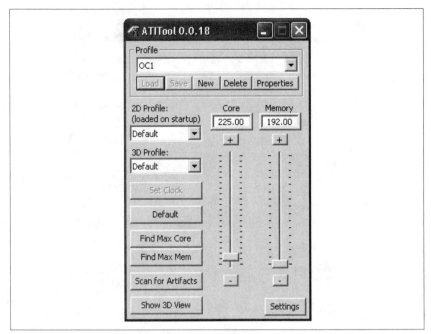

Figure 7-6. ATITool tests and sets video overclocking

It is available for download from *http://www.techpowerup.com/atitool/*. ATI-Tool is known to overclock cards with the ATI Radeon 9000, 9200, 9500, 9600, 9700, and 9800 chips, but it should work on other older ATI cards as well. ATITool will test your adapter for both the maximum core video processor speed and the highest memory speed your card will work at reliably. When it finds the fastest and safest values, you can store them away, lock them into the adapter, and have them set every time you boot your PC.

Before overclocking, an ATI Radeon 7000–based video card running at its default 183 MHz core and memory clock speeds in a 533 MHz Pentium III ran at an average of 13.6 fps. Overclocking by 10.3% to 202 MHz provided a performance increase of 12%.

HACK #74   Overclock Anything

Two different versions of PowerStrip have got your overclocking needs covered for almost any card from legacy to present day.

PowerStrip, shown in Figure 7-7, detects and allows overclock settings for dozens of different video adapters.

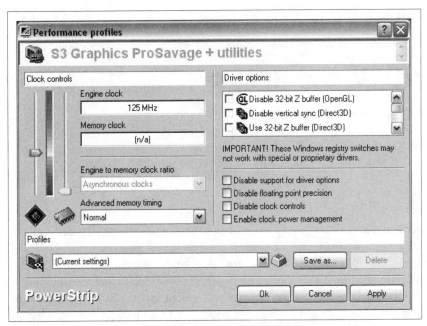

Figure 7-7. Dozens of video options can be set with PowerStrip

A trial version of PowerStrip is available for download from *http://www. entechtaiwan.net/util/ps.shtm*. The program runs resident and provides access to its settings through a right-click on its icon in the system tray. Myriad general video monitor and performance settings are available. Power-Strip Version 2.78 can soup up legacy video cards and chips, such as those from 3dfx, Number Nine, Cirrus Logic, Rendition, S3, and Tseng Labs.

Using PowerStrip to overclock an ATI Radeon 7000 card in a 2.1 GHz AMD Athlon system, I measured a 10% frame-rate performance increase for a 10% increase in clock speed. Overall performance changed only 2%, leading me to believe the card was already maxed out due to the high PC system speed.

## CHAPTER EIGHT

I/O Device Hacks
Hacks 75–84

As you travel through a PC system from the inside to the outside, you end up at the I/O, or Input and Output systems: serial, parallel, game, USB, and IEEE-1394 ports. There isn't a great deal here—just a couple of ports that slog along at what seems like a snail's pace compared to blazing CPU speeds and outrageous disk drive transfer rates—but what you do have can use some understanding and hacking to get them shipshape. By shipshape I mean working at the speeds they are supposed to, not conflicting with other devices or themselves, and operating in the correct mode for the peripherals connected to them.

While you shouldn't look for any spectacular performance boost in your I/O ports, they can be one of the most frustrating parts of a PC to deal with if things do not work right.

While the hacks in this chapter might not apply to your shiny new legacy-free laptop, they *will* help you out if you're working with an older PC used by a friend, school, or church, or trying to recycle an old system as a server or Linux system.

If you don't have enough ports, there are ways to add more—from bending the COM port configuration rules for connecting conventional I/O devices to expanding port availability with USB devices.

Rules? Do you mean to imply that there are actually *rules* you should abide by when configuring PC I/O devices? Of course—no computer system would work consistently if there were not a few rules lying around and being enforced. Indeed, computing is based on rules from the lowest level machine code that starts things up, to, um, the lowest level machine code that actually runs in the CPU.

Face it, the PC didn't just pop out of some guy's garage ready to run DOS, Windows, Linux, Solaris x86, BeOS, or whatever you can get to run on your system and drive's thousands of possible combinations of modems, video cards, network cards, sound cards, keyboards, mice, and disk drives. Somewhere, sometime, you will run into a device or port that needs a specific configuration when the PC stops cooperating. Knowing a few simple configuration rules and how to work around them may not make your PC run *faster*, but the right configuration can make a PC run properly if not better.

Basic PC Configuration Rules

The details of how the PC turned from a renegade project at IBM to a mega-industry go a long way toward explaining the limitations of the systems we have today. The basic PC configuration rules explain why even some new components consume both old and new resources.

The original IBM PC provided a meager hardware addressing range 400 bytes wide into which all the possible hardware (at the time) would exchange commands and data. In addition, eight *interrupt request lines* (IRQs) were available for hardware to signal the CPU and operating system that attention was needed. Further, it was anticipated that some devices would benefit from direct memory access (DMA) capabilities, and six *channels* were provided for that.

Within the PC, there are a few prescribed devices and functions that are absolutes no matter the generation, architecture, manufacturer, CPU, chipset, or peripherals involved. The system is destined to have timers, clocks, and a keyboard but no reservation for a display or I/O devices, which are optional.

The Bad Old Days

Shortly into the life of the PC, IBM and other vendors began to incorporate some new devices that led to the explosion of the PC into the consumer and business market. For the first three to four years of the PC's existence, the resources available for expansion and functionality were adequate, but in the years after that, they proved quite limiting. The resources, devices, and obvious limitations for expansion are listed in Table 8-1. This table represents the basic PC/AT (286 and higher) configuration, including many add-on components that were developed along the way, before PCI and Plug and Play began to change the PC platform. Note that several devices/functions, marked with an asterisk (*) in the "System device" column, are dedicated system devices—these represent resources and functions that cannot be altered.

Table 8-1. Standard legacy PC configuration

Device/function	Address	IRQ	DMA	System device
RAM refresh		0		*
System timer	40h	0		*
Keyboard	60h	1		*
Cascade (see note) for IRQ 8-15		2		*
COM2	2F8h	3		
COM4	2E8h	3		
COM1	3F8h	4		
COM3	2F8h			
LPT2	278h	5		
Sound card	220h	1, 3, or 5		
Diskette adapter	3F0h	6	2	*
LPT1	3BCh or 378h	7		
Real-time clock	70h	8		*
Reserved for 16-bit ISA		9		
ISA-bus network card	280h	10		
SCSI adapter	330h	11	3 or 5	
PS/2 mouse port	64h	12		*
Numeric coprocessor	F0h	13		*
Hard disk interface	1F0h	14		
Second hard disk interface	170h	15		
VGA card	3B0 or 3C0			

The "cascade" designation for IRQ 2 means that the second interrupt chip for IRQs 8–15 feeds or triggers the IRQ 2 signal in the first chip. The IRQ 2 signal line is not available for use by plug-in devices or other system board devices.

Most of the devices in early PCs, from essential system resources through hard drive interfaces and video cards, provided little or no hardware configuration options: they use fixed I/O addresses and IRQs, and anything you added to the system had to work around what was left. Even in a PC-AT system, you have only 16 total IRQs and 6 total DMA channels to choose from, with seven of the IRQs (0, 1, 2, 6, 8, 9, 13) taken by the system and another three taken by normal devices (hard drive using 14 and 15, and mouse port using 12). This leaves only six IRQ (3, 4, 5, 7, 10, and 11) lines to work with. With COM ports 1 and 2 present, even if those ports are not in use, IRQ 3 and 4 are spoken for, leaving four lines for expansion.

The PC-AT architecture ties up two IRQ lines, 2 and 9, to accommodate devices on the 16-bit ISA bus. IRQ2 has typically never been accessible on either 8- or 16-bit ISA I/O slots because it is the IRQ line used by the second IRQ chip that provides IRQs 8–15 to the 16-bit bus. Whether or not you can use IRQ9 for an add-in device has been an ongoing question for years because it was thought that the IRQ-handling code in BIOS and operating systems confused it with IRQ2. This seems not to be the case, and since the IRQ9 signal does appear on the 16-bit ISA bus connector, it seems that we can use it. Many have done so successfully and without problems. This increases the available IRQ count to five, but those five lines get used up quickly.

In the PC-AT architecture, a sound card and network adapter will use up another two IRQ lines (typically IRQs 5 and 10), leaving only three lines (IRQs 7, 9, and 11) for future expansion. If you want to get a total of four serial/COM ports working simultaneously [Hack #77], you need to figure out a way to use two of these IRQ lines, leaving only one available IRQ for expansion. If you add a SCSI host adapter, IRQ 11 gets used and you're out of expansion capabilities.

Toward a Modern Bus: VESA, PCI, AGP, and Beyond

It's easy to see under the older architecture that if you want to add a web camera, a connection to your PDA or cell phone, an external disk drive, or any other sophisticated device, you could run out of IRQ lines and be stuck. It was obvious to Intel and Microsoft that something had to be done to provide additional expansion capabilities. This revelation was coincident with the need for higher-speed peripheral connectivity; the old 16 MHz 16-bit ISA bus was not going to deliver adequate graphics or connectivity performance for the future.

The PC industry, including IBM, and later the Video Electronics Standard Association (VESA), saw the need for better performance, more configuration options, and easier configuration of the PC. Before the PC got the PCI bus (Peripheral Component Interconnect), it struggled through IBM's MicroChannel Architecture, EISA (Enhanced Industry Standard Architecture), and VESA's VLB (VESA Local Bus) enhancements on various PC models—mostly through the i80386 and i80486 generations of PCs. Intel, Microsoft, and others finally were able to create and drive to market the current PCI bus standard as well as support Plug and Play routines in the system BIOS and hardware devices.

The PCI bus provides a totally separate set of electronic circuits, addressing and data lines, and configuration capabilities to the PC. PCI removes issues of exclusive IRQ assignments, expands the hardware I/O addressing range, speeds up I/O data transfer rates, and provides for automatic, or at least more intelligent, hardware device configuration. In fact, it is virtually impossible to manually configure a PCI device because there are no jumpers or switches and very few devices support setting the configuration through software; configuration is done entirely through Plug and Play processes.

PCI is exactly what the PC needed to expand beyond the limitations of fixed hardware addressing and limited IRQ and DMA resources. While the premise behind PCI for reducing resource constraints still has advantages, PCI is limited in data throughput speed as a 33-MHz bus. This bus speed is not nearly fast enough for the demands of multimedia applications like games and full-motion video. The PCI bus is overdue for a speed enhancement. Just as ISA, MicroChannel, and EISA were not fulfilling the need for speed, the original PCI bus has all but outlived its ability to deliver data fast enough, leading to the evolution of PCI-X with 266 MHz and 533 MHz speeds provided in some systems.

From PCI evolved the Universal Serial Bus (USB) and Texas Instruments's IEEE-1394 (also known by Apple's brand name of FireWire and Sony's brand name of i.Link), high-speed interfaces for supporting additional new devices in PCs and Apple Macintosh systems.

USB removed any foreseeable restrictions on the number and type of peripheral device imaginable to date. Essentially consuming one PCI port but with a more direct interface to the CPU than the bus itself, USB 1.1 and 2.0 can accommodate up to 256 devices through a single I/O port, and USB 2.0 has achieved data transfer rates up to 57 megabytes per second (MBps), superceding the original IEEE-1394.

IEEE-1394 ports have been perceived as competition to USB 1.1, but it turns out they found a niche in high-end video and data storage uses, with speeds up to 50 MBps. Adoption and use of IEEE-1394 has been slow due to technology licensing fees that increase per-system costs that can only be justified in higher-priced, higher-performance devices.

While external I/O gained from USB and IEEE-1394, the inside of the PC didn't get a performance boost until the Advanced Graphics Port (AGP) was implemented, providing a dedicated path from the CPU to the video adapter. The AGP has experienced performance enhancements that take its data throughput to well above 800 MBps. Although AGP is fast, it's limited to being a single-purpose I/O path (graphics), so PCI-X is the contender for speeding up internal I/O expansion to multiple devices.

PCI, USB, IEEE-1394, and AGP provide the PC with higher performance capabilities but also free up critical resources that can be used for legacy/ISA devices if you can find a system board that still has an ISA bus slot or two.

I/O Speed

To give you an idea of the data throughput rates for various I/O technologies, I've provided a listing of I/O technologies and their data rates in Table 8-2. With the exception of devices connected through the PCI, USB, or IEEE-1394 interfaces, every I/O technology, including most IDE disk drive interfaces, requires legacy/ISA IRQ and possibly DMA configuration resources.

Table 8-2. The maximum transfer rates for various connections

Port	Maximum data transfer rate
Serial/COM port—8250	9.6 kilobits/s
Serial/COM port—16550A	115 kilobits/s
Standard Parallel/LPT port	115 kilobytes/s (10x faster than serial/COM)
10 Base/T Ethernet	10 megabits/s
USB 1.1	12 megabits/s
ECP/EPP parallel port	3 megabytes/s
8-bit ISA bus	8 megabytes/s
16-bit ISA bus	16 megabytes/s
IDE	3.3–16.7 megabytes/s
SCSI-1	5 megabytes/s
SCSI-2 (Fast SCSI, Fast Narrow SCSI)	10 megabytes/s
100BaseT Ethernet	100 megabits/s
Fast Wide SCSI (Wide SCSI)	20 megabytes/s
Ultra SCSI (SCSI-3, Fast-20, Ultra Narrow)	20 megabytes/s
UltraIDE	33 megabytes/s
PCI bus	33 megabytes/s
Wide Ultra SCSI (Fast Wide 20)	40 megabytes/s
Ultra2 SCSI	40 megabytes/s
Ultra ATA (IDE)	66–133 megabytes/s
IEEE-1394	100–400 megabits/s
USB 2.0	480 megabits/s
Wide Ultra2 SCSI	80 megabytes/s
Ultra3 SCSI	80 megabytes/s
1000BaseT Ethernet	1,000 megabits/s
Wide Ultra3 SCSI	160 megabytes/s

Table 8-2. The maximum transfer rates for various connections (continued)

Port	Maximum data transfer rate
FC-AL Fiber Channel	100–400 megabytes/s
AGP video bus	2.1 gigabytes/s (AGP 8x)

The speeds listed in Table 8-2 are from their respective maximum throughput specifications. Operating system, device driver, application, system hardware, cabling, and device overhead will impact the actual transfer speeds you obtain.

If you are feeling a bit of I/O-performance envy over the tremendous throughput of the AGP bus, you are not alone. Disk drive performance, perhaps the most significant PC performance bottleneck, could benefit significantly from higher bus and throughput speeds, but the industry is still waiting for economical disk drive technology that can accommodate higher data transfer rates.

HACK #75 Let Windows Tell You About I/O Card Conflicts

Find out if an I/O address, IRQ, or DMA signal is used by another card.

Early SCSI adapters and sound cards arrived in the PC market at about the same time. With only the known IBM PC design reference to go by, and no industry-standards group to keep track of who was developing what devices, none of the designers of various devices knew what the others were doing. In the face of limited available resources, everyone scrambled to establish a foothold and hoped they didn't get trampled.

It was not uncommon to encounter a SCSI host adapter and a sound card that both used the same address (often 220h or 330h). Obviously if both adapters used the same address this combination would not work. If software addressed the sound card, it would wrongly get the attention of the SCSI host adapter; if software addressed the SCSI host adapter, it would wrongly get the attention of the sound card.

In such battles, the device with more clout wins, and such was the case with the sound card. Many more people were buying sound cards than were investing in expensive SCSI devices, so makers of the SCSI adapters moved off to address 330h and the sound card manufacturers held the ground at 220h.

You need to know which devices use which addresses and configure them so there is no direct conflict. To find out if you have any device conflicts and drill down to what they are, open Windows Device Manager. If you see a yellow dot with an exclamation point in it, you have a conflict. If you see a red x, the device is disabled. Figure 8-1 shows a device in Device Manager with no conflicts; this is the picture you want to see. If you see a yellow dot, double-click it to open the Properties dialog for the device and then select the Resources tab. Any conflicts will be shown in the lower text box, identifying the conflicting device. To resolve the conflict, you must change the configuration of one of the devices.

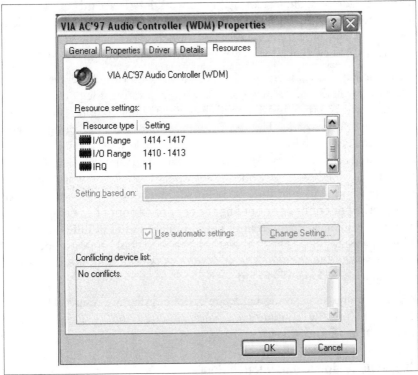

Figure 8-1. Properties for an I/O device with no conflicts

Sometimes resolving conflicts this way will not solve problems. In addition to making sure things don't collide, be sure to look out for 300h, the problem I/O address, and also make sure you're leaving enough room between addresses.

Avoid I/O Address 300h

Of the known IBM I/O devices, one significant but very rare device is often overlooked: the Prototype Card. IBM created and sold this special I/O card for hardware developers to use to hack together new I/O devices. An open

PC design and architecture has obviously been good for the existence of the PC business, but a few designers neglected to fully understand the PC design when they created new devices. IBM assigned or reserved I/O address 300h to the Prototype Card and accommodated recognition of the Prototype Card's presence in the BIOS, as did some DOS and Windows software. Engineers that ignored these facts caused no end of trouble for PC installers and users.

This bit of trivia usually isn't significant until you try to add an ISA device that uses address 300h, as many early network interface cards do. IBM had not accounted for network cards except their own for connection to Token Ring LANs and mainframes, and those devices did not use address 300h, because IBM knew that address was reserved for the Prototype Card.

This problem first came to light in the mid-90s with early Ethernet cards. A technician would install a new network card, unaware of the potential problem between the Prototype Card and the default configuration some of these cards used: address 300. The rest of the network card installation (drivers and related connectivity software) would seem to go well, connectivity with a server and other workstations could be established, and things seemed just fine—for a while. After "a while," some applications or network functions would cease to work and the trouble began; the network that worked once now worked intermittently. Finding the cause of the problem escaped technicians until some other network card, probably using a different default address, was installed. The card that was removed could appear to be OK in another system but ultimately would never work right until its address was changed to something other than 300h.

Be wary of and avoid using hardware addresses that are reserved for other devices, follow the configuration rules, and use the de facto standard addresses for your new devices.

Use an I/O Address with Enough Room

Most 8- and 16-bit ISA network adapters allow you to set the base I/O address to 340h. Since most adapters require an address range of only a few bytes beyond the base address, using address 340h is typically not a problem. If your network or other I/O adapter requires more address space, it may overlap onto another card's base address, specifically the LPT1/parallel port at address 378h [Hack #76], which will cause one or both of the adapters to stop working correctly.

In the case of most network adapters, you can reconfigure the card to use another base address (but not 300h!) to avoid colliding with another device. 280h is a typical alternative to try.

Be sure to research the complete addressing requirements of all your adapter cards and configure them so they do not overlap the address space of other adapters.

Break the Rules with LPT Ports

Get back the use of IRQ lines by changing your LPT port settings.

Even though none of the early standard LPT port implementations ever used an IRQ line, Windows still insists that IRQ 7 or 5 is assigned to an LPT port (Windows performs no actual test for this—it's a programmed assumption), so any other use of these IRQ lines causes Windows to erroneously flag such use as a conflict. Some of us are finicky about conflicts, and some programs may not accept port connections if a conflict exists.

Trying to use the same IRQ as the parallel port is a potential conflict only if both of these are true:

- The LPT port is configured for Enhanced Parallel Port or Extended Capabilities Port (commonly used modes for pre-USB printers and scanners).

- The device attached to the LPT port is capable of signaling the PC for attention.

If the parallel port is used as a standard or even bidirectional port for simply dumping text to a printer, you can ignore this conflict because the chipset and simpler printing devices that may be attached to it have no need to use the IRQ line. Thus, you gain a free IRQ line to use for other devices despite the apparent conflict.

If your printer attaches to your PC through a USB port, or is connected as a network device or shared on another computer, you do not need the LPT port at all. In this case, you can disable the LPT port to ensure that the IRQ is never used by the LPT port, and is available for other uses in the BIOS [Hack #14] and in Windows through Device Manager with these steps:

1. Right-click My Computer and select Properties.

2. Select the Hardware tab and then click the Device Manager button.

3. In Device Manager click on the plus (+) sign to the left of Ports (COM & LPT).

4. Right-click the Printer port entry and then select Disable.

5. Close Device Manager.

6. Shut down or restart the system and configure your other device to use the IRQ (typically IRQ 7) formerly used by the LPT port.

Break the Rules with COM Ports

HACK #77

Allow more than two COM ports to work simultaneously without conflicts.

We don't seem to use COM ports very much these days, but even new USB-connected devices emulate the tried-and-true methods of serial communications in today's technology. The plain old serial port is still imperative for communicating with most of the devices that make the Internet possible: modems, routers, switches, and headless servers.

In the design of the original PC, IBM created a deliberate conflict between COM ports that has never been resolved through any change of standards or design. The conflict is the IRQ assignments for COM1 and COM3, which both use IRQ4, and COM2 and COM4, which both use COM3. Apparently IBM never thought anyone would want to use more than two COM ports at the same time: you cannot use COM1 and COM3 at the same time, nor COM2 and COM4 at the same time.

This conflict came to light as early online pioneers started running bulletin board systems with multiple modems to allow multiple users access at the same time. Early communications software relied on the system BIOS for many hardware I/O functions, and serial communications was one of them. The BIOS, of course, was hard-coded to adhere to strict rules, and COM port configuration and IRQs were encompassed by them.

As time passed, developers determined the BIOS functions were not the only or best way to get the hardware to do what they wanted. Flexibility in software and hardware configurations came about to the advantage of users. They could work around the limitations of the BIOS by addressing system hardware directly, which worked well if it was certain that other hardware and software were not going to get in the way.

The first thing that got in the way of expanding the communications capabilities of the PC was the COM-port IRQ conflict. The conflict could only be resolved through some clever hacking of software and hardware to make things work. Software programmers had to know and provide for the many different addresses and IRQs that were likely to be available in the PC, and hardware makers or technically inclined users had to know how to get the hardware configured to their advantage.

Since the source of conflict with using multiple COM ports at the same time is the lack of a unique IRQ for each port, you need to scrounge for two more IRQ lines to give the COM3 and COM4 ports their own IRQs.

Even if you are not going to physically plug in additional COM ports, you may have to reconfigure the virtual COM ports created by USB-to-serial adapters and ensure that each has a nonconflicting setting to work with. See the steps at the end of this hack to make COM port settings changes.

Recovering an unused IRQ or two from one or more LPT ports **[Hack #76]** can be a rather fortunate coincidence. You can usually repurpose IRQ7 for one of the four COM ports. You may be able to repurpose IRQ5 as well, if a sound card or another device has not laid claim to it. With only IRQ 5, 9, 10, and 11 to choose from, you face another dilemma; most serial/COM port add-in cards use the 8-bit ISA bus form factor and thus lack any electrical connection or access to IRQs 8–15. This forces you to use IRQ5 for the fourth COM port expansion, which forces you to use a 16-bit ISA or a PCI-bus sound card.

Once you have determined that IRQs 5 and 7 are the only ones suitable and available to an 8-bit ISA serial/COM port expansion board, buy an expansion board that has jumpers or switches you can use to select these alternate IRQs, like the one shown in Figure 8-2.

The card shown in Figure 8-2 is available from Startech.com as part number ISA2S550 and provides an extended connection into a 16-bit ISA slot to pick up IRQs 9, 10, 11, 12, and 15. Startech also offers PCI-based serial I/O and many other hard-to-find cards for many different types of PC expansion.

It is often suggested that using a USB-to-serial adapter is the way to solve COM port limitations and avoid IRQ constraints. However, USB adapters create virtual COM ports, which must in turn emulate real COM ports, up to and including using their hardware addresses and IRQ signals.

Additionally, many USB drivers create these virtual COM ports with nonstandard COM port numbers (anywhere from COM5 and much higher), which are not traditional port numbers and may not be recognized by the programs you use to communicate with a COM-port-connected device.

In a worst-case scenario, the USB-to-serial adapters, like those offered for handheld-to-PC synchronization, are known to change the COM port number they assign to themselves between reboots, leaving you to have to reconfigure the adapter or your applications to find the new randomly assigned port. Sometimes you need a real and stable COM port to get your work done.

Figure 8-2. A new COM port card with jumpers to set optional IRQs

Follow these steps to reconfigure address or IRQ settings in Windows to match the actual COM port device you are using—a physical port or a virtual one such as a USB-to-serial adapter:

1. Right-click My Computer and select Properties.
2. Select the Hardware tab, then click the Device Manager button.
3. In Device Manager click on the plus (+) sign to the left of Ports (COM & LPT).
4. Right-click the COM port entry and then select Properties.
5. Select the Resources tab.
6. Unselect the "Use automatic settings" checkbox.
7. Double-click either I/O Range or IRQ to make changes to these values, then click OK.

8. Select the Port Settings tab, then click the Advanced button to access the COM Port Number setting if you need to change the logical port number to suit the software you are using.

9. Click OK to exit the dialogs, restart your PC, and your port is ready to go.

Rewire Your COM Ports

#78 Rewire an old COM port board to use available IRQs to run four ports simultaneously.

In this hack, we'll rewire the IRQ lines of an old 8-bit COM port card to configure COM3 and COM4 ports to use IRQs 5 and 7. Rewiring older I/O cards takes a bit of skill—specifically with hand tools and a soldering iron.

Figure 8-3 shows an obvious rewire of IRQ signals. Accomplishing this rewiring required opening the circuit traces from the IRQ 3 and 4 connection "fingers," then adding wires from the IRQ 5 and 7 "fingers" to the circuit traces that once connected to IRQs 3 and 4.

Figure 8-3. IRQ lines rewired on a COM port I/O card

If you decide to try this at home, you need to know the connector pin information to locate the respective IRQ circuit traces, which are:

Pin B21 = IRQ7
Pin B23 = IRQ5
Pin B24 = IRQ4
Pin B25 = IRQ3

The "B" designates the component side of the circuit board, as shown in Figure 8-3. Pins are counted from the bracket (off camera to the left) towards the end of the card. Pin B21 is the 21st pin from the left.

To perform this hack, you need the following tools:

- A 60-watt soldering iron or a temperature-controlled soldering iron with a small 700–800 degree tip
- Solder
- 2 to 3 inches of 22- to 26-gauge wire
- Wire cutters and strippers
- An X-ACTO or similar hobby knife

With the right tools at hand, follow these steps:

1. Power down the computer, unplug it, and remove the card.

2. Locate the circuit traces that lead from pins B24 and B25 and go into circuitry on the card—most likely to a switch or jumper block. You can decide to simply leave the respective switches or jumpers in their open condition rather than cutting the copper foil traces, but you do run the risk of inadvertently closing those connections and shorting two IRQ lines together.

3. Cut the foil traces using the pointed end of a small hobby knife, making sure the cut is clean and all the way into the circuit board material to ensure you completely open the foil trace.

4. Prepare two short pieces of wire (26-gauge wire-wrap wire is the traditional circuit board mending wire of choice) as long as needed to reach from the connector pins to the switch or jumper block you traced the cut IRQ 3 and 4 lines to. Strip about 1/8" of insulation off each end and tin (wet or soak with hot molten solder) the exposed wire ends with solder as necessary.

5. Locate and tin the very top edge of pins B21 and B23.

6. Attach one end of each wire to each connector pin.

7. Attach the other end of each wire to the point on the switch or jumper block that was connected to the copper traces for IRQs 3 and 4.

 Which end goes to which former IRQ line? Because COM1 uses IRQ4 and COM2 uses IRQ3, I stuck with convention and attached the wire for IRQ7 to where IRQ4 used to be connected and used it for COM3 (and configured the card accordingly) and used IRQ5 for COM4.

8. Make sure the connections are secure: add a dab of glue or tape to hold them in place.

9. Install the card in your system.

10. Boot up your system and configure Windows or your communications software to use the new settings. Your system BIOS and Windows should recognize the new COM ports, but Windows needs a little help in its configuration because it assumes COM3 and COM4 use IRQ4 and IRQ3, respectively, which needs to be changed to reflect reality. Windows allows you to manually change the COM port configurations in Device Manager. To do this:

   a. Launch Windows Device Manager (right-click on My Computer, click Properties, select the Hardware tab, and click Device Manager).

   b. Locate the Ports (COM & LPT) listing and expand it.

   c. Open the Properties dialog and select the Resources tab for each COM port in turn.

   d. Disable the "Use automatic settings" checkbox (clear the checkmark), then choose a new configuration setting in the "Settings based on" drop-down menu. As you change the selection, notice the I/O Range and IRQ values change in the "Resource settings:" box. When these values change to I/O Range = 3E8-3EF and IRQ = 7 for the COM3 port (to match the changes you made on the I/O card), stop and click OK.

   e. Repeat this process for COM4 until the resources indicate I/O Range = 2E8-2EF and IRQ = 5 (to match the changes you made on the I/O card), then click OK. Close Device Manager, and your new ports and Windows settings are ready for testing and use.

Boost COM Port Performance

If your PC has a COM port, tweak your state-of-the-art UAR/T chip through Windows settings.

Back in the olden days of the early PCs, getting online meant dialing in to CompuServe, Delphi, or The Source with a 300- to 1,200-baud modem, only to arrive at the legacy equivalent of Telnet—plain white characters on a green or black screen background, text menus (online servers were truly mainframes back then), and XMODEM downloads of "huge" 300 KB files. Back then, you could connect at 2,400 baud—or better yet 9,600—if your local node supported it, but this was a real challenge and a technical stress on PC serial ports. Generally, a PC built before 1990 couldn't communicate with the outside world any faster than 9,600 bits per second (bps).

The main component that made up the serial/COM port in the PC was a component called the 8250 Universal Asynchronous Receiver/Transmitter chip (UAR/T). The 8250 was capable of transferring data at a rate of 9,600 bps, roughly 960 ASCII characters per second. In the IBM PC-AT systems, the UAR/T was upgraded to the 16450 chip, which doubled the reliable throughput to 19,200 bps.

Both of these chips generated an interrupt signal to the CPU for every character of data or control information that came across the port. This was highly inefficient and bogged down the PC to a crawl, which didn't matter under single-tasking DOS but had a severe impact on the performance of multitasking Windows.

After becoming aware of this tremendous bottleneck, various chip makers created a new version of the UAR/T that provided 16 bytes of first-in/first-out (FIFO) data buffer, which held a chunk of data back until the buffer was full, reducing the need to interrupt the CPU significantly. The 16550 UAR/T was born. Unfortunately, the original 16550 had a design flaw: the buffer didn't work! Very quickly, the 16550A version of the chip was released in which the buffering *did* work. The result was a serial/COM port that could achieve 115 kilobits-per-second (kbps) transfer rates—a whopping 11.5 kilobytes per second (8 bits for data, 2 bits for data control information). Chip maker SMC created a combined serial/COM and parallel/LPT port chip to condense three ports into one smaller chip—a great idea, but the serial port didn't work right in some of its early production runs, so a special patch program was distributed to turn on all of the chip's features.

Later versions of this popular UAR/T chip came out: the 16650 UAR/T with a 32-byte FIFO, the 16750 UAR/T with a 64-byte FIFO, and the 16950 UAR/T with a 128-byte FIFO. For all their speed advantages, these have never seen the light of regular PC production: except for ISDN data connections, telephone and modem technology never exceeded the 53 kbps speed barrier so there was really no need for a serial port with data throughputs of 256–512 kbps. Instead, Ethernet ports, ISDN, DSL, and cable modems served the need for high-speed data connections, while USB ports handled higher-speed peripheral devices.

In support of these different UAR/T chip communications, software makers and Microsoft had to recognize the type of UAR/T chip present and be able to configure the chip for the best possible performance. Popular programs like Procomm Plus, shareware COM-AND, and Windows 95 were able to take advantage of the newer UAR/Ts and support the old if needed. Buffered 16550 UAR/T support was invisible in DOS and later Windows-based terminal programs; they simply set the device for maximum performance and went about their business. Windows, on the other hand, held back just a bit and limited port speed and buffer use so serial communications didn't visibly impact Windows performance.

Figure 8-4 shows the basic serial port configurations in Windows. Normally the "Bits per second:" parameter is set to 9,600, while optimum performance is achieved if the value is set to 115,200.

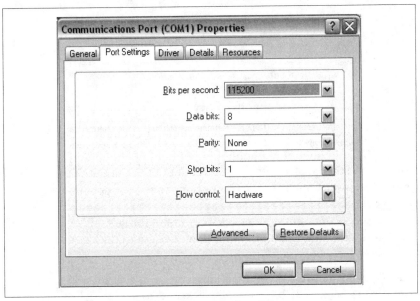

Figure 8-4. Basic serial port configuration in Windows XP

Figure 8-5 shows the advanced settings for a serial port. By default, Windows sets the receive buffer a notch lower than optimum so that communications do not disrupt overall Windows performance

Fortunately, Windows-based communications programs, from Hyperterm to Procomm Plus to the CompuServe and AOL services, could override the port speed value and set it to 38,400 or 57,600 themselves to accommodate 14.4, 28.8, and 56K modem technologies, but they did not tamper with the buffering value.

To achieve the best serial port performance, access each COM port's Properties, select the Basic Serial Port Settings dialog (Figure 8-4) through Device Manager, set the port speed as high as possible, and then select the Advanced button to access the UAR/T buffer settings (Figure 8-5) and set both Transmit and Receive buffers to their maximum values.

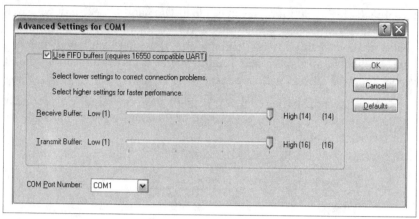

Figure 8-5. Advanced serial port configuration in Windows XP

HACK #80   New Uses for an Old Port

Select the correct LPT port settings to optimize the performance of Windows's Direct Cable Connection and third-party file transfer applications.

Your basic line parallel port is used for more than just sending text and graphics to your printer. Iomega and others found the port useful for connecting add-on disk and tape storage devices; Traveling Software, Symantec, AlohaBob, and others found the port useful for PC-to-PC file transfers; and Microsoft and others figured out how to use the port for PC-to-PC networking.

PC-to-PC file transfers and networking require a special cross-over cable (such as the Belkin F3B207 and F3D508 series) to get the right signals connected between two PCs, as well as the installation of appropriate software or the Windows Direct Cable Connection (DCC) feature. Microsoft provides easy-to-follow directions for setting up DCC at their web site: *http://support.microsoft.com/default.aspx?scid=kb;en-us;305621*. DCC can be used for Windows XP's Files and Settings Transfer feature to migrate data from an old PC to a new one, transfer applications and data with Aloha Bob's PC Relocator [Hack #96], and clone entire drives from one PC to another using Symantec's GHOST [Hack #95].

By setting the parallel port to ECP mode in the system BIOS on both PCs, a DCC connection between two PCs via parallel ports can be up to three times faster than a 10BaseT (10 megabits per second) Ethernet connection. Windows will detect mode changes in the parallel port settings and configure itself for you. Be sure you do not have any IRQ or DMA conflicts [Hack #75] or the connection may not work or will perform poorly.

Use USB for Peer-to-Peer Networking

HACK
#81

USB's versatility comes in handy for PC-to-PC data transfer as well as file and Internet sharing.

If you'd like to move data between systems more quickly than the parallel port allows, you can always step up to interconnecting PCs by USB. Belkin, Traveling Software, and other vendors sell USB transfer cables and accompanying software—effectively a crossover or null modem cable between two USB ports. In some cases, the cable becomes a private TCP/IP network connection and can be used for Internet connection sharing.

Using a USB-to-USB bridging cable is especially handy for systems without network adapters that need to communicate with each other in a peer-to-peer network.

A USB PC-PC interconnection cable costs about $30–40 and comes with appropriate drivers. (The cables contain USB devices that crossover the send and receive lines between PCs.) It is often packaged with software or wizards that help you establish connectivity between PCs.

> Keep your cables and software together as much as possible. USB "networking" cables and the software that comes with them are usually very specific to each other—that is, a cable from Company A will usually not work with the driver and software from Company B.

Get the Most out of USB

HACK
#82

Use separate USB ports to get the best performance out of your high-speed devices.

The USB port in your PC is designed to supply up to 12 (USB 1.1) or 480 (USB 2.0) megabits per second throughput to attached devices, but that is *total* throughput and must be shared with all connected devices. If you use two USB ports on your PC at the same time, it's best to have two USB controllers, each delivering the total throughput. Although this limitation is more noticeable with the slow USB 1.1 speeds, you'll certainly notice it if you do something I/O-intensive with USB 2.0, such as copying large files between two USB mass storage devices.

To check if you have two USB controllers, open Windows Device Manager and expand the Universal Serial Bus controllers branch in the list. If you have two separate controllers, they will be listed, as shown in Figure 8-6.

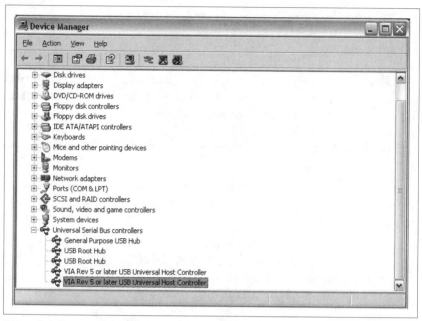

Figure 8-6. Device Manager lists two USB controllers

If you need to connect and use two high-speed USB devices at the same time, such as a scanner, external disk drive, video camera, or network adapter, connect them to different ports on your PC so neither one suffers from sharing bandwidth. If you need to support more than two high-speed devices operating at the same time, you will have to add a USB hub or install additional USB controllers, either with an add-in PCI card for your desktop or a PC card for your laptop. If you're going to install a new PCI-based USB interface, get a USB 2.0-compliant card to get two upgrades in one.

To see how much bandwidth is being used on your USB ports, expand the properties of the Universal Serial Bus controllers listing in Device Manager and select the Advanced tab. As shown in Figure 8-7, you will see how much of your USB bandwidth is consumed.

Monitoring the bandwidth used on a specific USB port can tell you if one device, such as your video camera or video-to-USB capture device, is hogging all the throughput and whether it's time to add another separate interface to share the available bandwidth across multiple ports.

Use USB-Powered Hubs for Stability

USB ports are supposed to be able to provide up to 500 milliamps (mA) of current to power-attached devices. No single USB device is supposed to

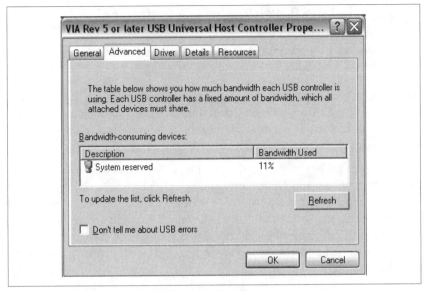

Figure 8-7. Windows keeps track of USB bandwidth used

draw more than 500 mA from a USB port, and if it needs more, it is required to provide its own power source. Some devices, such as a data connection to a PDA or cell phone, may not use any power from the port, but beware that many of these cables are now used to charge these devices as well.

Those cute little two- and four-port USB hubs are handy to expand the number of devices you can connect to your port, but obviously a single device, or combination of devices, that tries to draw more than 500 mA will overload your USB port and one or more devices will stop working due to lack of power.

If your USB devices only function intermittently, it is likely that power is your problem. Running a USB web cam, charging your PDA and cell phone, and using a USB mouse at the same time might change your Universal Serial Bus into an unusable serial bus. For around $20, you can get a powered USB hub with more than enough capacity to supply multiple power-grabbing devices without a glitch. Do the math when you buy it. For example, if you get a four-port powered hub, be sure the power supply that comes with it is rated for two amperes so you can get a full 500 mA per port.

H A C K
#83

Install the Driver Before You Install the Hardware

How not to "outsmart" Plug and Play and the Windows Add New Hardware wizard.

As brilliant and helpful as the concept and implementation of Plug and Play [Hack #18] has been, it is possible to confound it. This hack is almost too simple, and all too easily overlooked: install the drivers provided with your devices before you connect the device to your computer.

Why? As you probably know, when you connect a new device to your PC, Windows starts its Add New Hardware wizard and usually prompts you to provide the location of the drivers for the device. When the wizard runs, you have three choices: locate the disk or download location for the driver and let the wizard continue to install the driver and enable the device; let the wizard try to find new the driver on its own and possibly fail; or cancel the installation.

If you locate the driver and it installs, all is well. If the wizard cannot find a driver, it disables the device, remembers that the device is unconfigured, and marks it as an Unknown Device in Windows Device Manager. This is a fairly common situation for many USB devices, especially among anxious users who expect Plug and Play to "know all" and connect their devices, without following instructions. Windows needs to have the driver information available so it can detect the device by name and associate it with the right driver.

If you don't have the driver immediately handy but know you'll find it eventually, go back one step and cancel the wizard. Do not let the wizard mark the device as unknown or it will be dumped in "unknown device purgatory."

Once the device is remembered as being "unknown," no further attempts to install a driver will be made no matter how many times you disconnect the device, restart it, or reconnect it. The only way to get out of this condition is to uninstall the device using the Device Manager, as follows:

1. Disconnect the device so you do not end up in a vicious circle of failed installations.

2. Call up Windows Device Manager and note the presence of a yellow dot with an exclamation point inside, as shown in Figure 8-8.

3. Right-click the Unknown Device label and select Uninstall. Then you are free to reinstall the device, but only after you have found and installed the driver for it.

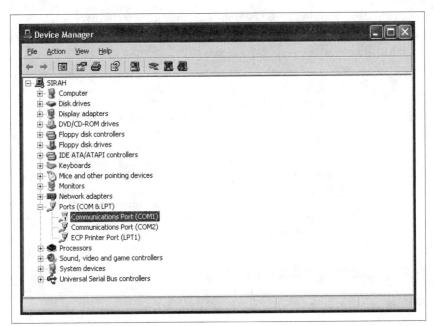

Figure 8-8. Windows marks devices that have conflicts with an exclamation point in a yellow dot

Very often you can "scrounge" through Windows device listings and find an acceptable alternative or generic driver to get you going, albeit with the loss of some features. A good example is the installation of a typical HP LaserJet printer. Most LaserJet printers respond to the same Printer Control Language (PCL) command set, so you can get away with picking the older LaserJet 4 driver to print to a new LaserJet 4100.

Printers that use the Adobe PostScript (PS) language will print with almost any generic or specific PostScript driver.

As simplistic as it sounds, taking a minute to read and follow the instructions will save you several minutes, hours, or days of frustration as you try to figure out how to resolve the problem. Install the drivers first and connect the device afterwards.

This type of problem has been the curse of PCs and technology advances for years, whether or not the technology is ISA, SCSI, Plug and Play, PCI, USB, or AGP. Most add-on devices are created and sold sometime after the hardware and operating system have been sold and installed, so there is no way Windows could have a driver for the device or know it existed beforehand.

Unfortunately, Windows Update does not support enough driver updates to be of much help here, so you are dependent on what ships in the box and the content of vendors' web sites to keep your hardware up to date.

> If you believe you need an updated driver for a hardware device visit the manufacturers' web sites for the latest versions that may or may not ever make it into the Windows Update service.
>
> In order for Windows Update to provide device drivers, the manufacturer of the device must submit their drivers to a lab for extensive testing to get Microsoft certification, and then to Microsoft for inclusion in Windows Update—an expensive and time-consuming process. You are much more likely to get the latest, greatest, and most stable driver directly from the manufacturer.

Please Continue Anyway

Digital signatures for device drivers and applications are a luxury we often have to do without.

You've seen the dialog box shown in Figure 8-9 pop up during a new driver installation: "The software you are installing for this hardware: Some Cool Device has not passed Windows Logo testing to verify its compatibility with Windows XP..." Yikes! It's enough to scare you out of hooking anything up to your PC.

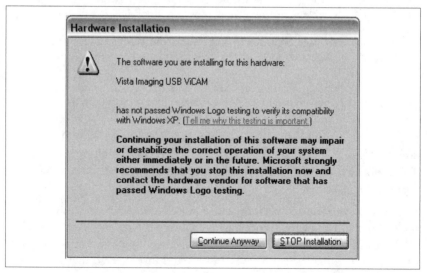

Figure 8-9. Windows Logo certification warning dialog

To solve this problem, locate and download a Windows-certified driver from the vendor's web site, assuming one is available. The risk of not doing so is minimal, but using a certified driver removes an element of potential surprise and disaster that may appear later on. Certified drivers will often be flagged with the words "WHQL Certified," as shown in Figure 8-10.

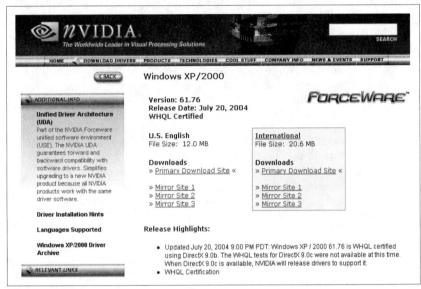

Figure 8-10. nVidia's driver feature web page listing WHQL certification

The warning dialog appears because the driver installation package did not come with a digital certificate that matches the one in Windows to let the installation process know the file was tested by a Microsoft-approved lab.

The intention is good: vendors have someone who knows the Windows environment very well review their drivers to ensure they are not consuming all the memory, stealing resources, or overwriting operating system files or other applications' files, and then they assure the public that things are OK. Then the vendor can deliver the assurance that all is well with the program or driver in the form of a digital certificate that matches the one Microsoft provided in the operating system. This is Microsoft's answer to the many cases of driver and program conflicts we all faced under Windows 95 and 98, when the Windows market was still relatively young and programmers ran wild trying to get cool new products into users' hands.

The scare tactic has some legitimate basis, especially if you're Microsoft and want hundreds of vendors to spend thousands of dollars on week-long visits to testing labs to get their wares certified as "not harmful to Windows." However, most companies can barely afford to do some of this Windows compliance testing in their own labs, much less risk the time and money sending their products to a distant lab hoping everything will pass with flying colors. Most products do not pass Windows Logo certification the first time and may not pass at all by the strict rules of the program. Passing the certification often requires the developer to plead their case and show the testing lab how their product really does comply with sound Windows programming and operation, despite Microsoft's rules and limitations, and ultimately get an approval by conditional and careful exemption.

> Microsoft certifications or compliance with their Authenticode program are intended to ensure applications or drivers are secure by protecting the files against tampering. However, the lack of these stamps of approval does not necessarily mean that the application or driver might carry a virus, is carelessly written, or is otherwise harmful; but it also means that no one but the original vendor or their developer has reviewed and tested them.
>
> If you have a choice, locate, download, and install certified drivers. If you do not, be prepared to remove the driver and device, and possibly even boot into Safe Mode or use System Restore to extract the offending code.
>
> You can access System Restore through Start→All Programs→Accessories→System Tools.

Today programmers have to try really hard to screw up Windows XP and Windows Server 2003—and certainly some of them do—but a clear majority of them, especially easily recognized brand name vendors, do not. Microsoft is a little better about documenting the tools and resources developers use, and developers are more mature and their employers are much more concerned about excessive support costs and product returns than making a quick buck.

You may see the compatibility testing warning dialog during one or two of approximately 20 installations of new hardware or programs, and only in one or two out of 100 cases will there ever be a problem. Fortunately, when you continue the installation, Windows Me and XP create a System Restore Point, saving the current, working preinstallation configuration that you can go back to if something does not work correctly. If your new hardware or software is from a reputable source, go ahead and select Continue Anyway: you have Windows System Restore and likely the vendor to help get you back to good working condition.

## CHAPTER NINE

Boot-Up Hacks
Hacks 85–94

Setting up your PC to be able to boot the operating system of your choice is a great way to conserve space and energy and is of great benefit to those who like to play games that must run under DOS or Windows 9x (and this chapter has a couple of hacks on improving the performance of these operating systems).

With a bit of preplanning and the right software, you can hack your PC to have multiple operating system personalities, including any operating system from DOS to Linux, as well as any and multiple versions of Windows. There is a variety of options for booting different operating systems on the same PC, with or without separate hard drives or partitions. Multibooting is a great solution for those who love DOS-based games that don't work at all under NT, Linux, or 2000 and work only marginally well under XP. You can keep a Windows 98 or Me installation around just for running those games.

With various multiboot techniques, you can allow different operating systems to share a common filesystem or let each operating system maintain its own unique partitions and filesystems. If you want to share files between operating systems, you have to determine which filesystems are common to all of the operating systems you want to use—in most cases that will be nothing more advanced than FAT-32 partitions—and realize that DOS does not support long (256-character) filenames. (For example, a file named *MicroSoft.txt* will be named *MICROS~1.TXT* in DOS.) Table 9-1 lists common operating systems and their respective filesystems to help you determine the file compatibility level to suit your needs.

Table 9-1. *Operating system versus filesystem compatibility*

Operating system	FAT-16	FAT-32	NTFS 1.2 (4.0)	NTFS 3.0 (5.0)	NTFS 3.1 (5.1)	Linux
DOS 6.22	X					
Windows NT 4	X		X	w/SP4		
Windows 95	X					
Windows 95 OSR-2	X	X				
Windows 98	X	X				
Windows 98SE	X	X				
Windows 2000		X	X		X w/SP3+	
Windows Me	X	X				
Windows XP		X	X	X	X	
Windows 2003		X	X	X	X	
Linux	X	X	Read-only (with experimental write support)	Read-only (with experimental write support)	Read-only (with experimental write support)	ext2, ext3, reiserfs, jfs, and more

It should be obvious from the data in Table 9-1 that the most common filesystems supported by the most common operating systems are FAT-16 and FAT-32. Earlier in the book, I discussed the inefficiencies of using the FAT-16 filesystem on large hard drives [Hack #40] and determined that the most efficient and common shared filesystem is FAT-32. However, FAT-32 is certainly not a showstopper; FAT-16 has some advantages over it. With FAT-16, you can partition some of your hard drive to accommodate DOS and everything else, which enables you to read files from it or write files to it from the other operating systems, but DOS/Windows 95 cannot read or write files in the FAT-32 partitions.

If you don't need to share files between operating systems, the choices become a lot easier; each operating system should use the most efficient partition and filesystem it can accommodate. This consideration is especially important if you must work in a native environment with all of the limitations or features of that environment, such as the file security provided by NTFS or the Linux filesystem. Your choices for multibooting in different ways are many.

Windows NT, 2000, XP, and 2003 natively support multiboot and require you to partition accordingly or accept using just the FAT-32 filesystem on a single drive and single partition providing shared, nonsecure file access. This means you will not get the benefits of NTFS filesystem security, and anyone can access the files on your hard drive after booting up with most typical startup diskettes. Linux also provides multiboot capability with the GRUB and LILO utilities.

Several utility-software vendors provide tools to manage different partitions and provide multiboot capabilities—most notable are V-Com (*http://www.v-com.com*), with their System Commander product, and PowerQuest, recently acquired by Symantec (*http://www.symantec.com*), with their PartitionMagic and BootMagic products. There is a handful of freeware and shareware software options, such as Smart BootManager (*http://btmgr.sourceforge.net/*) and Gujin (*http://gujin.sourceforge.net/*), available as well. With these multi-boot products (except BootMagic), your entire system is at the mercy of third-party software controlling your drive's boot capability rather than native operating system features.

If you're not into dabbling with various bits of software, there is a brute force method of using different operating systems on the same PC system hardware—using swappable hard drive bays. With this method, you have discrete hard drives formatted with the filesystem and loaded with the operating system and software of your choice. If you need to boot DOS to support game playing, simply power down, remove the Windows or Linux drive, plug in the DOS drive, power up, and go. In its simplest form, this method has the distinct disadvantage of not being able to share files between operating systems, but by adding a second hard drive used for data storage, any operating system that can read and write the second drive's filesystem can share files. A less expensive alternative to using a second installed hard drive is to use CD-RW media or a shared network drive on another system to store your files.

An option in between using a boot manager utility and using discrete hard drives is to install multiple hard drives and a boot manager to select which drive your OS of choice at the moment will boot from. Chances are you do not need a large hard drive for DOS-only booting, even for some of the larger game files, so dedicating a 2–4 GB hard drive as the boot manager and DOS drive may be a good choice, reserving a larger and probably faster hard drive for Windows operating systems, Windows applications, and datafiles.

Finally, if you do not want to fiddle with multibooting options, there is VMware (*http://www.vmware.com*), which is an operating environment that can spawn one or more operating environments or "virtual machines" under Windows NT, 2000, XP, or Linux. You install VMware as you would any other application, run it, and create virtual machine sessions to run DOS, Windows, or Linux in a window within your main operating system. While there are a few limitations as far as access to hardware, different disk partition types, and network resources that go along with a virtual operating system running inside another OS, VMware is pretty darned cool stuff.

In all cases except using discrete plug-in hard drives, VMware, or the PQBoot utility that comes with PartitionMagic, it is likely a few things will change in your system for each OS:

- The boot manager software you choose may modify the boot sector of your first active disk drive so that the boot manager software loads instead of a normal operating system to allow you to select an operating system. Your system can become totally dependent on the boot manager software, which—unless you are using Windows NT, 2000, XP, or GRUB/LILO to manage your boot selections—puts your system at the mercy of a third-party software vendor. If there is a problem with the third-party software, you could lose the ability to boot your system.

- Changing the active partition is no trivial undertaking: while you can change your Active boot partitions with the DOS FDISK program, it is a cumbersome process requiring you to boot to DOS first and you could mistakenly delete partitions. You do have several third-party options, such as PQBoot, for changing partitions, which this chapter explores.

- Each separate Windows installation ignores the software installed for any other operating system. This means you probably will not be able to run an application installed under one operating system from within another. Installing additional operating systems will require that you reconfigure or reinstall your application's software within each separate operating system so each operating system can use the data you may be sharing with other operating systems.

Choosing to set up your PC to use multiple operating systems begs and pleads for you to either back up your data and make sure you have the installation disks for all of your software, or experiment on a spare hard drive or entire PC system where your data is not at risk. Then, if you choose to configure your working PC for multiboot, by all means back up all of your data.

I know, backups are a pain in the butt and take up a lot of time and media, but they can also save your butt.

The quickest and easiest way to back up an entire drive or partition is to use either Symantec's Ghost or Acronis's True Image or any similar drive imaging utility to copy your complete hard drive to another of equal or greater space. You can also back up to a CD or DVD, which can take up a lot of time. With an image of your hard drive saved to another drive, you can get back up and running very quickly by imaging back to your original drive or using the drive you copied your original drive to. Image backups are probably not something you want to do every day, but they are expedient before doing maintenance tasks like messing with partitions and booting.

For all of the fuss, my personal preference is to use swappable hard drive bays and different hard drives for each operating system. Better yet, use separate PC systems for different operating systems and tasks. I do not expect to be doing my email or documentation on a PC set up for playing games under DOS or Windows 9x, and I won't be playing games under Windows 2000.

However, VMware and its ability to let me run multiple, separate operating systems at the same time on one PC is very compelling: I can game with DOS or Windows apps, dabble in Linux, test a piece of software under Windows 98, and fiddle with a mail server under Windows 2000 at the same time on the same PC, while I handle email and web browsing under Windows XP. Amazing!

PC Surgeon General's Warning: repartitioning, formatting, or adding boot management software can cause data loss.

PC "patients" who are susceptible, have adverse reactions, or are allergic to having their life's work destroyed are advised to protect their data at all cost, consult a qualified expert, or avoid these procedures altogether.

Make a Bare Disk Bootable

You're starting from scratch. What do you do first?

The original PC hard drive partitioning software comes with each Microsoft operating system—either as the DOS FDISK.EXE program or the installation and disk management utilities with Windows NT, 2000, and XP. Creating multiple partitions with FDISK can be a tedious and slow process that requires deliberate planning and keeping track of your work as you work your way through the process. Once you have completed the partitioning processes with FDISK, you then need to format each partition's filesystem or let the operating system installation process do that for you.

If you are setting up to multiboot to DOS or Windows 9x by adding Windows NT, 2000, or XP, you need only establish the first system partition and format it with DOS: the Windows setup processes take care of partitioning and formatting themselves, making the rest of the process much easier.

Complete documentation for FDISK can be found at Microsoft's web site at *http://support.microsoft.com:80/support/kb/articles/q255/8/67.asp)*. Additional tips for FDISK and alternative partitioning utilities can be found at *http://www.fdisk.com/fdisk/*.

The basics of partitioning are:

- Determine how much space you want to allocate for the primary DOS/ Windows 9x partition, which will be the foundation for multibooting using Windows's capabilities or a third-party boot utility. Two to four GB should be enough to hold the operating system and critical files for a few games.

- It is not necessary to use FDISK to partition the rest of the drive into an extended partition and various logical partitions within the extended partition because Windows 2000, XP, and Linux provide partitioning and formatting tools in their setup process and disk management utilities. However, if you do continue to create additional partitions, they will be FAT-32 partitions and need to be converted to NTFS if so desired (unless you are installing Linux and need to access the same file space).

- Create an extended partition to be used for additional operating systems and data storage space. You may create only one extended partition, which can be split into different logical partitions and drives.

- Determine how much space you want to preallocate for one or more additional operating systems—perhaps 10–30 GB for Windows 2000 and another 10–30 GB for Windows XP, depending on the size of your drive. Remember that 2000 and XP can share files on either FAT-32 or NTFS partitions, so you may wish to allocate a mere 4–6 GB to hold each operating system and leave the remainder of the drive for applications and data storage. Allow space for applications that may be unique to each operating system.

- Create logical drive areas in the extended partition for each operating system and for data storage as described in the preceding item.

Partitioning Quick Steps with FDISK

With the preplanning completed, you are ready to create your partition(s), format the drive, and then begin the operating system installation processes. The process is straightforward, but the changes are permanent.

1. Boot with a DOS diskette or bootable CD containing the *FDISK.EXE* program. Use a Windows 98 or Me boot diskette to get a version of MS-DOS and the FDISK and FORMAT programs that support large hard drives and FAT-32. At the DOS prompt, execute the FDISK program. Select large-disk support, as shown in Figure 9-1. If you elect not to enable large-disk support, DOS and your partitions will be limited to 2 GB in size and you will not be able to create extended partitions.

```
Your computer has a disk larger than 512 MB. This version of Windows
includes improved support for large disks, resulting in more efficient
use of disk space on large drives, and allowing disks over 2 GB to be
formatted as a single drive.

IMPORTANT: If you enable large disk support and create any new drives on this
disk, you will not be able to access the new drive(s) using other operating
systems, including some versions of Windows 95 and Windows NT, as well as
earlier versions of Windows and MS-DOS. In addition, disk utilities that
were not designed explicitly for the FAT32 file system will not be able
to work with this disk. If you need to access this disk with other operating
systems or older disk utilities, do not enable large drive support.

Do you wish to enable large disk support (Y/N)..........? [Y]
```

Figure 9-1. Select large-disk support for FAT-32 partition support

2. At the FDISK menu, shown in Figure 9-2, select option 4 to view any existing partitions: note what you find for DOS and non-DOS partitions including volume labels.

> If your PC lacks a diskette drive to boot from, you can use Symantec GHOST or Ahead's Nero program to create a bootable CD from a bootable DOS image containing the programs you need.
>
> Many variations of DOS diskette images are available from *http://www.bootdisk.com*. Another alternative is the Ultimate Boot CD, *http://www.ultimatebootcd.com*, which contains many useful disk utilities.

3. If there are existing partitions, you will need to delete them so you have a clean slate to work from. Press Escape to go back to the main FDISK menu and select option 3 to delete any and all existing partitions, as shown in Figure 9-3. This may be an iterative process performed until there are no more partitions on the hard drive. Next, return to the main menu.

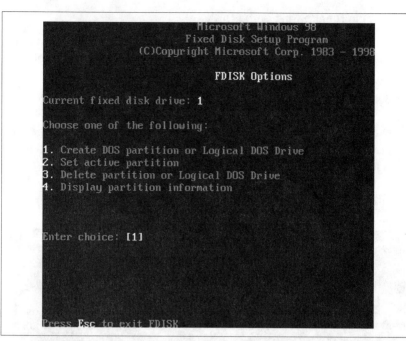

Figure 9-2. FDISK main menu

Figure 9-3. Choices for deleting partitions

If you have some partitions that FDISK refuses to recognize, boot from the rescue disk mentioned in "Fix GRUB or LILO Boot Problems" [Hack #50], use that disk's utilities to delete the sticky disk partition, shut down, and reboot into DOS when you are done.

4. Select option 1 to create a primary DOS partition. You do not need and probably do not want to make one partition using the entire drive, so instead make a modest-size DOS-only partition, as in Figure 9-4. FDISK will let you select the size of the partition by percentage of the whole drive or a specific number of megabytes. When you have created the primary DOS partition, return to the main FDISK menu.

```
                        Create Primary DOS Partition

Current fixed disk drive: 1




Total disk space is 10237 Mbytes (1 Mbyte = 1048576 bytes)
Maximum space available for partition is 10237 Mbytes (100% )


Enter partition size in Mbytes or percent of disk space (%) to
create a Primary DOS Partition.................................: [10237]




Press Esc to return to FDISK Options
```

Figure 9-4. Creating a primary DOS partition

> If you will be multibooting and one of your operating systems will be DOS or Windows 9x-Me, that operating system must be installed on the first partition.

5. Select option 2 and make the first partition active/bootable, as in Figure 9-5. You may quit FDISK at this point, leaving the rest of the partitioning up to subsequent Windows or Linux installation processes. If you decide to stop here, restart the system so you can format the primary partition.

6. If your alternate operating system will be Windows 9x–Me and use the rest of the drive, select option 1 to create an extended partition in the remaining drive space. You may skip this step and Step 7 if your second and subsequent operating systems will be Windows NT, 2000, XP, or Linux, since they can partition and format when they are installed.

7. Create logical drives within the extended partition—one logical drive using a fraction of the remaining space per operating system. Return to the main FDISK menu when finished.

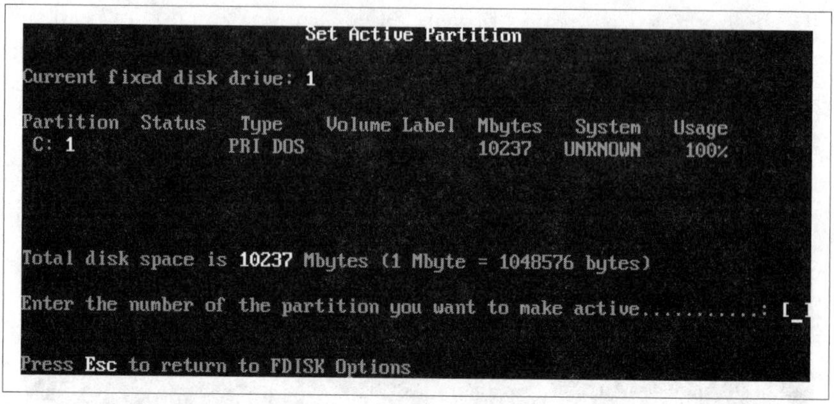

Figure 9-5. Making a partition active

8. Exit FDISK and reboot your PC from diskette so you can format the primary partition.

Formatting

Once the primary partition is created and you are through with any additional partitioning, you need to establish a bootable filesystem in the first/primary/active partition as a place for the boot manager to start from.

The DOS FORMAT program is very simple (see Figure 9-6). To format a hard drive and make it bootable, use the following command:

```
FORMAT C: /S
```

That's it. You're formatting drive C: to be a bootable system partition (with the /S). When the formatting is finished, drive C: will be bootable but will contain nothing more than boot information and the main DOS program *COMMAND.COM*.

I recommend making the partition bootable with /S for these reasons:

• In case you want to try booting from the hard drive to make sure things are OK.

• Some versions of Windows setup check for the existence of a bootable drive before installing.

• In case you want to copy Windows installation files to the hard drive and install from there [Hack #88].

• If you are installing an upgrade version of Windows that checks to see if DOS exists before proceeding.

At this point, you can leave the partition as is, copy more DOS files onto the drive, or install Windows 95, 98, or 98SE and then any applications or

```
DRIVE C: WILL BE LOST!
Proceed with Format (Y/N)?y


Formatting 2,055.15M
Format complete.
Writing out file allocation table
Complete.
Calculating free space (this may take several minutes)...
Complete.
System transferred

Volume label (11 characters, ENTER for none)? DOS-PART

2,150,768,640 bytes total disk space
      323,584 bytes used by system
2,150,445,056 bytes available on disk

        4,096 bytes in each allocation unit.
      525,010 allocation units available on disk.

Volume Serial Number is 1C65-15DB

A:\>
```

Figure 9-6. Formatting a 2 GB partition for DOS

games you prefer. The next step is to install other operating systems (such as Windows NT, 2000, XP, or Linux) in the unpartitioned or unformatted space on the drive.

> If you choose to multiboot with separate disk drives, follow the steps in this hack for your DOS/Windows 9x drive, then let Windows NT, 2000, or XP install onto your second hard drive. The initial boot files will be installed on the first hard drive and the second operating system itself on the second drive. The second drive will not be bootable, so the first drive must remain in the system. If the first drive fails or is reformatted, you will have no access to the operating system(s) on the second drive.

HACK #86 Configure a Multiboot System

Windows NT and later provide multiboot capabilities supporting DOS and Windows.

Windows NT, 2000, and XP natively support multiboot capabilities, on one or more disk drives. This capability allows you to retain DOS or an older version of Windows, install Windows NT, 2000, or XP, and be able to select between DOS/old Windows and the later operating system of your choice. Assuming you want to retain "good old DOS" or an older version of Windows, there is a requirement that the system (typically the first) partition of your hard drive already be formatted as FAT-16 or FAT-32 and have a working version of DOS (6.22 or 7.0 from Windows 95/98/Me) already installed, and optionally that Windows 95/98/Me is functional on that partition before installing NT, 2000, or XP.

> Windows's multiboot process works by placing a special boot loader program called NTLDR in the boot sector of the hard drive's active/bootable partition. NTLDR reads and acts upon boot disk, partition, and operating system information found in a hidden configuration file named *BOOT.INI*. After reading *BOOT.INI*, NTLDR loads and executes the appropriate boot code for the operating system you have chosen.

To begin the NT/2000/XP installation, boot from a diskette (or CD-ROM) that includes CD-ROM support and start from a DOS prompt. Assuming your CD-ROM drive is drive D:, issue the following command:

```
D:\i386\winnt
```

You may also boot from the NT/2000/XP installation CD, which starts installation automatically. Either way starts the setup process in non-Windows mode and provides all of the options necessary to configure for a multiboot installation. During the installation process, Windows NT/2000/XP prompts you to select the drive and directory you want to install the new OS on, as shown in Figure 9-7.

```
Windows XP Professional Setup

    The following list shows the existing partitions and
    unpartitioned space on this computer.

    Use the UP and DOWN ARROW keys to select an item in the list.

        • To set up Windows XP on the selected item, press ENTER.

        • To create a partition in the unpartitioned space, press C.

        • To delete the selected partition, press D.

    10237 MB Disk 0 at Id 0 on bus 0 on atapi [MBR]

        C:  Partition1 (DOS-PART) [FAT32]        2055 MB (  2039 MB free)
            Unpartitioned space                  8182 MB


    ENTER=Install   D=Delete Partition   F3=Quit
```

Figure 9-7. Select which space to use for Windows installation

NT, 2000, and XP will install on the same partition as your older operating system, but you may not want to do this if you don't want to risk doing something in DOS that may trash your Windows installation. If you elect to use the same partition, the directory that NT/2000/XP installs on should be different than the one containing DOS or Windows 9x, so your selection will probably be to \WINNT (NT, 2000) or to \WINDOWS (XP and later) as the target directory.

As you consider the installation possibilities, keep in mind the following tips from Microsoft for combined NT and XP installations:

- Because of differences in NTFS versions, using NTFS for Windows XP and Windows NT is not recommended unless you install all of the service packs for NT. If NTFS is used, file corruption or the inability to read or write files from the other operating system can result.

- Windows NT 4.0 should be updated with the latest released Service Pack before installing Windows XP.

In general, when NT/2000 and Windows XP are involved in the same system, follow these guidelines:

- Install NT/2000 and XP on separate partitions.

- Install applications separately on separate partitions for each operating system if necessary.

- If the multiboot PC is to be used on a LAN, the network name for the computer must be different for each operating system because authentication and security credentials are tied to the name of the machine as well as some internal details specific to each install. Otherwise, your other machines get confused about the identity and credentials of the multiboot PC.

> Only 2000 and XP support Dynamic disks—that is, RAID, removable, or other media that is likely to go offline or change from run-time to run-time. Check your disks and partitions in Control Panel→Administrative Tools→Computer Management→Disk Management. Change any Dynamic disks to Basic disks if you want all operating systems compatible with the common filesystem to be able to access them.

If you elect to install the new operating system on the drive and partition with an existing operating system, you don't want to let the installation process format the partition as FAT or NTFS (Figure 9-8) or you will lose the original operating system and possibly any data contained on the drive. You are, of course, free to delete an expendable partition and then create and format a new partition for the new operating system. The screen prompts and warnings are obvious with a couple of "are you sure" chances so you can back out and rethink the process.

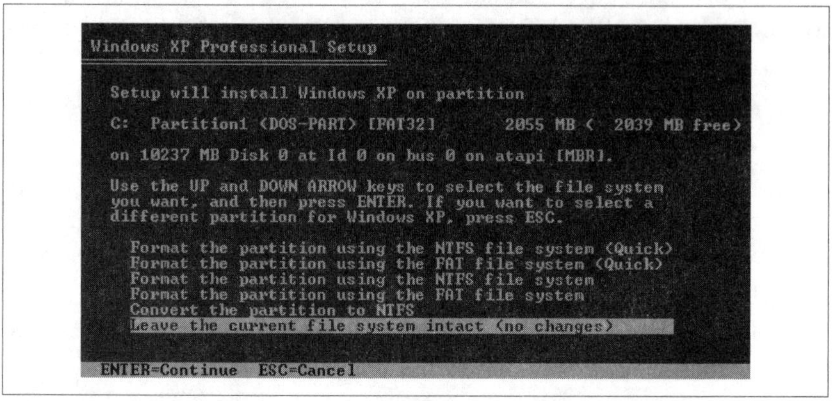

Figure 9-8. Windows 2000 setup asks whether to format the selected partition

The installation process will create a *BOOT.INI* file **[Hack #94]** in the root directory of the system/boot partition of the first active disk drive. *BOOT.INI* contains the information read by the NTLDR boot-up application and presents it at startup in the form of a text menu from which you select the operating system you want to run.

When the installation of the new operating system completes and you restart the system, you will be presented with a new boot menu (Figure 9-9) that allows you to select your previous operating system or the new one. The process works the same when adding a third operating system to unused disk space on the existing drive or a separate new drive.

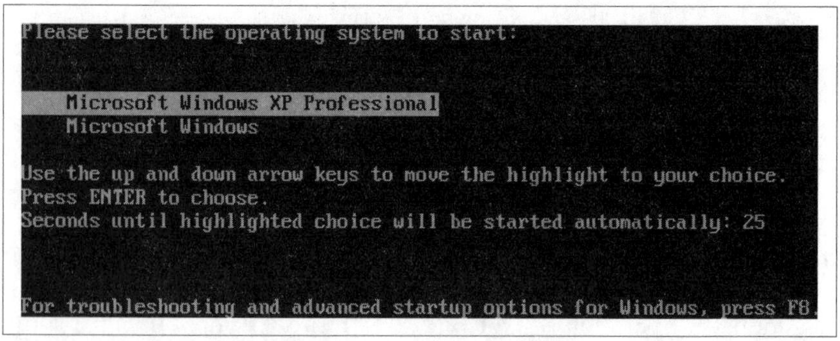

Figure 9-9. Multi-boot menu for Windows and Windows XP

Follow the same basic steps to add partitions, additional disk drives and partitions, and more operating systems. They will all be dependent upon the NTLDR program and boot information on the first hard drive's partition.

> Multibooting with Windows requires that DOS and Windows 9x–Me be present first, adding NT/2000/XP later because DOS and 9x–Me do not natively support multiboot. Adding DOS or 9x–Me to an existing NT/2000/XP installation requires the use of a third-party multiboot utility, or taking advantage of the OS-within-OS virtual machine capabilities of VMware.

The Hardware Solution

The absolute simplest (no partitions or menu choices) and safest (no filesystem compatibility issues) way to use different operating systems is to change out the hard drive in the PC. Admittedly the thought of opening the case of your PC and wrestling with all the cables and screws to change the OS from DOS to Windows XP to Linux does not sound very appealing, even to hardcore techies. The solution to this dilemma is to use a product called a *swappable drive carrier*. Swappable carriers allow you to easily and safely remove and change hard drives without opening your PC's case. They also provide a good method to secure your drive(s) somewhere away from your PC, such as in a fireproof safe.

This device, shown in Figure 9-10, comes in two pieces—a removable carrier to hold and connect to a 3.5" hard drive, and a host bay that installs in the system and gets connected to power and IDE or SCSI cable (depending on the version you buy).

The carrier and bay provide mating connections for power and data. To use this method, you must have an open 5.25" half-height drive slot to hold the connection bay. Remove your hard drive from the PC, configure the jumpers on your hard drive so it is the Master, connect the hard drive to the power and data cables, insert the drive into the carrier, and secure it with screws. Install the connection bay in a 5.25" drive slot and connect the data and power cables. Slide the drive carrier into the connection bay and boot up.

Obtain additional drive carriers from your dealer, install hard drives in them, and configure each for your operating system(s) of choice. If you need to share data across operating systems, install a second hard drive as the "Slave" in the system and copy your data from each of the operating system drives onto this second "data" drive. Make sure the "data" drive is using a

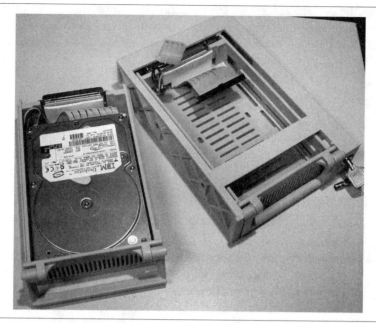

Figure 9-10. IDE drive carrier and connection bay

filesystem that is supported by all of the operating systems you'll be using. If you want to secure your data away from your PC, use a second drive carrier/connector bay to allow you to remove the "data" drive to a secure location as well.

 Be sure to obtain the correct style of drive bay for your hard drives. There is a style available for older, slower, non-DMA/ATA-66 IDE drives and one for newer, faster UDMA/ATA-100/ATA-133. Buying the older style will reduce the performance of your faster hard drives. Buying the newer style is recommended for all drive types. In all cases, using an 80-wire IDE cable is recommended to maintain optimal data transfer performance of any drive type.

Multiboot with Third-Party Utilities
Use a third-party partitioning and boot utility to extend multiboot support beyond DOS and Windows.

A third-party boot management utility provides simpler configuration, significantly more options, and a friendlier user experience than FDISK and an NT-based text menu for operating system selection. These utilities are intended to be installed on a working Windows system before you add any other operating systems. Setting up partition and boot managers is not well documented in the two most popular products: Symantec's PartitionMagic and BootMagic combination, and V-Com's Partition Commander and System Commander.

To use these utilities effectively, you must install them on the first active partition of the first hard drive, and that partition should be FAT-32 and boot to DOS. Installing them on the first partition running DOS or Windows 9x allows them control over the boot process.

The third-party utilities cannot properly manage boot control if you add them after you've set up an NT-based multiboot configuration. This is because the NT-based boot loader (NTLDR) and menu (*BOOT.INI*) take over the boot process for the first drive and partition no matter what initial or additional operating systems or boot managers are installed. In such a scenario, you will see the third-party boot manager's menu with only one selection, typically DOS/Windows 9x. When you make that selection, the NTLDR process starts and presents the operating system selection from the contents of *BOOT.INI*, from which you choose DOS/Windows 9x or Windows NT, 2000, or XP.

Plan Ahead

Start with one or more hard drives that are large enough to be partitioned to hold the operating systems and data you will be installing and using. If you're using DOS 6.22 or Windows 95 (Retail or OSR1), remember that they use the FAT-16 filesystem, which limits partition size to 2 GB. Windows 2000 or later operating systems cannot reside on FAT-16 filesystems. You can start with DOS, then add another partition for Windows 95, another for Windows 95 OSR2, another for Windows 98, then 98SE, then Me, and so on.

It is recommended that the first partition on the first drive should be partitioned and formatted as a FAT-32 volume with Windows 95 OSR2, 98, or 98SE. If you require the security of NTFS under NT/2000/XP, these operating systems will have to be installed in a separate partition and formatted for NTFS. Then, if you have files under NTFS that you need to share with an OS that uses FAT-32, you'll have to copy those files to the unsecured FAT partition or use "Access NTFS Files from Other Operating Systems" [Hack #89].

If you are going to share datafiles between this DOS/Windows installation and other operating systems, make the partition large enough to hold all of your DOS and Windows 9x applications and the shared data.

Subsequent partitions may be partitioned for the NTFS filesystem. NTFS is much more efficient and secure, but native access to NTFS partitions is limited to Windows NT, 2000, or XP. Assuming you choose to follow these recommendations, the steps in the following sections will take you through adding Windows 2000 or XP to your system with PartitionMagic and System Commander, respectively.

> If you have or add a second hard drive to your system after these utilities are installed and that drive is not recognized, you will have to boot to the original installation operating system and set the hardware options to allow recognition of the new drive. Even after this, partitioning software may not allow you to select the second drive as a target for a new OS installation but will let you set the drive to Active so you can proceed with the install.

Adding a New Operating System with PartitionMagic

PartitionMagic and its companion program BootMagic require separate configurations to support installing and booting additional operating systems.

1. Install PartitionMagic and BootMagic under Windows on the first partition of the first hard drive. Configure the boot manager so it is active and restart the system. The boot manager should appear after the Power On Self Test but before the original operating system starts.

2. Accept the selection to boot into your original operating system. When Windows is running, start BootMagic.

3. Select Add and configure BootMagic for the additional operating system(s) you will be installing. BootMagic does not need to know where the additional operating system is located. Exit BootMagic.

4. Start PartitionMagic. Select "Install another operating system" from the menu choices at the left, as in Figure 9-11. Note the instructions that appear and then click Next.

5. Choose the operating system you wish to install, as in Figure 9-12, and then click Next .

6. Choose the location (disk and partition) for your new operating system, as shown in Figures 9-13 and 9-14, and then click Next.

7. Set the desired partition size, label, and filesystem type, as in Figure 9-15, click Next, and then indicate if you will be installing the new operating system now or later (Figure 9-16) and click Next.

8. Review and confirm the changes to be made, as in Figure 9-17, and click Finish.

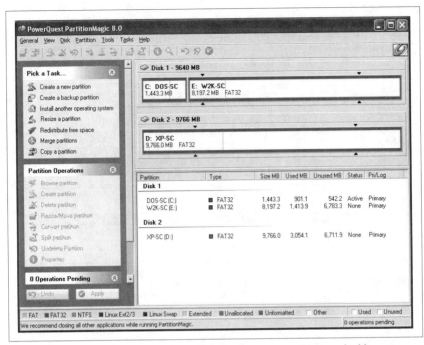

Figure 9-11. PartitionMagic provides options for changing partitions and adding a new operating system

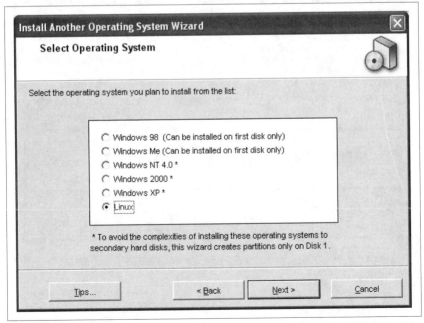

Figure 9-12. Selecting which new operating system to install with PartitionMagic

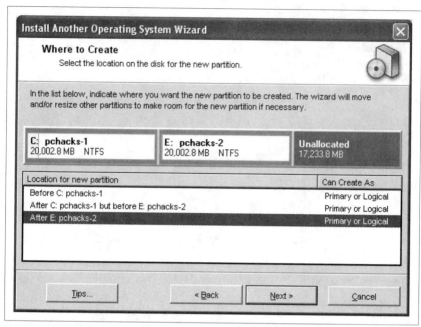

Figure 9-13. Selecting the location for a new operating system in PartitionMagic

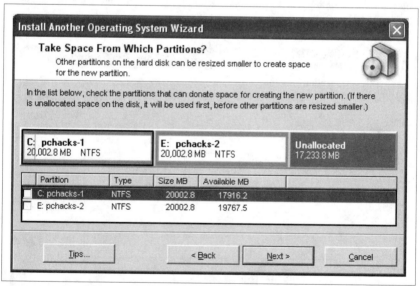

Figure 9-14. Selecting which partition will provide disk space for a new OS in PartitionMagic

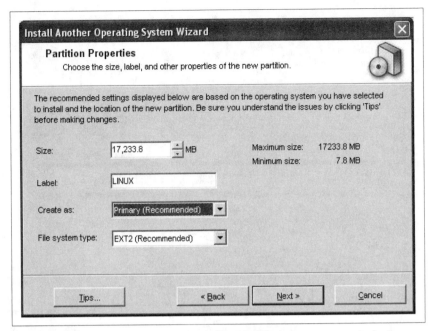

Figure 9-15. Setting partition parameters in PartitionMagic

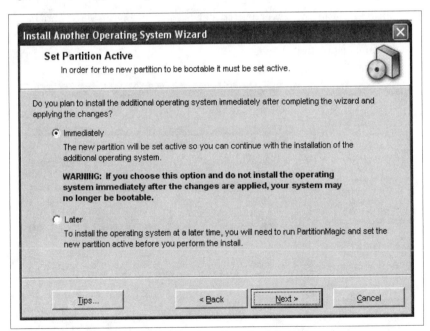

Figure 9-16. PartitionMagic lets you defer the installation of a new operating system

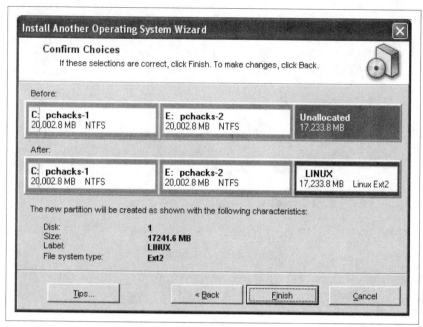

Figure 9-17. Reviewing changes PartitionMagic will make

9. Click Apply in the lower left corner, shown in Figure 9-18, and PartitionMagic will reconfigure your disk drives and prepare the system for the new installation.

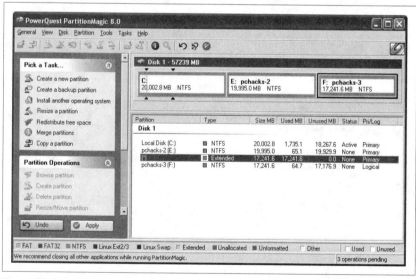

Figure 9-18. PartitionMagic with changes pending for a new OS installation

10. If you are installing Windows 2000 or XP, insert the installation CD in your CD-ROM drive and restart the system. Watch for the "boot from CD" prompt and press any key to start the OS install. If you cannot boot from your CD-ROM (for Windows 9x–Me installations), let PartitionMagic come up and then choose to boot from your A: drive. Let the system boot with a DOS diskette with CD support. At the DOS prompt begin the new installation from the CD—typically with this command (replace *D* with the drive letter of your CD-ROM):

    `D:\i386\winnt.exe`

11. Proceed through the Windows installation as usual. When the installation prompts to restart, remove the bootable diskette if you used one and then restart the system.

12. When the BootMagic menu appears, select the new operating system you are installing. The installation process will boot and proceed from that point.

13. When the installation is complete, remove any diskettes or CDs from their drives and restart the system. Your OS selections should work as expected, though you may wish to edit the *BOOT.INI* [Hack #94] file for any of your NT/2000/XP installations to set the TIMEOUT= value to 0 and make sure the DEFAULT= setting indicates the new operating system so you do not have to wait through these delays.

Adding a New Operating System with System Commander

V-Com's System Commander is a pioneer in supporting multiple operating systems on one PC. It is an effective but not always intuitive program to use, so I'll take you through the steps of adding Windows 2000 to a system running Windows 98.

 The instructions given in both the System Commander program and on V-Com's web site are incomplete and may seem misleading for this installation scenario. Working around the pitfalls is discussed in the steps below.

1. Install System Commander under Windows. Configure it so it is enabled and restart the system. The boot manager should appear after the Power On Self Test but before the original operating system starts. (If your mouse does not work in these screens, you can navigate and select with the Tab, Space, arrow, and Enter keys.)

2. At the upper left in the menu bar, select the OS Wizard.

3. Select "New installation" and then click Next.

4. The default new OS selection is Windows, so click Next.

5. Select the specific OS you will be installing (Windows 2000) and click Next.

6. Choose New install and then click Next.

7. For the location of the new OS, select "Isolated by itself" and click Next.

8. Select the drive and partition size you would like to use for the new OS and click Next. Follow the prompts to proceed. System Commander will make any necessary partition changes, then provide a set of directions for installing the new operating system. At this point, the new partition is marked Active and will be the target for your installation. If you have selected Windows 2000 or XP, the instructions tell you to have your bootable installation CD ready and insert it when prompted.

   Your system must support booting from CD or you will need a bootable DOS diskette with CD-ROM support

9. Insert the installation CD in your CD-ROM drive and restart the system. Watch for the "boot from CD" prompt and press any key to start the OS install. If you cannot boot from your CD-ROM, let System Commander come up and then select booting from your A: drive. Let the system boot with a DOS diskette with CD support. At the DOS prompt begin the new installation from the CD—typically with this command (replace *D* with the drive letter of your CD-ROM):

   ```
   D:\i386\winnt.exe
   ```

10. After the first pass of the installation, you will be prompted to remove the boot diskette and restart, so do so now. System Commander will start and advise that it needs to update partition records—let it do so.

11. You will then see the OS Selection menu. Choose the operating system being installed, in this case Windows 2000. The Windows boot menu will appear and you will need to accept/select Windows 2000 installation.

12. Proceed through the installation process. In the second setup screen you will see a selection for the drive/partition as the target for this installation. Drive E: will be the disk/partition of your prior OS and drive C: will be the active target for this installation—select this to proceed.

13. You will be asked to reboot once during the installation, then you will receive the boot sector/partition update prompt from System Commander, and then the OS Selection menu again. Select Windows 2000 and proceed.

14. Follow the remaining Windows installation instructions, fill in the information required, and complete the new installation. At the prompt to

restart, you are finished and can use System Commander to select your desired operating system. Your OS selections should work as expected, though you may wish to edit the *BOOT.INI* [Hack #94] file for any of your NT/2000/XP installations to set the TIMEOUT= value to 0 and make sure the DEFAULT= setting indicates the new operating system so you do not have to wait through these delays.

Speed up Operating System Installation and #88 Maintenance

Save yourself time by making Windows installation files available on your hard drive.

We know you've had this problem: you install a new mouse, change a network setting, do almost anything that upsets the delicate balance in Windows and you're prompted to insert the Windows so-and-so CD. Where is it? Did you grab the right one?

If you have a lot of free disk space (about 700 MB), take a cue from the major PC makers and copy the files from your Windows CD to your hard drive. In fact, it's not a bad idea to copy the files before you install Windows so the resulting installation automatically knows where to find the files later—thus no prompting to insert a CD later.

PC manufacturers have typically placed the Windows 95, 98, 98SE, and Me files in a *C:\WINDOWS\OPTIONS\CABS* folder, and Windows NT, 2000 or XP files into *C:\i386*.

Before you do any of this, I suggest you load SMARTDRV [Hack #65].

You can emulate this pattern for Windows 9x–Me by creating these folders on your hard drive from a DOS prompt, then copying the files from the CD (assuming this is drive D:) as follows, from the A:\> DOS prompt:

```
A:\>C:
C:\>MD WINDOWS
C:\>MD \WINDOWS\OPTIONS
C:\>MD \WINDOWS\OPTIONS\CABS
C:\>CD \WINDOWS\OPTIONS\CABS
C:\ \WINDOWS\OPTIONS\CABS>COPY D:\WIN98\*.*
```

Start the Windows installation from this folder by typing:

```
C:\ \WINDOWS\OPTIONS\CABS>SETUP
```

If you feel that the \WINDOWS folder is too vulnerable a place to put your Windows installation files, try \WINDOWSCD or something similar.

For Windows NT-XP:

```
A:\>C:
C:\>MD i386
C:\>CD i386
C:\I386>COPY D:\i386\*.*
```

Start the Windows installation from this folder by running this command:

```
C:\I386>WINNT
```

The next time Windows needs a file from the installation CD it will automatically look in the appropriate folder, copy the file, and move on.

HACK #89   Access NTFS Files from Other Operating Systems

Read files on an NTFS partition from a non-NTFS operating system with these free tools.

The folks at Sysinternals have created a series of utilities that allow us to access files and program in NTFS partitions from non-NTFS operating systems. Two of them, NTFSDOS and NTFSWIN98, are free to download from *http://www.sysinternals.com*. NTFSDOS is intended for use under DOS, Windows 3.1, and Windows 95, and NTFSWIN98 is used for Windows 98 and Me. To access files on an NTFS volume, you'll need a user account and password to access any secured NTFS partitions, but you won't have to boot up the entire NT/2000 or XP operating system to do it.

If you require write access to files in an NTFS partition, you will need to purchase professional versions of these programs or Sysinternal's Administrator's Pak.

You can access NTFS from most current versions of Linux simply by mounting the NTFS filesystem as root (the -o ro option specifies read-only mode):

```
# mount -o ro /dev/hda1 /mnt
# mount | grep ntfs
/dev/hda1 on /mnt type ntfs (ro)
debian:~# ls -l /mnt/boot.ini
-r-------- 1 root root 230 Aug  8 17:32 /mnt/boot.ini
```

In some cases, you may need to load the NTFS module first:

```
# modprobe -v ntfs
insmod /lib/modules/2.6.6-local/kernel/fs/ntfs/ntfs.ko
```

If the NTFS module is unavailable (you'll see the error message "FATAL: Module ntfs not found"), you'll need to obtain a newer kernel or download (see *http://www.kernel.org*), compile, and install one, making sure that the NTFS module is enabled.

> NTFS support is generally limited to read-only access. NTFS write support under most kernels is experimental, but the 2.6 kernel series supports limited write access to NTFS.

Give Your XP Installation Access to the Recovery Console

Add this essential recovery tool to your boot menu to save time saving your system.

If you cannot boot your Windows XP installation, the Recovery Console is an important tool for regaining access and restoring bootability. (Chapter 5 has several hacks that discuss the Recovery Console.) You can install the Recovery Console, which is essentially a command-line utility for restoring Master Boot Records and replacing lost boot files, so that it appears as an option on your XP boot menu.

Typically, system administrators and savvy users run the Recovery Console from the Windows XP installation CD and select Recovery Console as one of the boot options. Adding it to the current installation and Start menu is invaluable, especially if you cannot locate your XP CD in a crisis. To install the Recovery Console, follow these steps:

1. With your Windows XP installation CD in a CD-ROM drive, click Start and then Run.

2. Type **d:\i386\winnt32.exe /cmdcons**, where *d* is the drive letter for the CD-ROM drive containing the XP CD.

3. A Setup Dialog Box will appear. Click Yes to continue the installation.

4. When the installation has finished, restart the computer. "Microsoft Windows Recovery Console" will appear on your boot menu.

For help using the Recovery Console, simply type **help** at the Recovery Console command prompt. This will give you a list of commands and instructions.

Hack the Windows 95/98/Me DOS Startup

#91   Gain more control and boot faster by customizing this DOS configuration file.

In this hack, you'll learn ways to customize how DOS boots and to make booting up faster.

A Typical MSDOS.SYS File

Windows 95, 98, and Me use a file called *MSDOS.SYS* to configure the initial boot process. *MSDOS.SYS* resides in the root folder of the boot drive with Read-Only, System, and Hidden file attributes. The *MSDOS.SYS* file contains sections of information pertaining to the Windows installation and boot options. The [Paths] section of the file lists information about Windows' files (the Windows folder and location of the Registry), and the [Options] section holds information about customizing bootup.

> Under DOS 6.22 and earlier, *MSDOS.SYS* is a binary program file critical to basic DOS operation and is not editable. Only with the DOS supplied in Windows 95 and higher is the *MSDOS.SYS* file an editable text file.

To view and edit the contents of the *C:\MSDOS.SYS* file, you must first remove the Read Only and Hidden file attributes. To do this, get to a DOS prompt (in Windows, open MS-DOS Prompt or go to Start→Run, type in **COMMAND.COM**, and then click OK) and issue the following commands:

```
X:\>C:
C:\FOO>CD \
C:\>attrib -r -h -s MSDOS.SYS
```

> When you are done editing *MSDOS.SYS*, restore its attributes with **attrib +r +h +s MSDOS.SYS**.

Note that there are spaces between the -r, -h, and -s in the previous command. The file is now ready to be viewed or edited with a plain text editor like DOS Edit, Windows Notepad, or similar. The contents of the file may look like this:

```
;FORMAT
[Paths]
WinDir=C:\WINDOWS
WinBootDir=C:\WINDOWS
HostWinBootDrv=C
```

```
[Options]
BootMulti=1
BootGUI=1
DoubleBuffer=1
AutoScan=1
WinVer=4.10.1998
;
;The following lines are required for compatibility with other programs.
;Do not remove them (MSDOS.SYS needs to be >1024 bytes).
;xxxxxxxxxxxxxxxxxxxxxxxxxxxxxxxxxxxxxxxxxxxxxxxxxxxxxxxxxxxxxxxxxxxxxxa
;xxxxxxxxxxxxxxxxxxxxxxxxxxxxxxxxxxxxxxxxxxxxxxxxxxxxxxxxxxxxxxxxxxxxxxb
;xxxxxxxxxxxxxxxxxxxxxxxxxxxxxxxxxxxxxxxxxxxxxxxxxxxxxxxxxxxxxxxxxxxxxxc
;xxxxxxxxxxxxxxxxxxxxxxxxxxxxxxxxxxxxxxxxxxxxxxxxxxxxxxxxxxxxxxxxxxxxxxd
;xxxxxxxxxxxxxxxxxxxxxxxxxxxxxxxxxxxxxxxxxxxxxxxxxxxxxxxxxxxxxxxxxxxxxxe
;xxxxxxxxxxxxxxxxxxxxxxxxxxxxxxxxxxxxxxxxxxxxxxxxxxxxxxxxxxxxxxxxxxxxxxf
;xxxxxxxxxxxxxxxxxxxxxxxxxxxxxxxxxxxxxxxxxxxxxxxxxxxxxxxxxxxxxxxxxxxxxxg
;xxxxxxxxxxxxxxxxxxxxxxxxxxxxxxxxxxxxxxxxxxxxxxxxxxxxxxxxxxxxxxxxxxxxxxh
;xxxxxxxxxxxxxxxxxxxxxxxxxxxxxxxxxxxxxxxxxxxxxxxxxxxxxxxxxxxxxxxxxxxxxxi
;xxxxxxxxxxxxxxxxxxxxxxxxxxxxxxxxxxxxxxxxxxxxxxxxxxxxxxxxxxxxxxxxxxxxxxj
;xxxxxxxxxxxxxxxxxxxxxxxxxxxxxxxxxxxxxxxxxxxxxxxxxxxxxxxxxxxxxxxxxxxxxxk
;xxxxxxxxxxxxxxxxxxxxxxxxxxxxxxxxxxxxxxxxxxxxxxxxxxxxxxxxxxxxxxxxxxxxxxl
;xxxxxxxxxxxxxxxxxxxxxxxxxxxxxxxxxxxxxxxxxxxxxxxxxxxxxxxxxxxxxxxxxxxxxxm
;xxxxxxxxxxxxxxxxxxxxxxxxxxxxxxxxxxxxxxxxxxxxxxxxxxxxxxxxxxxxxxxxxxxxxxn
;xxxxxxxxxxxxxxxxxxxxxxxxxxxxxxxxxxxxxxxxxxxxxxxxxxxxxxxxxxxxxxxxxxxxxxo
;xxxxxxxxxxxxxxxxxxxxxxxxxxxxxxxxxxxxxxxxxxxxxxxxxxxxxxxxxxxxxxxxxxxxxxp
;xxxxxxxxxxxxxxxxxxxxxxxxxxxxxxxxxxxxxxxxxxxxxxxxxxxxxxxxxxxxxxxxxxxxxxq
;xxxxxxxxxxxxxxxxxxxxxxxxxxxxxxxxxxxxxxxxxxxxxxxxxxxxxxxxxxxxxxxxxxxxxxr
;xxxxxxxxxxxxxxxxxxxxxxxxxxxxxxxxxxxxxxxxxxxxxxxxxxxxxxxxxxxxxxxxxxxxxxs
```

The contents are typical of a default Windows 9x–Me installation. It says that Windows is installed in and runs from the C:\WINDOWS folder on drive C:, it is possible to interrupt the boot process to stop at a DOS prompt rather than load Windows without interruption, the Windows GUI is loaded, the Double Buffer setting is asserted if the disk drive interface needs it, and Scandisk is run with prompts if the system was not shut down properly before.

A variety of other parameters is set by default but not shown under the [Options] section of the file. These are:

```
BootDelay=2
BootKeys=0
BootMenu=0
BootMenuDefault=1
BootMenuDelay=30
BootSafe=0
DblSpace=1
DrvSpace=1
LoadTop=1
Logo=1
Network=0
```

These parameters mean that:

BootDelay=2, BootKeys=0

You have two seconds during which "Starting Windows" is displayed to press one of the F-keys to alter the boot process (except that the F-keys are disabled).

BootMenu=0

No boot menu is presented.

BootMenuDefault=1

The default selection for the boot menu, if it is presented, is 1 (the normal operating system).

BootMenuDelay=30

If the boot menu is presented, it will show for 30 seconds before the default selection is used.

BootSafe=0

The system will not boot into Safe mode.

DblSpace=1, DrvSpace=1

The DblSpace and DrvSpace disk compression drivers will load.

LoadTop=1

DOS and drivers will load at the top of DOS memory.

Logo=1

The Windows startup logo will be displayed.

Network=0

No network is configured, so you won't get a "Safe mode with networking support" option on the boot menu.

To give you more control over the optimization of the boot process, the following settings can be changed or added under the [Options] section of the file:

```
BootDelay=5
BootKeys=1
BootMenu=1
BootMenuDelay=5
DblSpace=0
DrvSpace=0
Logo=0
Network=1
```

Adding BootDelay=5 gives you more time to respond with any boot key selections. BootKeys=1 shows you the F-key options for bootup at the bottom of the screen. BootMenu=1 turns on the boot menu. BootMenuDelay=5 lets the menu stay on the screen for only 5 seconds instead of 30. DblSpace=0 and DrvSpace=0 specify that these drivers will not be loaded. Logo=0 mandates that the Windows startup logo will not be displayed. Finally, if you have a network setup you can have support for it if you start Windows in Safe mode by adding `Network=1`.

The advantages to these changes are that you can exercise more control over bootup, the menu doesn't hang around forever, and you do not tie up resources loading and displaying the Windows logo.

The Details of MSDOS.SYS

The [`Paths`] section of *MSDOS.SYS* may contain the following information (default values for each parameter follow the parameter's name in parentheses):

`HostWinBootDrv=Root of Boot Drive` (C)
> The location for the root of the boot drive.

`UninstallDir=Root of Boot Drive` (C)
> Specifies the location of the *W95undo.dat* and *W95undo.ini* files. These files are necessary to uninstall Windows 95.

`WinBootDir=Windows Folder (usually` C:\Windows)
> The location of the necessary files for booting.

`WinDir=Windows Folder (usually` C:\Windows)
> The location of the Windows folder

The [`Options`] section of *MSDOS.SYS* may contain the following information:

`AutoScan=Number` (1)
> Specifies if ScanDisk is to be run after a bad shutdown. 0 does not run ScanDisk; 1 prompts before running ScanDisk; 2 runs ScanDisk but prompts before fixing errors if any are found. This setting is available to Windows 95 OEM Service Release 2 and later.

`BootDelay=Seconds` (2)
> The amount of time the "Starting Windows" message appears before Windows continues to boot. BootDelay is not supported in Windows 98.

`BootSafe=Boolean` (0)
> 1 forces Windows into Safe mode.

`BootGUI=Boolean` (1)
> 1 forces Windows to load. 0 disables the loading of Windows.

`BootKeys=Boolean` (1)
> 1 enables the use of the function keys F4, F5, F6, F8, and CTRL to override other settings. 0 disables the function keys during boot.

`BootMenu=Boolean` (0)

Comment: 1 enables the DOS startup menu. If 0, you must press F8 when "Starting Windows" appears to use the Startup menu.

`BootMenuDefault=Number` (1 or 3)

Comment: Use this setting to set the default menu item for startup. The default parameter is 1 if the system is running correctly and 3 if the system hung in the previous instance

`BootMenuDelay=Number` (30)

Comment: The number of seconds your system shows the Startup menu. After this time expires, the `BootMenuDefault` is used and the system boots with it. `BootMenu=1` must be set for this to work.

`BootMulti=Boolean` (1)

Comment: 0 disables the ability to select your previous operating system (typically DOS).

`BootWarn=Boolean` (1)

Comment: 0 disables the Safe-mode boot warning and the Startup menu.

`BootWin=Boolean` (1)

Comment: 1 forces Windows's GUI to load.

`DoubleBuffer=Boolean` (0)

Comment: 1 enables double-buffering for disk adapters that need it (most SCSI and some SCSI-like IDE disk adapters). 2 enables double-buffering regardless.

`DBLSpace=Boolean` (1)

Comment: 1 allows loading the *DBLSPACE.BIN* disk compression driver. 0 disables it. Set 0 if you do not have compressed drives.

`DRVSpace=Boolean` (1)

Comment: 1 allows loading the *DRVSPACE.BIN* disk compression driver. 0 disables it. Set 0 if you do not have compressed drives.

If you don't need it (I don't know anyone who has used the DOS disk compression feature in over 12 years), loading the disk compression driver wastes time and memory.

To disable the disk compression driver from being loaded, set both `DBLSPACE=0` and `DRVSPACE=0`.

One way to tell if a drive has been compressed is to boot to DOS without loading the compression drivers, then get a directory listing of the hard drive with DOS's `DIR`. You will see a large file named either *DBLSPACE.000* or *DRVSPACE.000*, which contains the contents of the compressed drive. You cannot format or partition a compressed drive because it is merely a large file containing the data that was on the previously uncompressed drive.

LoadTop=*Boolean* (1)

> 1 causes *COMMAND.COM* and, if enabled, *DRVSPACE.BIN* and *DBLSPACE.BIN* to load at the top of DOS's 640K memory space.

Logo=*Boolean* (1)

> 1 causes the Windows boot logo to appear. 0 does not show the logo and can fix problems with some memory managers.

Network=*Boolean* (0)

> 1 tells DOS a network is or was installed and adds the "Safe mode with network support" option to the Start menu.

The "Junk" at the End of the MSDOS.SYS File

The *MSDOS.SYS* file also contains a large section of filler characters that are necessary to keep the file large enough for programs that expect the *MSDOS.SYS* file to be at 1,024 bytes or larger. Leave this block of characters as is to ensure proper operation of your applications.

Hack the MS-DOS Configuration File
#92

Tailor DOS's *CONFIG.SYS* file to optimize memory use, load device drivers, and set the DOS environment.

The *CONFIG.SYS* file resides in the root directory of your boot drive (typically C:\) and contains commands that configure your computer's hardware components (memory use and device drivers) and operating system during bootup. The contents of the *CONFIG.SYS* file are read and processed before DOS loads. *CONFIG.SYS* is a text file you can edit with DOS EDIT.COM, Windows Notepad, or any text editor program. *CONFIG.SYS* is used by DOS 6.22 and earlier and Windows 95–Me, but is not used by Windows NT, 2000, XP, or 2003.

> You can bypass *CONFIG.SYS* and *AUTOEXEC.BAT* files if BootKeys=1 is configured in *MSDOS.SYS* [Hack #91]. To use this feature, press the F5 key when you see the "Starting MS-DOS..." or "Starting Windows..." notice at startup.
>
> You can also "walk through" and accept or reject individual *CONFIG.SYS* and *AUTOEXEC.BAT* commands by pressing the F8 key instead of F5.

Under Windows 95 through Me, a few basic *CONFIG.SYS* parameters are preset within the *IO.SYS* boot file. These are:

```
DOS=HIGH
Device=HIMEM.SYS
```

```
SETVER.EXE
FILES=60
BUFFERS=30
LASTDRIVE=Z
STACKS=9,256
FCBS=4
```

These parameters aren't nearly adequate or ideal to get a typical PC with a CD-ROM drive running efficiently, so we need to create or hack our own *CONFIG.SYS* file to suit our needs. A typical and often more suitable *CON-FIG.SYS* file reads as follows:

```
Device=HIMEM.SYS /TESTMEM:off
Device=EMM386.EXE ON RAM ROM
DOS=HIGH,UMB
FILES=99
BUFFERS=6,2
STACKS=0,0
DEVICEHIGH=C:\CDROM\CDROMDRV.SYS /D:MSCD001
```

This new *CONFIG.SYS* file alters some of DOS's default parameters and includes a few new parameters to give your system more resources to work with and slightly better performance. The significance of each parameter is explained below:

Device=HIMEM.SYS /TESTMEM:off
> Loads the HIMEM.SYS Extended memory driver but, to save boot time, does not allow the memory test to run.

Device=EMM386.EXE ON RAM ROM NOEMS
> Loads the EMM386 LIMS-EMS memory driver and creates Upper Memory Blocks with no LIMS-EMS available (to save RAM) that can be used to contain some loaded device drivers and part of DOS.

DOS=HIGH,UMB
> Loads DOS into high and Upper Memory Blocks (UMB)

FILESHIGH=99
> Allows up to 99 files to be opened at the same time and stores the information about them (not the files themselves) in upper memory.

BUFFERSHIGH=6,2
> Creates six disk buffers using a total of approximately 3 KB of RAM to hold incoming disk data, and tells DOS to read ahead two sectors of data. This parameter is intentionally set well below the DOS default recommendations of 30, in anticipation of using SMARTDRV or another disk caching utility loaded under DOS through AUTOEXEC.BAT [Hack #93]. The buffer region is created in upper memory to save DOS RAM.

```
STACKS=0,0
```

Turns off the creation of processor stacks to handle hardware interrupt requests. The default value is fine in some cases and causes crashes in others. No stack or application problems have been seen in several years of using this setting.

```
DEVICEHIGH=C:\WINDOWS\COMMAND\ANSI.SYS
```

Loads the *ANSI.SYS* enhanced character set and display color-attribute driver into upper memory. *ANSI.SYS* is needed by some programs to support multicolor display versus the plain white-on-black DOS color scheme.

```
DEVICEHIGH=C:\CDROM\CDROMDRV.SYS /D:MSCD001
```

Loads a hardware driver for a CD-ROM into upper memory. *MSCD001* is just an example. Your actual driver filename will be different and may be stored in different folder.

Try this *CONFIG.SYS* sample on your system and see how you like it for quicker booting and faster performance.

 ## Hack the MS-DOS Startup File

#93 Set up DOS environment parameters and load utilities and virus protection before Windows takes over your PC.

The *AUTOEXEC.BAT* file resides in the root directory of your boot drive (typically C:\) and contains commands that configure the appearance of DOS and loading of transient or terminate-and-stay-resident (TSR) programs at bootup. The DOS command processor, *COMMAND.COM,* loads and looks for and reads *AUTOEXEC.BAT* after the contents of the *CONFIG.SYS* file are processed. *AUTOEXEC.BAT* is a text file you can edit with DOS EDIT.COM, Windows Notepad, or any text editor program. *CONFIG.SYS* is used by DOS 6.22 and earlier and Windows 95–Me, but is not used by Windows NT, 2000, XP, or 2003.

Under Windows 95 through Me, a few basic DOS parameters are preset within the *IO.SYS* boot file. These consist of the DOS prompt (C:\>) and the PATH to DOS and Windows files.

 You can bypass *CONFIG.SYS* and *AUTOEXEC.BAT* files if `BootKeys=1` is configured in *MSDOS.SYS* **[Hack #91]**. To use this feature, press the F5 key when you see the "Starting MS-DOS..." or "Starting Windows.." notice at startup.

You can also "walk through" and accept or reject individual *CONFIG.SYS* and *AUTOEXEC.BAT* commands by pressing the F8 key instead of F5.

If you are running Windows 95–98SE, WIN.COM is loaded by default, although it doesn't appear in *AUTOEXEC.BAT*. Windows Me does not load DOS or process a *CONFIG.SYS* or *AUTOEXEC.BAT* file at startup but will bypass loading Windows and run DOS if you use a boot menu or press the F5 key when the system boots up. Unless you use the F5 or F8 keys, or put a PAUSE statement anywhere or as the last command in the *AUTOEXEC. BAT* file, Windows will load. Beyond that you are on your own and can do all sorts of things in the *AUTOEXEC.BAT* file.

The most common chores to let DOS do within *AUTOEXEC.BAT* are more environmental than functional. You can set environment variables for programs that require them, enhance the PATH statement so programs can be found without including drive and path information on the command line, and load any special drivers that cannot be loaded in *CONFIG.SYS*, such as those for disk caching, CD-ROM designations, and pointing devices.

"Out of the box," the basic environment variables *IO.SYS* sets can be set equivalently by having the following lines in an *AUTOEXEC.BAT* file:

```
PROMPT=$P$G>
TEMP=C:\WINDOWS\TEMP
TMP=C:\WINDOWS\TEMP
PATH=C:\WINDOWS;C:\WINDOWS\SYSTEM
```

This set of parameters is pretty benign and ignores a lot of desirable features I'd like to have working in my favor. If I'm working only in DOS, and I want it to be fast and functional, I add a few commands to make a complete *AUTOEXEC.BAT* file that looks like this:

```
ECHO OFF
CLS
C:\WINDOWS\SMARTDRV C+
PROMPT=$P$G>
TEMP=C:\TEMP
TMP=C:\TEMP
PATH=C:\WINDOWS;C:\WINDOWS\SYSTEM;C;\DOS;C:\
LH C:\WINDOWS\COMMAND\DOSKEY /INSERT
LH C:\WINDOWS\MSCDEX /D:MSCD001
LH C:\MOUSE\MOUSE.EXE
```

Here's a breakdown of what each command does:

ECHO OFF

Keeps every subsequent command from echoing its invocation and output to the screen. It makes things neater, but you can omit it if you want to see the BATch file run to be sure everything looks OK.

CLS

This means "clear screen" and gives a clean palette to view as *AUTOEXEC.BAT* runs.

`C:\WINDOWS\SMARTDRV C+`

Starts the SMARTDRV disk caching program providing delay-write/ write-cached performance enhancements to drive C:. Add D+, E+, etc. for additional hard drives. The DOS copy of SMARTDRV is replaced by Windows's VCACHE driver after Windows loads.

`PROMPT=$P$G>`

Ensures the DOS prompt shows the current drive and folder.

`TEMP=C:\TEMP`

You have to create the *C:\TEMP* folder (with **MD TEMP** at the C:\> prompt) to use this, but it keeps the temporary files from cluttering the *C:\WINDOWS* directory structure.

`TMP=C:\TEMP`

Same as above. TMP is declared for compatibility with older DOS and Windows programs.

`PATH=C:\WINDOWS;C:\WINDOWS\SYSTEM;C:\WINDOWS\COMMAND;C:\`

Adds the DOS folder and root directory so commands entered at the DOS prompt can find their required programs. Feel free to add `C:\DOS` in the path if you have such a folder and some fond memories of it, or specific DOS programs you want to be able to access readily.

`LH C:\WINDOWS\COMMAND\DOSKEY /INSERT`

Once you've experienced the ability to use the up and down arrow keys to recall previously entered commands at the DOS prompt, you'll never go back. DOSKEY remembers a series of command-line entries and can play them back by scrolling through them using the up arrow key. The /INSERT parameter allows you to edit the current and previous command-line entries without erasing what was there. DOSKEY features remain intact and available under Windows.

`LH C:\WINDOWS\MSCDEX /D:MSCD001`

MSCDEX is DOS's way of assigning a logical drive letter to a CD-ROM drive. Although Windows provides its own version of MSCDEX and makes this line inactive, you will need it for DOS. LH is an abbreviation for LOADHIGH, which places the program in upper memory. MSC-DEX functions are required for Windows 95 but are displaced by Windows drivers when 98 or Me load and run.

`LH C:\MOUSE\MOUSE.EXE`

This is an example of loading a mouse driver into high memory. DOS's mouse driver or a mouse driver supplied with a pointing device is used for DOS but ignored in Windows, which provides its own driver.

AUTOEXEC.BAT can be used to set up other parameters or load resident programs as applications may require. Occasionally your applications may require additional PATH declarations or set their own environment variables, such as SET SYBASE=C:\SYBASE, which, with a large number of these parameters being set, can exceed the size of DOS's memory pool for such variables. If the total of your DOS environment variables exceeds 256 characters, you need to make an addition at the end of your *CONFIG.SYS* [Hack #92] that reads:

```
SHELL=C:\COMMAND.COM /E:512
```

This tells DOS to set aside and use 512 bytes for all of the DOS environment data. The number after the /E: sets the numbers of bytes for DOS environment data. You can replace 512 with 1024 for a larger environment. It's not unusual for this number to need to be as high at 2,048 bytes.

AUTOEXEC.BAT is a pretty versatile tool, permitting most DOS programs to be loaded and run, as well as letting you call other batch files to do work for you and then returning to where you left off and completing the sequence of events in the file. There are two ways to run batch files from within batch files. The first is to simply specify a second batch file to be run, usually at the end of a current batch file. When processing of the first batch file gets to a reference to another, the rest of the first batch file is ignored and control is turned over to the second batch file. If you want to run another batch file from the first and then return to complete the first batch file, add CALL before the reference to the next batch file. When the second batch file has finished running, then the first batch file will pick up where it left off. For example:

```
ECHO OFF
CLS
C:\WINDOWS\SMARTDRV C+
PROMPT=$P$G>
TEMP=C:\TEMP
TMP=C:\TEMP
PATH=C:\WINDOWS;C:\WINDOWS\SYSTEM;C;\DOS;C:\
LH C:\WINDOWS\COMMAND\DOSKEY /INSERT
LH SMARTDRV C+
rem the next line calls a second batch file
rem after the second.bat file is done
rem this batch file resumes after the next line
CALL C:\SECOND.BAT
LH C:\WINDOWS\MSCDEX /D:MSCD001
LH C:\MOUSE\MOUSE.EXE
```

In the above example, everything up to and including the loading of SMARTDRV runs, then *SECOND.BAT* is "called" and run, and then control is returned to this batch file so that MSCDEX and MOUSE are loaded.

Hack the Windows NT/2000/XP Boot Loader

HACK
#94

Customize what and how you boot using the *BOOT.INI* file.

The *BOOT.INI* file was introduced with Windows NT and lives on through Windows 2000, XP, and 2003 as a means to provide preboot reference to where the operating system is located and control over which operating system will be used. It allows users to select the DOS environment or the Windows NT environment (which does not support many of the applications and direct hardware access that DOS does). *BOOT.INI* can also be modified to support the addition of another drive that has an operating system installed (perhaps unknown to the operating system on the first/original disk drive), giving you multiboot support to a non-Microsoft OS.

BOOT.INI is a plain-text file (equivalent to DOS's *IO.SYS* and *MSDOS.SYS*) that resides in the root directory of your boot disk and is read by the NTLDR program when the system is starting up. It is saved with Read-only, System, and Hidden attributes, requiring you to remove these attributes before reading or modifying the file.

BOOT.INI Contents

The contents of a typical *BOOT.INI* file are shown below. The parameters in the file are few—essentially specifying the time that the boot loader waits for user input before processing the default selection, the default operating system to boot if there is no user selection, and a list of possible operating systems and the disk parameters indicating where the operating systems are stored.

```
[boot loader]
timeout=3
default=multi(0)disk(0)rdisk(0)partition(1)\WINDOWS
[operating systems]
multi(0)disk(0)rdisk(0)partition(1)\WINDOWS="Microsoft Windows XP
Professional" /fastdetect
```

In this example, only one operating system is presented, Windows XP, and the computer will wait for three seconds after the menu appears before loading the default operating system. Windows XP is installed in partition 1 on the first physical disk, rdisk(0), on an ATA or SCSI device that is recognized by the system BIOS (the multi(0) parameter).

The following sample shows the [operating systems] section of a *BOOT.INI* file on a computer with two operating systems, Microsoft Windows XP and Microsoft Windows 2000. It has two boot entries, one for each operating system.

```
[operating systems]
multi(0)disk(0)rdisk(0)partition(1)\WINDOWS="Microsoft Windows XP
Professional" /fastdetect
multi(0)disk(0)rdisk(0)partition(2)\WINNT="Microsoft Windows 2000
Professional" /fastdetect
```

These entries reveal that Windows XP and 2000 are installed on two different partitions of the same physical disk drive. The operating system location information uses the Advanced Risk Computing (ARC) naming convention for the physical and logical information about the disk and partition where the operating system resides. ARC paths use the formats described in the following sections.

Editing BOOT.INI with a Text Editor

BOOT.INI starts out with System, Read-only, and Hidden file attributes. To find the file in Explorer or at a command prompt, you need to remove at least the Hidden attribute. To edit the file, you need to remove the Read-only attribute. You can remove all of the attributes at a command prompt with the following steps:

1. Open a command prompt window through Start→Run, type in CMD, and then click OK.

2. Change to the root directory of the boot disk and remove the attributes (System, Hidden, Read-only):

   ```
   X:\Foo>C:
   C:\Bar>cd \
   C:\>attrib -s -h -r boot.ini
   ```

With the attributes removed, you can use EDIT, Notepad, or a similar text editor to view and make changes to the file. NTLDR can use the *BOOT.INI* file with any attributes set, but to protect the file when done editing, restore the attributes at a command prompt with the following steps:

1. Open a command prompt window through Start→Run, type in CMD, and then click OK.

2. Change to the root directory of the boot disk and restore the attributes:

   ```
   X:\Foo>C:
   C:\Bar>cd \
   C:\>attrib +s +h +r boot.ini
   ```

ARC Disk and Partition Syntax for BIOS Drives

The *BOOT.INI* syntax discussed is used for all controllers that provide BIOS INT-13 support for ATA and SCSI disks. Table 9-2 provides details about these parameters.

Table 9-2. BOOT.INI syntax for IDE devices

Parameter	Description
multi(0)	The drive controller number, typically 0.
disk(0)	Always 0; not used with IDE drives
rdisk(0)	The physical hard disk attached to drive controller. For ATA controllers, this number is typically between 0 and 3. For SCSI controllers, this number is typically between 0 and 7, or 0 and 15, depending on the adapter type.
partition(0)	The partition number.

ARC Disk and Partition Syntax for Non-BIOS Drives

The following syntax tells Windows that the startup device is attached to a SCSI host controller that does not support BIOS INT-13 disk access and that bootup requires the *NTBOOTDD.SYS* device driver. SCSI host adapters built into servers, many of which support a variety of RAID and disaster recovery functions, avoid using the BIOS for disk access and must use either a custom disk access driver or the boot driver of Windows to support all of the features available in the special hardware. Table 9-3 describes the syntax used in *BOOT.INI* for SCSI devices.

Table 9-3. BOOT.INI syntax for SCSI devices

Parameter	Description
scsi(0)	The drive controller, typically 0.
disk(0)	The SCSI disk drive device number, between 0 and 7, or 0 and 15, depending on the host adapter.
rdisk(0)	The SCSI logical unit, typically 0.
partition(0)	The partition number the operating system resides on.

You can use this syntax to specify which SCSI disk to boot from by following these steps:

1. Take a disk drive with an operating system already installed.

2. Install it as the second disk drive in a system that has another NT-based operating system installed on its disk drive.

3. Modify the *BOOT.INI* file on the first drive and adjust all of the lines containing selections of which operating system to boot.

The unmodified *BOOT.INI* on both drives may initially read as follows:

```
[boot loader]
timeout=3
default=multi(0)disk(0)rdisk(0)partition(1)\WINDOWS
[operating systems]
multi(0)disk(0)rdisk(0)partition(1)\WINDOWS="Microsoft Windows XP
Professional"
```

After installing the second drive, the *BOOT.INI* file on the first drive should be modified to look like:

```
[boot loader]
timeout=3
default=multi(0)disk(0)rdisk(0)partition(1)\WINDOWS
[operating systems]
multi(0)disk(0)rdisk(0)partition(1)\WINDOWS="Microsoft Windows XP on 1st
Drive"
multi(0)disk(0)rdisk(1)partition(1)\WINNT="Microsoft Windows 2000 on 2nd
Drive"
```

Add the second operating system choice, "Microsoft Windows 2000 on 2nd Drive" and indicate that it resides on the first partition, partition(1), of the second disk, rdisk(1).

Then modify the *BOOT.INI* file on the second drive to look like:

```
[boot loader]
timeout=0
default=multi(0)disk(0)rdisk(1)partition(1)\WINNT
[operating systems]
multi(0)disk(0)rdisk(1)partition(1)\WINNT="Microsoft Windows 2000 on 2nd
Drive"
```

This provides the operating system location reference for the operating system on the second drive.

> Remember to make backups of these files before you change them so you can restore them if you make a mistake. You can copy the original file back into the text-based Recovery Console, which you can access by running Windows setup and choosing to recover an existing installation.

Booting Linux

You can boot Linux from *BOOT.INI* with a little trickery. The first step is to install a Linux bootloader, such as GRUB or LILO, onto your Linux partition. So, supposing your Linux root partition is */dev/hda6*, you'd set up the GRUB bootloader with these commands:

```
# grub

GNU GRUB  version 0.95  (640K lower / 3072K upper memory)

 [ Minimal BASH-like line editing is supported.  For the first word, TAB
   lists possible command completions.  Anywhere else TAB lists the possible
   completions of a device/filename. ]

grub> root (hd0,  <TAB>
 Possible partitions are:
```

```
Partition num: 0,  Filesystem type unknown, partition type 0x7
Partition num: 2,  Filesystem type is fat, partition type 0xc
Partition num: 4,  Filesystem type unknown, partition type 0x82
Partition num: 5,  Filesystem type is ext2fs, partition type 0x83

grub> root (hd0,5)
 Filesystem type is ext2fs, partition type 0x83

grub> setup (hd0,5)
 Checking if "/boot/grub/stage1" exists... yes
 Checking if "/boot/grub/stage2" exists... yes
 Checking if "/boot/grub/e2fs_stage1_5" exists... yes
 Running "embed /boot/grub/e2fs_stage1_5 (hd0,5)"... failed (this is not
fatal)
 Running "embed /boot/grub/e2fs_stage1_5 (hd0,5)"... failed (this is not
fatal)
 Running "install /boot/grub/stage1 (hd0,5) /boot/grub/stage2 p /boot/grub/
menu
.lst "... succeeded
Done.

grub> quit
```

> Note that GRUB uses a different numbering scheme than the rest of Linux. Linux numbers partitions starting at 1, but GRUB starts at 0. So /dev/hda6 is (hd0,5) in GRUB.

After you set up the bootloader, you need to grab it and save it into a file with the dd command:

```
# dd if=/dev/hda6 of=grub.bin bs=512 count=1
```

Now you need to copy *grub.bin* over to the root of your boot partition, typically the Windows C: drive. If your Windows C: drive is formatted as NTFS, you probably won't be able to write *grub.bin* to it from Linux, so you'll need to use a FAT-32 partition, a floppy disk, a directory on another computer, or some other means to transfer it over.

Boot back into Windows, edit your *BOOT.INI* as directed earlier in this hack, and add the following line to the [operating systems] section:

```
c:\grub.bin="Linux"
```

If you reinstall your Linux boot loader, you'll need to use dd to extract the boot loader and copy it to your C: drive again. The advantage of using GRUB instead of LILO is that GRUB does not need to be reinstalled each time you install a new kernel (simply edit the GRUB configuration file, usually */boot/grub/menu.lst*).

Booting DOS or Windows 9x–Me

Configuring the *BOOT.INI* file to allow you to boot to DOS or Windows 95–Me is done automatically by the setup program if, when you install Windows NT–2003 including XP, you choose to leave your current filesystem intact (it must be a FAT-16 or FAT-32 partition) and install the new operating system in a different directory or on a different disk drive (which could be NTFS).

If you want to add DOS/95/98/Me to an existing NT–2003 installation, it is easier to do so by adding a second hard drive setup with a FAT-16 or FAT-32 filesystem and modifying the *BOOT.INI* file to provide the option to boot to the second drive. The steps in a nutshell are:

1. Disconnect the first hard drive that contains Windows NT–2003.
2. Connect the drive you want to use for DOS–Me as the first/only hard drive.
3. Install DOS or Windows 95–Me.
4. Reconfigure the hard drives so that the Windows NT–2003 drive is the first/"Master" drive and the DOS–Me drive is the second/"Slave" drive.
5. Boot into Windows NT–2003.
6. Modify the *BOOT.INI* file on the second drive to look like:

   ```
   [boot loader]
   timeout=5
   default=multi(0)disk(0)rdisk(1)partition(1)\WINNT
   [operating systems]
   multi(0)disk(0)rdisk(1)partition(1)\WINNT="Microsoft Windows 2000"
   d:\="Windows 98"
   ```

The line containing d:\="Windows 98" provides the boot-time option and operating system location reference for the operating system on the second drive.

## CHAPTER TEN

Configuring a New PC
Hacks 95–100

You're wondering how the heck to get all the "stuff" from the old PC to the new one. Unless you've got all of the installation disks for your software and want to reinstall all of it—and have backed up datafiles to another tape, CD, disk, or network—you've got a big chore ahead.

The next series of hacks presents applications you can use to copy files, settings, and even some applications from one PC to another.

Previous chapters showed you dozens of ways to tune up a PC, and of course you'll apply the most appropriate hacks to this new PC. You built it, configured it, got it set up just the way you like it, and you probably don't want all that work on your new PC to go to waste. The programs and data you work with are invaluable to your life and your occupation. Leaving them and your whole PC at risk makes as much sense as leaving your car or home unlocked in a high-crime neighborhood. The Internet is as much a "friendly global village" as it is a seething hotbed of malicious activity covering everything from questionable marketing methods to multimillion dollar identity theft and fraud scams.

In my anxiety to tinker with fresh PC installations, I have let unprotected Linux and Windows systems connect to the Internet and subsequently come under attack or become infected within a matter of seconds. It is not a pretty or pleasant sight. An essential part of setting up a new PC is making sure it becomes and stays safe and stable. This three-tiered approach to protecting yourself, your family, and your employer can save you hours of work and potentially thousands of dollars of personal or corporate worth:

Virus protection
>   Whether you prefer AVG, Trend, F-Prot, McAfee, Norton, or Panda, you simply must have virus protection on your PC. Even if you download little or nothing to your PC, exchange files with no one or only

with people you trust, and don't use Outlook or Outlook Express for email, a virus will find its way to your PC eventually.

Network protection

I include both hardware and software firewalls as well as anti-malware [Hack #98] protection in this category. What you do with your PC is your business—you didn't buy it or build it just to let someone else take control of it. Hardware firewalls block most if not all undesirable incoming traffic, and software firewalls protect you from what may get through a hardware firewall and from programs running on your own PC, including some malware. Malware protection is necessary to eliminate hidden applications that may circumvent the firewalls and consume your resources without your knowledge.

Backups

Backing up your data is considered long-term protection, but a failure can happen at any time and may be self-induced as you're hacking your way through this book. Whether you make a complete image of your PC's hard drive or merely copy your documents to a CD, you owe it to yourself to perform some kind of backup.

> The first thing you *must* do when setting up a new Windows, Linux, Unix (the list goes on and on!) PC is to get the latest operating system updates. On Windows, you can do this with Windows Update (available off of Internet Explorer's Tools menu). On Linux, Unix, and other operating systems, the method varies. *Apply these updates early; apply them often.*
>
> Every new install involves a bootstrapping problem: you can't securely connect to the Internet without running the updates; you can't get the updates without connecting to the Internet. The solution to this is simple: get a firewall [Hack #99].

H A C K   Clone Your Hard Disk
#95

Disk imaging software is one quick way to move all of the contents of your old hard drive to your new one.

Getting a shiny new PC is a wonderful experience, but a new computer won't have the lived-in feel of your familiar old PC. If your old PC is just the way you want it but not fast enough, won't accept as much RAM as you need, can't take a better video adapter, or doesn't have a big enough hard drive space, then cloning it onto a new hard drive is easy.

Most of your PC's "personality" is on the hard drive—all of the desktop settings, browser preferences and history, and, of course, datafiles. You can transfer and retain that personality on a new PC or simply on a new hard drive with disk imaging software like Symantec's GHOST or Drive Image (*http://www.symantec.com*) or Acronis's True Image, (*http://www.acronis.com*).

> Have your device driver installation disks handy if you are cloning to a new PC that's different from your previous one. The biggest trouble comes when the new PC has a totally different motherboard. (Windows will usually forgive other hardware changes.) If you're staying with the same chipset manufacturer (Intel, Via, etc.) but only leaping a chipset generation or two, it should go smoothly. A big jump, such as from a Pentium II system to an AMD64 system, is probably not going to work. Even a seemingly small jump, such as from a Pentium 3 to a Pentium 4, could be troublesome. Your mileage may vary.
>
> This process is acceptable but not "perfect" when used with Windows XP and marginally acceptable with Windows 2000. This technique is not recommended for use with Windows 9x–Me because their installations lack the device drivers and robust "new hardware found" forgiveness of 2000 and XP to accommodate the new system hardware. Linux is generally much more forgiving than Windows, but I suggest you switch to a generic kernel (one compiled for Intel 386 architecture) before the upgrade and then install a kernel compiled for your processor architecture after you've confirmed that the upgrade is working well.
>
> If you're just upgrading your hard drive, this should work with any operating system.

GHOST is a DOS-based program, installed first on your hard drive and run from a DOS prompt, or it can be transferred to diskette as needed. If you run GHOST from within Windows, it will create a temporary DOS partition **[Hack #40]** somewhere in the unused space on your hard drive and reboot into PC-DOS to do its thing. For this reason, GHOST for Windows requires that you have one free partition slot left. (For example, if you've set up three primary partitions and one logical, GHOST will refuse to run.)

If something goes awry with GHOST during this time, you could end up with strange little DOS partitions whose cylinders overlap with an existing partition. I have found that you can safely delete this partition by booting into a Linux rescue CD **[Hack #50]** and using Linux FDISK. But this is dangerous territory, and if you find yourself here, it may be best to contact Symantec support.

Because this is such a horrible kludge, I do not suggest that you run GHOST from within Windows.

Drive Image, shown in Figure 10-1, and True Image, shown in Figure 10-2, work from within Windows. Each of these programs allows you to transfer partitions or entire drives from one to the other or create an image file of a hard drive that you can read with a special explore program to retrieve individual files from within the image file.

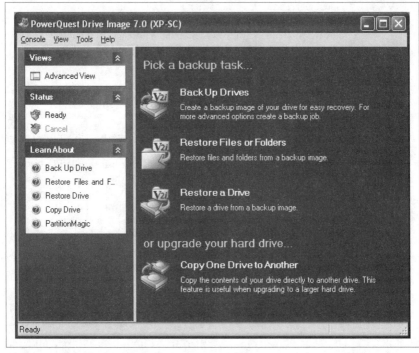

Figure 10-1. Drive Image performs imaging and disk copying within Windows

Drive cloning is best done with both drives connected to the same PC but can be done over special parallel port cables or even a local network. Transferring the contents of an entire disk drive to another, including the boot files, operating system, directory structure, and files is the purest and simplest "one-shot" process to get your existing PC personality up and running on a new drive or PC.

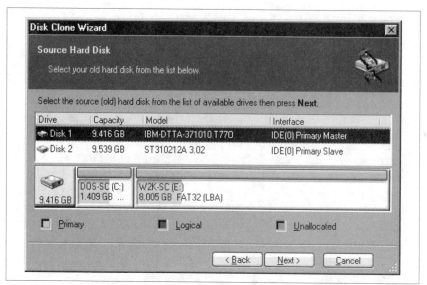

Figure 10-2. True Image drive-cloning selections

Symantec's GHOST and Drive Image and Acronis's True Image aren't the only utilities available for copying the contents of one hard drive to another. A small handful of other products are readily available as well, two of them specific to Linux systems:

For Linux

> ghost4unix at *http://rfhs8012.fh-regensburg.de/~feyrer/g4u/*
>
> QTparted at *http://qtparted.sourceforge.net/*

For Windows

> HDClone at *http://www.miray.de/download/sat.hdclone.html*
>
> Farstone's DriveClone at *http://www.farstone.com*

> You may have to reactivate Windows XP or 2003 with Microsoft if you transfer it to a new hard drive, especially into a new PC system or after a motherboard swap. Windows detects significant hardware changes and determines that enough system components have changed that the installation may be an attempt to pirate a copy of the operating system. Have no fear; if you are not trying to pirate the OS, reactivation by phone is a very simple process.

Move Applications and Settings from One PC to Another
HACK #96

It's not hard to get essential PC "personality" information from your old PC to your new one.

Microsoft anticipated the old-to-new PC transition and has tried to make it easier and desirable to upgrade your PCs by including a tool to copy desktop settings and preferences as well as your datafiles.

Using the Files and Settings Transfer Wizard, shown in Figure 10-3, is about as simple as can be. It sets up the process on the Windows XP system and creates the diskette needed to connect the two PCs together to allow the data transfers to "fly by wire." The connection between both PCs may be over a serial cable (very slow), a Direct Cable Connection between parallel ports, or through files saved from the old PC to disks or a network drive.

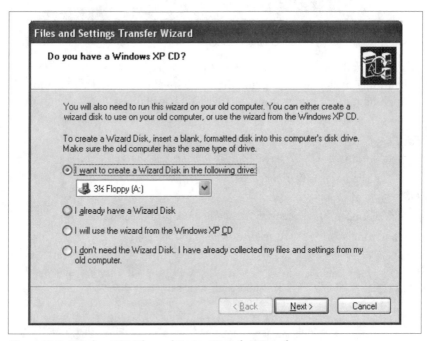

Figure 10-3. Windows XP Files and Setting Transfer Wizard

The program will automatically find your Windows settings and default document file locations on the old PC and let you choose which documents and other datafiles you want to transfer to the new PC. To reduce software piracy and avoid potential compatibility problems, this tool does not let you transfer program files to another PC. You will have to reinstall and, where required, reactivate your applications.

Of course, Microsoft included this feature in XP only after other companies had created and marketed products to address the issue of PC migration. Several vendors provide equal or better features to get your "stuff" onto your new PC, including:

- AlohaBob's PC Relocator (*http://www.alohabob.com*)
- Acronis MigrateEasy (*http://www.acronis.com*)
- Spearit Software's Move Me (*http://www.spearit.com*)
- Detto IntelliMover (*http://www.detto.com*)

Of these, Aloha Bob's PC Relocator is my favorite. From Day One, Aloha-Bob's has been the only migration program to transfer not only settings and files but also application programs—it simply works for me.

Aloha Bob's PC Relocator

Cloning an entire hard drive is certainly quick and easy, but if you're going from an old Windows 9x system to a new Windows XP system, cloning the old hard drive [Hack #95] wipes out your XP installation. Transferring only your data and Windows settings leaves the new PC's operating system intact but leaves you having to reinstall your applications on the new PC.

Covering the middle ground is the PC Relocator utility, which is capable of transferring not only Windows settings and data but also your installed application programs. PC Relocator, shown in Figure 10-4, can transfer items from your old PC to the new one by special parallel port data transfer cables, network connections, USB transfer cable, or disk storage.

Since most users have just one hard drive for everything from operating systems and applications to data, it's easy for PC Relocator to reestablish the old PC's environment on the new PC. One thing PC Relocator cannot do is resolve locations of applications and data if the old PC uses multiple partitions and the new one uses just one partition. Instead of guessing where applications and data from various drives are supposed to go, PC Relocator makes folders representing and containing the contents of the old PC's partitions, which you have to sort out on the new system's drive after completing the transfer. If you encounter this situation, you will probably have to reinstall some applications and move datafiles around to suit the configuration of your new PC.

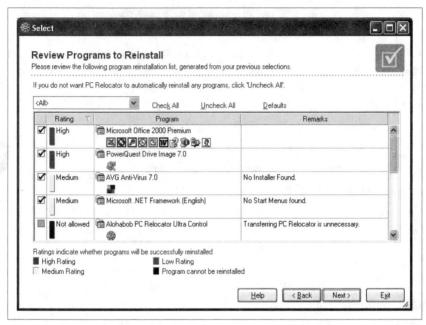

Figure 10-4. PC Relocator moves application programs as well as datafiles

HACK #97 Protect Your PC from Viruses

Stop incoming and outgoing viruses before they begin to tear apart your new system.

It happens to all of us. You will get at least one virus infection on your PC whether you like it or not. Whether or not that virus does any damage is mostly up to you and a little bit of software. A significant new virus is distributed every week or so, and yet there are thousands if not millions of PCs that have outdated virus protection, or none at all.

Ultimately it matters little which virus protection product you choose; you simply need to be protected. Ideally you want to use a virus protection product that does little, if anything, to get in your way and slow down your work and covers your email, web browsing, and the files on your hard drives as well as other writable media.

Almost every maker of virus protection software offers a free trial version for download, and most new PCs and motherboards come with a full or partial version of one product or the other. Be aware that a big brand name does not necessarily mean the fastest, most, or best protection. You can download and try each product to see which you like best, removing the previously installed product(s) through Add/Remove Programs and even using

System Restore points to go back to preinstalled conditions. Check the license and subscription terms as well as the cost to determine if you'll be stuck buying the same product at nearly full price year after year.

If you need good virus protection quickly, I highly suggest AVG from Grisoft (*http://www.grisoft.com*). They offer Version 6 of their product line free. I've sold more friends on AVG than any other PC product around because many other products hog memory, disk space, and CPU time. AVG "gives them their PC back." After switching to AVG and turning off the other products, users typically experience Windows running as if they'd just increased their CPU speed, doubled their RAM, and installed a faster hard drive. You may also want to check out AntiVir Personal Edition (*http://www.free-av.com/*).

Paying for Virus Protection

As you might expect, one reason to pay for AVG is that you get support, not that you need much, if any, but Grisoft is very responsive, and heck, the product is so good that you'll feel you really ought to pay for it.

I also use "the other" products both personally and commercially in enterprise settings and find them to be adequate to the task of protecting your system. Don't feel you need to shy away from off-the-shelf commercialware, because you do have some good choices of where to spend your money with these top three virus protection products:

- PC-cillin from Trend Micro (*http://www.trendmicro.com*)
- Norton AntiVirus from Symantec (*http://www.symantec.com*)
- VirusScan from McAfee (*http://www.mcafee.com*)

HACK
#98

Protect Your PC from Malware

Rid your PC of dozens of performance-robbing pop-up and search bar annoyances with a few free programs.

Viruses and malicious hackers are bad, but you may find yourself under considerably more threat from software that has a way of sneaking onto your computer, such as:

Adware
Software that pops up advertisements while you are using your computer.

Spyware
Software that gathers data on what you do with your computer and reports that information back to its maker.

Malware
> Software that is designed to cripple your computer or open a back door for malicious attackers. Often used as a catch-all term for adware, spyware, and any other bad software you didn't knowingly install.

Such "badware" gets onto your system in many ways:

- Through browser plug-ins that you agree to install despite a security warning from Windows.
- By installing applications that promise to "speed up and enhance your web experience."
- By installing free versions of popular software applications (often file-sharing programs) that include accompanying adware or spyware.
- By installing some programs that claim to prevent infestation from such malware!

The long-standing adage, "If it sounds too good to be true, it probably is" definitely applies here. Certain types of freeware, particularly file-sharing applications and free games, are actually "paid for" by companies that provide advertisement and search-enhancement add-ins and who in turn get paid by advertisers. Those advertisers get their ads distributed in the form of pop-ups from ad services like GAIN/Gator/Claria and DoubleClick.

Figure 10-5 shows a signed ActiveX program permission screen from Internet Explorer 6 under Windows XP. (This is the pre–Windows XP Service Pack 2 warning. See "Surround Yourself with a Firewall" **[Hack #99]** for more information on Service Pack 2.) If you select the "Always trust" checkbox and then click Yes to trust this vendor you will *never* be asked permission to trust or install their applications again, no matter how they try to get onto your system. This is the only such warning you will receive if you download directly from the software publisher. It is best to *never* select the "Always trust" checkbox. Instead, you should verify downloads on a case-by-case basis.

If you install a piece of ad-sponsored software, such as one of the many versions of the popular DivX media player (*http://www.divx.com*), you may be presented with a dialog revealing that you will be getting ad software, shown in Figure 10-6. You may also see a dialog with a lengthy license agreement, as in Figure 10-7, amidst the installation of the program you really wanted to use. This particular installation, and many like it, do not tell you exactly which pieces of software will be installed along with the product you want. In this case, two different pieces of GAIN/Gator software get installed.

2934

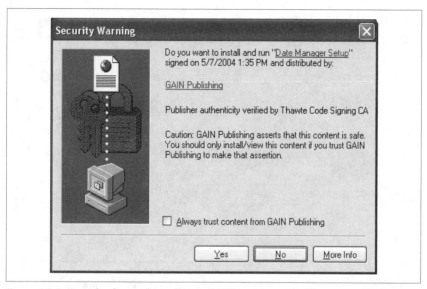

Figure 10-5. Downloading and installing a GAIN program asks for your permission to trust them for all future installations

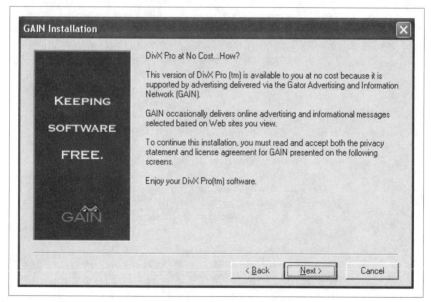

Figure 10-6. Some software installations will tell you that adware comes with the product

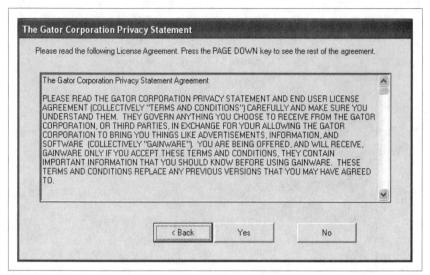

The Gator Corporation Privacy Statement

Please read the following License Agreement. Press the PAGE DOWN key to see the rest of the agreement.

The Gator Corporation Privacy Statement Agreement

PLEASE READ THE GATOR CORPORATION PRIVACY STATEMENT AND END USER LICENSE AGREEMENT (COLLECTIVELY "TERMS AND CONDITIONS") CAREFULLY AND MAKE SURE YOU UNDERSTAND THEM. THEY GOVERN ANYTHING YOU CHOOSE TO RECEIVE FROM THE GATOR CORPORATION, OR THIRD PARTIES, IN EXCHANGE FOR YOUR ALLOWING THE GATOR CORPORATION TO BRING YOU THINGS LIKE ADVERTISEMENTS, INFORMATION, AND SOFTWARE (COLLECTIVELY "GAINWARE"). YOU ARE BEING OFFERED, AND WILL RECEIVE, GAINWARE ONLY IF YOU ACCEPT THESE TERMS AND CONDITIONS, THEY CONTAIN IMPORTANT INFORMATION THAT YOU SHOULD KNOW BEFORE USING GAINWARE. THESE TERMS AND CONDITIONS REPLACE ANY PREVIOUS VERSIONS THAT YOU MAY HAVE AGREED TO.

[< Back]   Yes   No

Figure 10-7. You must be patient and have good eyes to read through the entire license agreement for GAIN software

Read the fine print. It might not be so bad if you got just one easily identifiable piece of spyware, but these things tend to propagate like weeds throughout your system; start with one piece of spyware today and in a week or two, your system could be overwhelmed with 10 or 20 of their "friends."

The End-User License Agreement (EULA), or installation dialogs, for some freeware may contain either obvious or subtle indications that software from partners will be installed along with the software you really want to use. Some software requires the presence of the tag-along spyware as a condition of using the program for free. For example, the popular file-sharing program Kazaa (see *http://www.kazaa.com/us/privacy/index.htm*) requires the presence of Cydoor (displays ads, records which were viewed and for how long) and GAIN (displays ads based on your web surfing habits).

Unless you *really* need the specific spyware-laden version you downloaded, stop the installation and search for a friendlier alternative. I find it preferable to pay $30 for spyware-free software than to have to spend hours cleaning up the pop-up, executable, and DLL mess many insidious spyware programs leave behind. For example, the makers of Kazaa offer an ad-free version for $29.95.

In reality, most of the generic search-assistant programs have nothing to do with the top search engines such as Google, Yahoo!, Lycos, MSN, or AltaVista and using them doesn't do you any good at all. Those selective "targeted" ads that supposedly focus on *your* personal interests seem to be the same ads everyone else gets regardless of preferences, needs, or buying habits. The search bars or toolbars provided by Google and Yahoo! are legitimate and safe, and both come with pop-up-blocking features. You may be wondering where the other search assistants came from. Perhaps you or someone using your computer clicked OK or Yes when a security alert appeared. It's very difficult for these applications to get on your computer without someone's consent, but the request for consent is often sneakily worded.

The sinister aspect to badware is that you really have no idea what the programs are doing, what information they are sniffing for or sending out across the Internet, or how they affect you other than hogging the performance of your system, altering your browser settings (Netscape 4.x and Internet Explorer mostly; Opera and Netscape 7 seem to be left alone for now), and delivering more mind-numbing pop-ups than any 100 people can tolerate.

> Using personal/desktop firewall software [Hack #99] can help you identify and block spyware that attempts to make outbound connections to the Internet, although most spyware program use the features and identity of Windows or IE and get a free ride through the firewalls.
>
> If you wish to use a personal firewall to block spyware programs from making connections back to their "mother ship," you will have to configure your firewall to block zones of domains and URLs, many of which change IP addresses often to foil this blocking technique.

These free programs available on the Web, each of them operating a bit differently, are a good combination to sniff out, clean up, and "immunize" your system from badware:

* Definitive Solutions's BHODemon (*http://www.definitivesolutions.com*)
* Patrick Kolla's Spybot Search & Destroy (*http://www.spybot.info*)
* Javacool Software's SpywareBlaster (*http://www.javacoolsoftware.com*)
* Lavasoft's Ad-Aware, (*http://www.lavasoft.de*)

BHODemon, shown in Figure 10-8, is a "quick and dirty" application that shows you which Browser Helper Objects, otherwise known as ActiveX controls, are automatically loaded with Internet Explorer (and thus Windows Explorer).

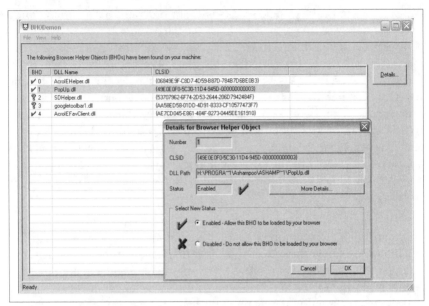

Figure 10-8. BHODemon provides details about installed ActiveX controls

BHODemon allows you to disable any of the programs it finds. You can perform a similar task by investigating all of the files in the *C:\Windows\ Downloaded Program Files* folder, which is the ActiveX program cache, and you may have to look into that folder from time to time to see if there are files that BHODemon does not show. If you right-click on any of the files and then select Properties, you will see the originator of the file and can determine if the file is legitimate or not. In fact, you could delete all of the files found as needed, and in theory, the critical ones for the operating system will be replaced.

Spybot Search & Destroy, shown in Figure 10-9, performs four critical functions. First, it can scan your system for existing spyware. Second, it allows you to remove the bad programs it finds, digging deep into the Windows Registry to unearth stubborn files. Third, it provides an "immunization" function, installing its own ActiveX application to watch for and stop the installation of spyware programs. Fourth, it allows you to disable the ability of other programs to change your browser settings. Covering over 12,400 different variations of spyware, this is a very handy and robust tool to use.

SpywareBlaster, shown in Figure 10-10, does not scan for the presence of spyware or remove it, but it offers myriad techniques to block badware from getting your browsers, acting as a very specific firewall against dozens of known spyware sites. It also provides a way to block the installation of Macromedia's Flash ActiveX control so you can avoid many of those annoying

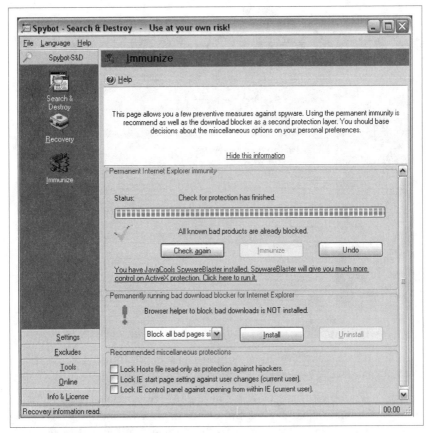

Figure 10-9. Spybot Search & Destroy blocks spyware

animated ads that never seem to stop. (Unfortunately, blocking Flash also robs you of being able to take advantage of many web sites that insist on forcing you into Flash-enabled pages instead of good old HTML content.)

HACK #99 Surround Yourself with a Firewall

Protecting yourself from incoming and outgoing threats is easy with personal firewall software.

The great thing about the Internet is that it allows connectivity between millions of users anywhere in the world at any time. The bad thing about the Internet is that it allows connectivity between millions of users anywhere in the world at any time. Expecting your Internet Service Provider (ISP) to protect your PCs from the Internet's hacker community is like expecting your local police and fire departments to prevent burglaries, speeding, traffic collisions, and house fires—it is simply not going to happen. ISPs and Internet

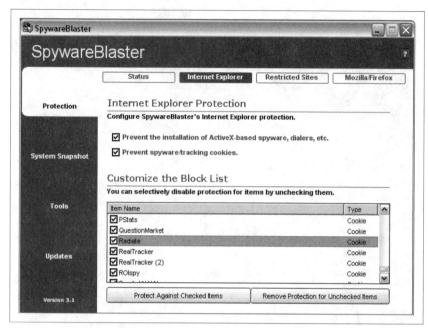

Figure 10-10. SpywareBlaster blocks the installation of spyware cookies

users are on the defensive; there are too many opportunities for bad things to propagate on the Internet for them to be effectively proactive.

Personal/desktop firewalls exist to filter a variety of connections, applications, and content from getting into or out of your PC. Windows XP (pre-Service Pack 2) comes with a firewall of its own, the Internet Connection Firewall (ICF), but it is perhaps the least documented, least understood, and least effective PC network protection tool created. ICF does not provide significant control over types of connections (client or server features) nor over abuse by programs that want to get out to the Internet. You deserve better.

> XP Service Pack 2 adds a Security Center to Windows that contains a new Windows Firewall that is more robust than ICF, providing the ability to block assorted inbound and outbound connections, application security that alerts you when new programs want to install and run (Figures 10-11 and 10-12), and a pop-up blocker, shown in Figure 10-13, for Internet Explorer.

Despite their vested interest in the success and reliability of the XP operating system, Microsoft's only risk if their firewall fails is an already questionable reputation for security. Because their efforts at secure computing are

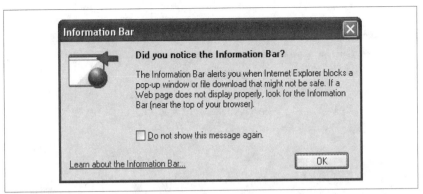

Figure 10-11. XP Service Pack 2's Security Center alerts you to blocked pop-ups

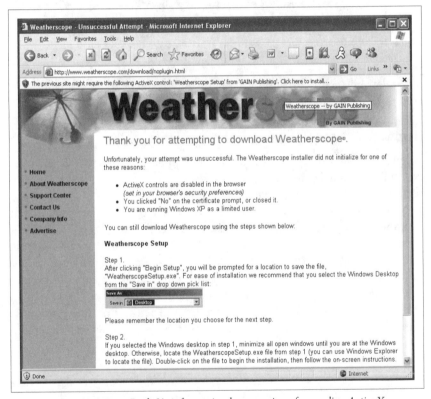

Figure 10-12. XP Service Pack 2's information bar warning of a pending ActiveX installation

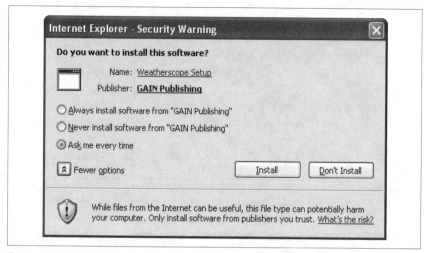

Figure 10-13. XP Service Pack 2's Security Center provides choices about ActiveX installations

still relatively new and unproven, I do not recommend that anyone rely solely on Microsoft for system protection and data security just yet.

Hardware Firewalls

A hardware firewall, typically built into an appliance that serves as a router and hub for your DSL or cable connection to the Internet, offers some protection against incoming threats to your PC or local network. However, you may be amazed at what can get through them to clog up your network. (For example, if a malicious web page causes Internet Explorer to put up a security warning and you ignore it and click OK or Yes, a hardware firewall will not protect you from what you just let in.) Hardware firewalls provide no protection from programs or threats inside your PC or local network getting out to the Internet, which is how your data and perhaps your money gets to someone it shouldn't. Still, a hardware firewall is the first line of defense against remote attacks that don't rely on tricking the user into accepting something he shouldn't.

> Even if you're on dial-up, consider getting a router (such as the D-Link DI-824VUP) that bridges your home network and a dial-up network through a backup external modem port. (One model of the Apple AirPort Extreme Base Station, which works fine with PCs, has a built-in 56k modem.) The advantage of such a router is that it is somewhat future-proof: you can plug it into a broadband connection if and when you get it, and it supports wired and wireless home networks.

Software Firewalls

Highly configurable and more comprehensive firewall protection for your PC desktop can be found in products like ZoneLab's ZoneAlarm (*http://www.zonelabs.com*), shown in Figure 10-14, Norton Internet Security (*http://www.symantec.com*), and Sygate's Personal Firewall (*http://www.sygate.com*). Windows XP Service Pack 2 also includes a comprehensive firewall (see Figure 10-15) that can be configured through the new Security Center control panel.

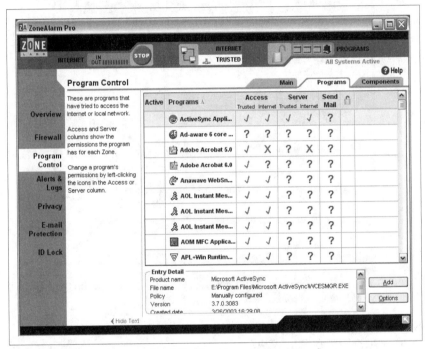

Figure 10-14. ZoneAlarm tracks applications that use your network

Using a combination of hardware firewall protection to reduce unnecessary "chatter" on your local network and software firewall protection on individual desktops creates a secure environment in which you can feel safe and compute more safely. Using a desktop firewall on each system on your network can also reduce the chances of cross-pollination of malware [Hacks #97 and #98].

With a desktop firewall, you can know immediately if a program is trying to sneak something out of your PC to persons unknown on the Internet and stop the activity before it happens. Your hardware firewall and your ISP simply do not care; they do not know and cannot decide what you want to

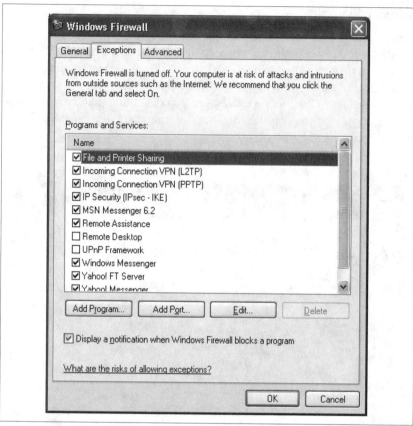

Figure 10-15. Windows Firewall in XP Service Pack 2 provides program and port control for inbound and outbound connections

share over the Internet and what you do not. This level of discretion and protection is your responsibility.

HACK Do Your Backups
#100
Reduce long-term risk when starting out with a new system—backing up is not hard to do.

Admittedly, backing up your datafiles is not the coolest thing you could be doing with your PC. Backups rank right up there with cleaning out the rain gutters, giving the cat a bath, calling your ISP for support, and having a root canal. That said, spending an hour or so setting up the right backup process and then launching it manually or letting it run at a scheduled time will be a blessing sometime in the future.

Depending on the method and software you choose, your first backup may be a whopper—but the subsequent ones, *incremental* or *differential* backups, may take very little time or trouble.

Windows provides its own limited backup program—sending files off to diskettes, tape drives, or other logical drives, including network drives. Apparently the developers of Windows XP had not counted on using the included backup program with CD-ROMs as a media of choice to hold the backup files. At least you can back up to a network drive on a file server.

More versatile programs such as Stomp's BackUp MyPC (*http://www. stompinc.com*) and Newtech Infosystems NTI Backup Now! (*http://www. ntius.com*) support placing backups on CD and DVD media as well as tape drives and other logical disk drives. BackUp MyPC's wizard and scheduler are as simple as can be to get you going, and after your first backup, it's almost a set-and-forget process—just make sure you leave your PC on and have writable media ready to accept the data.

You can also back up with disk imaging/cloning software **[Hack #95]**, making it much easier to recover from a totally dead disk drive on a replacement drive. Whichever method you choose, even if it is as primitive as copying your datafiles to diskettes, Zip drives, CD-ROMs, or DVDs, consider adding backups to your new PC's configuration.

If your backup media choices are limited to a program like Windows Backup, then the simplest and fastest way to store your data is to add a second hard drive to your PC and use it only for backups. If you clone your first hard drive to your second and then store backups on the second drive, you have a bootable spare with all your programs and data in one place. You can put the second drive in a removable hard drive tray (see the hardware solution under "Configure a Multiboot System" **[Hack #86]**) and use it to back up other PCs as well. Backing up to another hard drive is the fastest method of saving your data, but I do not recommend leaving the backup drive in a system or running anywhere all the time. Disconnect your backup device to save it from mechanical wear and tear, as well as possible electronic damage if you experience a power surge.

The second, bootable hard drive concept is available in an off-the-shelf product from CMS (*http://www.cmsproducts.com*) called the Automated Backup System, or ABS. The ABS is available in desktop and portable/laptop models. The ABS software can make the backup media bootable as a clone of your main hard drive and then perform full or incremental backups of your data in the background with very little impact on system performance. After the first full backup and careful selection of the files and folders you want to back up in the future, you'll never even know the ABS is there.

Index

Numbers

1x (AGP cards), 169
2D performance testing, 168
2x (AGP cards), 169
3D performance testing, 168
3DMark test suite, 168
40-wire cable, 151
4x (AGP cards), 169
80-wire cable, using for hard drive, 151
8x (AGP cards), 169

A

ABS (Automated Backup System), 269
Acronis True Image, 209, 251, 252
Active partition, 111
ActiveSMART (disk monitoring tool), 145
ActiveX controls, 261
    details about, provided by BHODemon, 262
Ad-Aware, 261
Adware, 257
AGP (Advanced Graphics Port)
    bus, 167
    AGP USB, 28
    aperture size, setting, 170
    built-in video adapter, upgrading from, 170
    choosing correct AGP mode, 172
    communication speed, 60
    internal I/O performance boost, 182
    replacing legacy I/O devices, 26

speed of, CPU hacking and, 54
    upgrading to AGP-based video adapter, 169
AIDA32, identifying your CPU, 53
air bubbles between the CPU and heat sink, 63
Aloha Bob, PC Relocator, 255
alpha channel, 168
AMD CPUs
    benchmarking speed of Athlon XP 2600+ Barton series, 58
    FSB speeds, 72
    hacking, 54, 56
    heat sink, necessity of, 61
AMI BIOS, 17, 19
anti-malware, 250
ATA specifications, 147
ATI Radeon
    overclocking, 175
    overclocking with PowerStrip, 177
atomic clock programs, 15
AT-style system board, 24
ATX-style system board, 24
AUTOEXEC.BAT file, 237, 239–242
Automated Backup System (ABS), 269
AVG virus protection software, 257
Award BIOS, 17
    CPU hacking and, 57
    version numbers, 18
AwardMod program, 11
    boot-up graphic, adding to BIOS, 12
AWDFLASH.EXE program, 11

We'd like to hear your suggestions for improving our indexes. Send email to *index@oreilly.com*.

B

Colophon

Our look is the result of reader comments, our own experimentation, and feedback from distribution channels. Distinctive covers complement our distinctive approach to technical topics, breathing personality and life into potentially dry subjects.

The tool on the cover of *PC Hacks* is a screwdriver. A mainstay of the household toolbox, the screwdriver is a device composed of a handle and a metal head, used to thread screws into material. The screws act as fasteners and come in a variety of shapes and sizes. A typical screw has a cylindrical or conical shaft ingrained with a helical groove and is topped with a head specially shaped to interlock with the head of the screwdriver.

While the ancient Greeks allegedly used wooden varieties of the screw as early as the first century B.C. as part of their wine presses, the screwdriver itself is a more modern invention. Witold Rybczynski's venerable cultural history of the screwdriver, *One Good Turn*, dates the first evidence of the tool's existence back approximately 500 years, when it was believed to have been used to thread metal screws into fifteenth-century armor.

Sanders Kleinfeld was the production editor and proofreader for *PC Hacks*. Jane Ellin was the copyeditor. Emily Quill and Claire Cloutier provided quality control. Ellen Troutman-Zaig wrote the index.

Hanna Dyer designed the cover of this book, based on a series design by Edie Freedman. The cover image is from the *Just Tools* collection of the CMCD Library. Clay Fernald produced the cover layout with QuarkXPress 4.1 using Adobe's Helvetica Neue and ITC Garamond fonts.

Melanie Wang designed the interior layout, based on a series design by David Futato. This book was converted by Joe Wizda to FrameMaker 5.5.6 with a format conversion tool created by Erik Ray, Jason McIntosh, Neil Walls, and Mike Sierra that uses Perl and XML technologies. The text font is Linotype Birka; the heading font is Adobe Helvetica Neue Condensed; and the code font is LucasFont's TheSans Mono Condensed. The illustrations that appear in the book were produced by Robert Romano and Jessamyn Read using Macromedia FreeHand MX and Adobe Photoshop CS. This colophon was written by Sanders Kleinfeld.